"Lyndon Shakespeare brings remarkable erudition to his argument for the recovery of the body of Christ as an ecclesial designation. As part of that argument he makes clear that we must recover an understanding of the body that challenges the managerial body that so dominates contemporary literature."

—STANLEY HAUERWAS, Gilbert T. Rowe Professor Emeritus of Divinity and Law, Duke University

"Being the Body of Christ in the Age of Management isn't just a critique of how the church thinks when it loses confidence in theology, nor is it only an excavation of the philosophy behind managerialism. It's a joyful mediation on the church as the body of Christ, with a life that's received from, animated by, and ordered towards God. The detailed analysis is meticulous, and the large-scale message could not be more timely."

—ANDREW DAVISON, Starbridge Lecturer in Theology and Natural Sciences, University of Cambridge

"Lyndon Shakespeare's book is a timely and intriguing response to the crisis of confidence in practical theology. Rooted in a thorough awareness of the latest management fads, the demands of pastoral ministry, and a wise application of the traditions of Christian theology, Shakespeare is able to navigate a way forward that reflects both reality and a prophetic challenge to the nostrums of our day. Highly recommended."

—JUSTIN LEWIS-ANTHONY, Associate Dean of Students and Director of Anglican Studies at Virginia Theological Seminary

"To govern the church by neoliberal criteria of supposed 'efficiency' is surely a mode of 'corpolatry' that substitutes the body of an idol for the body of Christ, just as 'idolatry' substitutes the face of an idol for the face of God in Christ. This new book makes such a case in a very powerful manner, while also explaining why the grasp of secular organization-theory by current church leaders is rather poor in any case. Shakespeare issues, in effect, a clarion call to all seriously able and visionary clergy and theologians to now find ways to seize the initiative from the semi-talented and conformist liberal careerists who are so sadly to the fore in the churches, obscuring the real Christian cultural and intellectual revival that is underway in Europe and the Americas."

— JOHN MILBANK, Professor of Religion, Politics, and Ethics, University of Nottingham

"This book is a gift. It is a gift for people who sing in churches, people who write about churches, people who stand up and speak about the Bible in churches, and anyone who loves someone who loves a church. Lyndon Shakespeare has engaged the various schemes for saving mainline-Christianity with patient lucidity. The book takes seriously ideas that have saturated my own denomination, helping anyone who has sat through a strategy or mission-marketing meeting to name their unease. Management-think is not an inevitable, natural evolution of human ingenuity. This way of describing and prescribing has a context and a history. Shakespeare's close reading of Thomas Aquinas is beautiful and clear: to divide up the Body of Christ into niche-markets is not only to make a category error, but to dismember ourselves. To paraphrase Karl Barth, mainline marketing strategies have taught us to trade our inheritance of infinite grace, flowing in abundance at Holy Communion, for a set of pre-packaged granola bars. This book reminds Christians where we are when we worship God—held together mysteriously, un-accountably, and immeasurably the Body."

—AMY LAURA HALL, Associate Professor of Christian Ethics, Duke University.

Being the Body of Christ in the Age of Management

VERITAS
Series Introduction

"... the truth will set you free" (John 8:32)

In much contemporary discourse, Pilate's question has been taken to mark
the absolute boundary of human thought. Beyond this boundary, it is often
suggested, is an intellectual hinterland into which we must not venture. This
terrain is an agnosticism of thought: because truth cannot be possessed, it
must not be spoken. Thus, it is argued that the defenders of "truth" in our day
are often traffickers in ideology, merchants of counterfeits, or anti-liberal.
They are, because it is somewhat taken for granted that Nietzsche's word is
final: truth is the domain of tyranny.

Is this indeed the case, or might another vision of truth offer itself? The
ancient Greeks named the love of wisdom as *philia*, or friendship. The one
who would become wise, they argued, would be a "friend of truth." For both
philosophy and theology might be conceived as schools in the friendship of
truth, as a kind of relation. For like friendship, truth is as much discovered as
it is made. If truth is then so elusive, if its domain is *terra incognita*, perhaps
this is because it arrives to us—unannounced—as gift, as a person, and not
some thing.

The aim of the Veritas book series is to publish incisive and original
current scholarly work that inhabits "the between" and "the beyond" of theology and philosophy. These volumes will all share a common aspiration to
transcend the institutional divorce in which these two disciplines often find
themselves, and to engage questions of pressing concern to both philosophers and theologians in such a way as to reinvigorate both disciplines with a
kind of interdisciplinary desire, often so absent in contemporary academe. In
a word, these volumes represent collective efforts in the befriending of truth,
doing so beyond the simulacra of pretend tolerance, the violent, yet insipid
reasoning of liberalism that asks with Pilate, "What is truth?"—expecting a
consensus of non-commitment; one that encourages the commodification
of the mind, now sedated by the civil service of career, ministered by the
frightened patrons of position.

The series will therefore consist of two "wings": (1) original mono-
graphs; and (2) essay collections on a range of topics in theology and philosophy. The latter will principally be the products of the annual conferences
of the Centre of Theology and Philosophy (www.theologyphilosophycentre
.co.uk).

Conor Cunningham and Eric Austin Lee, *Series editors*

Being the Body of Christ in the Age of Management

LYNDON SHAKESPEARE

CASCADE *Books* · Eugene, Oregon

BEING THE BODY OF CHRIST IN THE AGE OF MANAGEMENT

Veritas 19

Cascade Books
An Imprint of Wipf and Stock Publishers
199 W. 8th Ave., Suite 3
Eugene, OR 97401

www.wipfandstock.com

PAPERBACK ISBN: 978-1-4982-3210-4
HARDCOVER ISBN: 978-1-4982-3212-8
EBOOK ISBN: 978-1-4982-3211-1

Cataloguing-in-Publication data:

Names: Shakespeare, Lyndon.

Title: Book title : Being the body of Christ in the age of management / Lyndon Shakespeare.

Description: Eugene, OR: Cascade Books, 2016 | Series: Veritas 19 | Includes bibliographical references and index.

Identifiers: ISBN 978-1-4982-3210-4 (paperback) | ISBN 978-1-4982-3212-8 (hardcover) | ISBN 978-1-4982-3211-1 (ebook)

Subjects: LCSH: Church | Church management | Thomas, Aquinas, Saint, 1225?–1274

Classification: BV600.3 S41 2016 (print) | BV600.3 (ebook)

Manufactured in the U.S.A.   AUGUST 24, 2016

For Amie, Xavier, Madeleine, and Aidan

Contents

Acknowledgments

I AM GRATEFUL FOR the many people and communities that made this book possible. In particular, I wish to thank Andrew Davison who provided wise counsel, pastoral sensitivity, and above all, friendship, during the writing of my thesis, which forms the basis of this work.

The parishes of All Saints' Navesink, St. Paul's, K-Street, and St. Francis, Great Falls, and my time at Washington National Cathedral provided the context for research, writing, and the testing of many of the ideas and arguments in these pages. This book would have been impossible without the generosity of these communities.

Finally, the support of my Mum and Dad, the friendship of Gary, Daryl, Jan, and Gina, and the care and patience of Amie, Xavier, Madeleine, and Aidan, was invaluable to seeing this project move from a question I found myself unable to shake after a particularly difficult vestry meeting many years ago to a completed thesis and now a published book.

List of Abbreviations

Introduction

Core Thesis and Aims

This is a work of ecclesiology, an essay in theological reasoning that explores the life of the church as part of God's divine economy. As ecclesiology, this work assumes the existence of people who identify as Christians, who for two millennia have gathered to worship, commemorate, and experience God as revealed in Jesus of Nazareth. Moreover, this work assumes that there are countless ecclesiologies, all of which attempt in one form or another to provide an account of what (or who) constitutes the church, and perhaps, address why there is a church in the first place. As a work of ecclesiology, this book attempts to add something to the ongoing deliberation and *traditioning* that has defined the church since its inauguration on Pentecost.[1]

The ecclesiology articulated and defended in this book accepts as a starting point that humans are social animals who strive, but often fail, to live as members of a sustainable community. Whatever community we try to set up by purely human means, whether it is as citizens of a particular country or members of a well-managed organization, we fail to reach real unity. Nevertheless, such an admission does not preclude all possibilities of a sustainable, loving community as such. What the church

---

1. The "traditioning" process is how the church over time lives from tradition as a community shaped in worship of God, and how the church struggles to discern and express various traditions as reflected in Scripture and theological reasoning. See Russell, "Why Bother with the Church?" 249. Russell's point reflects Alasdair MacIntyre's concept of *traditioned* reason wherein all reasoning is understood to take place within the context of some historical mode of thought, transcending, through argument and invention, the limitations of what had hitherto been reasoned. For MacIntyre, a tradition is, "a historically extended, socially embodied argument, and an argument precisely in part about the goods which constitute that tradition." MacIntyre, *After Virtue*, 222.

declares is that through the life, death, and resurrection of Jesus Christ, human community and human unity is possible.

Christ is the unity of the church. That is, the church, the people of God, consists of those who are in him. Being "in Christ" is an expression of a certain kind of membership, one made possible through the activity and agency of God; one that we use the phrase "the body of Christ" to describe. Such activity includes the clothing of material things with sacred meaning. This is the realm and role of the sacraments. As this book will argue, the church is nothing but the community that sacramentally foreshadows the life for which God has destined all human beings.

It is a characteristic of communities, ecclesial and otherwise, that there be a level of organization that sets the conditions for how the community exists. The guiding questions for this study focus on what organizational conditions are appropriate to the church as a particular kind of community. If the church is understood as the body of Christ, what parallel does it have to other organized, social bodies? In an era when the benefits of organizational and management theory are thought to bring greater efficiency and effectiveness to organizations, what is gained and lost when applying such logic to the church? This book addresses what I see to be an uncritical willingness within sectors of the church to operate as if the church is simply a religious organization in need of proper (and faithful) management. I contend that such an approach gives implicit priority to a metaphysic of the human body that coincides with the metaphysics of physicalism.[2] The argument in these pages is that a managerial account of the social body, resting on the metaphysical assumptions of physicalism, distorts the holism and unity implicit to a vision of the church as Christ's body.

In order to provide an alternative to an ecclesiology that privileges a managerial logic, this work makes an argument for the church as the body of Christ using the work of Thomas Aquinas as a resource and guide. A retrieval of Aquinas for contemporary analysis begs the question: which

---

2. For the purposes of this study, *metaphysics* (of the body or otherwise) is defined as the inquiry in which the concern is with the study of being as being (*ens secundum quod ens*). See Aquinas, *Aristotle's Metaphysics*, Book IV, Lect. 1, n. 532. What attention to metaphysics makes possible is a focus on what is common to all existing things and what constitutes their connectedness to the universe as a meaningful whole. "It is the ultimate framework or horizon of inquiry," W. Norris Clarke suggests, "into which all other investigations, including all the sciences, fit as partial perspectives." Clarke, *The One and the Many*, 5–6.

interpretation of Aquinas is being retrieved?[3] For the purposes of this study, the influence of Anglo-analytic readings by the likes of Brian Davies, Herbert McCabe, Eleonore Stump, and Anthony Kenny will be evident.[4] While not exclusively, these authors provide the basis for how this work reads and applies Aquinas's insights, with specific attention to his anthropology, Christology, and sacramental theology.

Contemporary studies of the church vary in how they address the principle question of ecclesial identity and purpose. Many studies begin with the likely questions: what is the church, or why the church? They go on to provide a description of church history or architecture, or the revealed character or scriptural warrant for the existence of the church, or more recently, models or images for understanding what constitutes the church.[5] These questions and paths of study are legitimate and important. However, I come at the reality of the church in the same way Aquinas comes to the reality of any existing thing, through examining the particular way the items in the world and our understanding of what constitutes our world (i.e., how we talk about it as existing and having a purpose) hangs together in a coherent way. To examine the church, on this account, requires exploring a range of topics (e.g., anthropology, Scripture, and sacramental theology) that inform our understanding of what we mean when we talk of the church as a particular kind of thing in our world.

I am particularly concerned to investigate Aquinas's use of the biblical image of the "body of Christ" as a description for the church. Following the classic Christian tradition, Aquinas uses the word "body" *analogously*, since he is committed to speaking in a number of ways about

3. In a phrase used by John Webster, this book employs a "theology of retrieval." Webster notes that theologies of retrieval try to "stand with the Christian past which, precisely because it is foreign to contemporary conventions, can function as an instrument for the enlargement of vision." See Webster, "Theologies of Retrieval."

4. As Fergus Kerr makes clear, the reception of Thomas Aquinas's work has given rise to a variety of interpretations that began in Thomas's own day, and continue through various "Thomisms" in current research and debate. For Kerr's analysis of "Thomisms," see, Kerr, "The Varieties of Interpreting Aquinas."

5. For example, see, Jenson and Wilhite, *The Church*. Chapters 1 and 2 address the question, what is the church, by means of models and historic "marks" of the church. Another recent survey by Veli-Matti Kärkkäinen outlines particular elements of ecclesial identity by means of comparing published statements and documents about the church by major ecclesial groups. See Kärkkäinen, *An Introduction to Ecclesiology*. Avery Dulles's classic text on ecclesiology uses "models" or "types" to analyze and describe the church's character over time, see, Dulles, *Models of the Church*.

the central body in Christian tradition, the body of Christ. When explicating how to understand the use of the word "body" in reference to the natural body of Christ, the Eucharist, and the church, Aquinas is careful to keep all his "body" language in balance, so as not to conflate or confuse the body of Christ as the social body of the church, the historical human body of Jesus, or the consecrated elements of the Eucharist. He is not unique in this use or care, but his analysis is particularly rich, especially in how he works the analogy of the body out in his primary texts, as well as his shorter treatises and biblical commentaries. In addition, Aquinas's account is significant because of the way his understanding of the "body of Christ" hangs not simply on his scriptural exegesis or his synthesis of theological work from over the previous generations, but on his explication of human anthropology, divine agency, and his overall argument for human well-being. As such, Aquinas is led to ask: what kind of body is a human body? What is the goal of human living? Was Jesus a human, in the ordinary sense? How do humans share in the divine life? How is Christ an instrument of divine grace?

In other words, it matters to Aquinas what we mean when we use the word "body" in the phrase, "the body of Christ," because a body—and here we are talking about a *human* body—is a particular kind of thing in our world. When we speak of a human body—its nature, its *quiddity*[6]— we provide a definition and description that ought to shape our use of the "body of Christ" in understanding Christ himself, the Eucharist, and the church. Moreover, the particular way we give account of the human body matters in ways we do not always fully recognize. For instance, the influence of a certain mechanized understanding of the human body can reduce what constitutes a living human to the mere functions of the spleen or brain or nervous system. A related reductionist move is evident when the only description of the human body is as an unfortunate and limiting vessel for what truly matters, the disembodied soul. For Thomas,

6. "Quiddity" being the essential quality that makes something what it is. This is an important term in medieval philosophy, including that of Thomas Aquinas, and will be explored with more depth below. For the purposes of this section, it is worth noting that for Thomas, to speak of the quiddity of a human being, is to define what constitutes humanity as a species (i.e., what makes human beings to be human beings), but not in terms of an individual human. Aquinas says, "we do not define the species of anything by the matter and properties peculiar to it as an individual. . . . 'Human nature' names the formative element in human beings; for what gives a thing definition is formative with respect to the matter that gives it individuality" (*ST* 1a.3.3). See Aquinas, *Summa theologiae*, 33–34.

the soul is the *form* of the body,[7] or to borrow from the philosopher Ludwig Wittgenstein, the body is the best image we have of the human soul.[8] Under this description, there is more to human life than the operations of the physical body.

This work will argue that the way we define (ask: *what* it is) and describe (ask: *how* it is) the human body will influence how we understand the church as the body of Christ. It is my contention that the particular definition and description of the social body that emerges from managerial theory displays an account of the human body that fits within the general empirical theories of materialism or *physicalism* that form part of the legacy that extends over 400 years from the late scholastic period of Francis Bacon and René Descartes to contemporary neuroscience and philosophies of mind. In brief, a physicalist understanding of the body provides the metaphysics for an understanding of organizational life as the privileging of the managerial practices of efficiency, calculability, predictability, and control. When applied to the church, such an account proves erosive to a more holistic and unifying understanding of the church as the body of Christ, where sacramental participation by individuals entails connection and membership in the glorified humanity of Christ.

The implicit connection and influence of physicalism and managerialism that this book seeks to elucidate requires some initial explanation. Physicalism in all its various schools looks at the human body and asks: how does a human body work? What pieces make up a body, and how do they relate? Physicalism postulates the human body is just a material thing, a complex and often mysterious thing, but simply an organic thing with moving parts and an organizing system that we call the brain and nervous system. It assumes that everything we do as humans is ultimately explainable via physical operations or states. To have a living body, according to the proponents of physicalism, is to possess a particular kind of organism whose behavior and purpose is governed solely by the laws of biology, physics, and chemistry, in short, the physical sciences.

Aquinas, operating as he was within a medieval intellectual environment, employed an understanding of the physical sciences that lacks the modern sophistication of recent technological advancement. Nevertheless, his general approach to the operations of the human body

7. Aquinas, *Commentary on Aristotle's De Anima* 2.1.234. (*quod anima sit forma corporis*).

8. Wittgenstein, *Philosophical Investigations*, 178.

and an understanding of the world in general is, in an important sense, scientific.[9] Taking a position that displays his scientific *and* metaphysical commitments, Aquinas thinks it is one thing to describe a body by reference to the physical makeup of the human body and something else to account for what it means for a human body to be alive and to have a particular purpose in light of being alive.[10] Consequently, Aquinas begins his account of the living human body with an analysis of what it means to say we are alive (as opposed to a lump of organic stuff or a corpse).[11] To be alive, whether as a human or a cat, is first to be *animated* (or to

9. See Velde, *Aquinas on God*, 25–27. Aquinas states in the opening lines of the *Summa Theologiae* that he seeks to provide a scientific account of matters pertaining to God and the world. Following Aristotle, Aquinas analyzed and employed the word "science" (*scientia*) in two ways. First, a science may proceed from principles immediately known as true in the natural light of the intellect. This constitutes a "normal" human science based on self-evident principles, *principia per se nota*. Aquinas, for example, expressed interest in the movements of the stars (in *De Iudiciis Astrorum*) and the function of the heart (in *De Motu Cordis*) as part of his overall scientific approach to the world.

Second, Aquinas suggests the possibility of a subaltern science, which proceeds from principles known by the light of a higher science. Optics, for example, is subaltern to geometry because some propositions that serve as principles in the *scientia* of optics are not self-evidently known, but are conclusions demonstrated in the higher *scientia* of geometry. One might say that the *scientia* of optics borrows its principles from the higher science of geometry in which their truth is ascertained. In this sense, a *scientia* need not be a logically self-sufficient whole based on principles which are, as such, known to be true; it may depend for its principles on a higher science, which guarantees the truth of these principles and, consequently, of all that can be concluded from these principles. According to this model of a subaltern science, Aquinas contends that theology (*sacra doctrina*) can be understood to be a *scientia*, since its conclusions are based on principles known by the light of a superior *scientia*, namely the *scientia* of God. These principles, from which the *scientia* of faith proceeds, are identified by Thomas as the articles of faith, the concise summary of Christian faith, which form the basic truths of sacred doctrine.

10. See *ST* 1a.91.1 & 3. In his discussion on the creation of human beings, Aquinas describes the elements that make up the human body, and how a description of the elements alone is insufficient to account for the fullness of human life and activity.

11. See Bishop, *The Anticipatory Corpse*. Drawing on the analysis of Foucault, Bishop claims that the human corpse has become epistemologically normative for contemporary medicine via the development of anatomy and pathological medicine. Death has become "the fundamental ground of medical knowledge" (p. 59). Moreover, Bishop argues that late eighteenth-century medicine precludes formal and final causation from its understanding of the body, thereby elevating material and efficient causation. With this epistemology of death, "the resulting metaphysics of efficient causation allows mastery over the living body as a machine, as dead matter in motion" (p. 60).

have an *anima*, soul).[12] Aquinas insists that the body (whether human, cat, or otherwise) needs a soul, where a soul is understood as the causal agent or power (i.e., substantial form) that is the actual life of the body (it *actualizes* the matter). In other words, to talk of an animal having a soul is to recognize that activities like seeing and eating involve organic parts of the animal that operate in reference to the whole of the animal. The animal, Aquinas would say, is not simply a collection of individual parts (or instruments) doing certain jobs on their own. What these parts are doing would not be these jobs (e.g., seeing or eating) unless the tasks they perform were parts of the behavior of the *whole* animal and representative of the *purpose* for the particular animal.[13]

Second, to then consider what it means for a living human body to be alive (e.g., to be a particular kind of embodied soul) is to say that we humans are a certain kind of self-moving and complex organism able to transcend our individual materiality.[14] This transcendence is recognized through such things as the learning and use of a common and public language and the understanding and planning of urban architecture (as operations of the soul), as well as by the less lovely path of bigotry and genocide.[15] Badgers do not build weapons of mass destruction, but neither do dolphins build cities. We would be amazed if they did. When Aquinas defines what it means to be human, he accounts for both our

12. In his commentary of Aristotle's *De Anima*, Thomas speaks of the soul or life-principle (*anima*) as what all living things have in common (*Commune autem omnibus rebus animatis est anima: in hoc enim omnia animata convenient*). See Aquinas, *Commentary on Aristotle's De Anima*, 2.

13. McCabe, "The Immortality of the Soul," 298. This view has its source in Aristotle, who argued that to say that, "the soul (*psuchē*) is angry is as if one were to say that the soul weaves or builds. For it is surely better not to say that the soul pities, learns or thinks, but that a man does these with his soul." Aristotle, *De Anima*, 115.

14. Stump, *Aquinas*, 201.

15. See Hacker, *The Intellectual Powers*. Working from within an Aristotelian-Thomistic framework, Hacker associates language use with the possession of rational powers of intellect and will that only human beings possess. To know how to use language and communicate with other language uses, Hacker maintains, is to have learned a vast range of "forms of action and activity and of reaction and response to speech (and, in literate societies, to writing) and of response to circumstance which are constitutive of a human form of life" (p. 103). An example of a human form of life that language makes possible is the symbol making and communication that forms the basis for human culture.

biology and the way we surpass our individuality through purposeful activity.[16]

Before turning to a brief overview of managerialism, it is worth summarizing the conceptual legitimacy of moving between notions of the human body and that of a social body. Anthropologist Mary Douglas is helpful in this matter. Douglas argues that in the Western imagination, the social body constrains the way the physical body is perceived. Similarly, the physical experience of the body, always modified by the social categories through which it is known, sustains a particular view of society. There is a continual exchange of meanings between the two kinds of bodily experience, so each reinforces the categories of the other. Because of this interaction, the body itself is a highly restricted medium of expression.[17] The forms it adopts in movement and repose express social pressures in manifold ways. Therefore, how we define and describe the human body modifies how we define and describe the body social, and vice versa. Douglas notes by way of example how the parts and functions of the human body (e.g., feet, heart, mouth, and even sexual organs) express the relevant patterns of position and function within families, organizations, and governments. For Douglas, the social categories of bodily experience shape our understanding of the physical and vice versa.[18]

Managerialism, as a form of social practice and categorization, wants to define and describe social bodies by their operations and purposes in much the same way as that of physicalism. Managerialism occurs when the implicit principles that govern the political, social, and economic ordering of a social body, be it a single organization or an entire nation-state, operate by means of the predetermined generic ends of efficiency, effectiveness, and predictability and the subsequent control of the social body through manipulating the function and purpose to meet only these ends.[19] In such an arrangement, formal calculations are aligned with creating efficiencies, effectiveness, and value-free law-like generalizations aimed at producing measurable results.

Managerialism asks: how can the parts of an organization work better to make the organization more efficient and effective? And, what

16. Peter Geach summarizes the general argument of Aquinas on this matter when he notes that a human alone, "has a world; an animal has only an environment." Geach, *Truth and Hope*, 29.

17. Douglas, *Natural Symbols: Explorations in Cosmology*, 66–70.

18. Ibid., 74.

19. Enteman, *Managerialism*, 30–31.

organizational strategies or techniques are needed to overcome any real or perceived disorganization in society? It seeks to provide a kind of rational order that presumes as normal the goals of expansion and specialization via increased organizational structure and bureaucracy. What matters is the use of better techniques for a more efficient system in order to reach a higher level of effectiveness as an organization. Within managerialism, social bodies are an amalgam of individual positions arranged in numerous ways to perform particular tasks. This social arrangement is presented as value-free.[20] Managerialism, proponents suggest, is simply a means to coordinate the allocation of resources among different spheres of an organization. There is little metaphysical intrigue here, and even less need to appeal to anything outside the social body itself. For the managed organization, what matters is that all the right parts are placed in the right order so a particular outcome can be reached: an outcome shaped by the principles of efficiency, calculability, predictability, and control. Such principles animate a managerialist logic that has little purpose other than increased growth and status for the corporate or social body.[21]

When applied to the church, the managerialist logic introduces a set of conditions for understanding church life that is satisfied with corporate-like results through the exercise of managerial-inspired leadership, strategies, and techniques.[22] Some forms of modern ecclesiologies, for example, acquiesce to a reconfiguration of the church that mirrors the modern managed corporation. Such a reconfiguration seeks the future survival of the church through adopting an organizational structure dedicated to a well-marketed and efficient delivery of a product in limited (because privileged) competition with other outlets in the spiritual marketplace. All of this can be measured, analyzed, and reported out, and all

20. Don Browning refers to the apparent value- or theory-free assumptions in the practice and theory of modern modes of inquiry like managerialism as an illusion. See Browning, *A Fundamental Practical Theology*.

21. Pollitt, "Mangerialism Revisted," 47.

22. The concern of this book is with managerialism as *a governing logic* in the church, not with organizational thinking or practice in general. *Organizing* is the general category in which management is one form. As a form, however, management, cautions Christopher Pollitt, has emerged as the "standard" form for organizing. The assumption of managerialism is that organizing always requires a particular set of individuals to be doing something called "managing," and that those people have special skills and training that are necessary for an organization or institution to operate more effectively and efficiently. See Pollitt, *Managerialism and the Public Services: The Anglo-American Experience*, 1–27.

of it orders the church towards a vision of corporate-like success through growth (profit) or privilege (power). The kind of vision of the church that I critique embraces the view that efficiency and effectiveness are the principal virtues, thereby, the guiding question is not are the methods of managerialism *true* but do the methods *work*?[23]

The account of the church provided in Aquinas operates as an alternative to the effectiveness-orientation and limited purposefulness of management-inspired ecclesiologies. For Aquinas, the church is more than simply an organization that reflects in speech and action particular beliefs about God and the world. Aquinas comes to the social body of the church with an organic, theologically derived imagery of the "body" in mind. We see this in two principles Aquinas holds in relation to human life and human community. First, Aquinas believes human bodily life to be the means by which our desire to be a real human community is made possible. Our bodies are how we relate with others (i.e., our bodies are the source of our communication with each other) and when we are with others in community, we truly transcend our individuality through the learning and sharing of language, the experience of culture, and the enjoyment of an occasional good whiskey. The kind of bodies we are—as meaning-making and symbol-sharing, embodied souls—allows us to become *more* of what it means to be human, the more we are present to each other.[24]

Second, Aquinas argues that although we form one human race because our bodies are linked with those of our common ancestors, our destiny and proper end is to belong to the new human race through our bodies being linked with the risen body of Christ.[25] To be linked with Christ, to be the body of Christ is not, for Aquinas, simply a "brand" or "slogan" used to denote the unique identity of the church among other organizations. The church, in a very literal sense, is the body of Christ, enacted and made material through the sacrament of the Eucharist.[26] The sacraments, for Aquinas, are regarded as mysteries of human community

23 Sargeant, *Seeker Churches*, 128. The category of "effectiveness" will be explored further in relation to the work of Alasdair MacIntyre and his critique of managerialism.

24. *ST* 1a2æ.4.5 & 8.

25. *ST* 3a.61.1.

26. The notion that the Eucharist is the basis for the church is exemplified in the past century by the theology of Henri de Lubac, in particular, Lubac, *Corpus Mysticum*, and more recently in the work of Paul McPartlan, particularly his McPartlan, *The Eucharist Makes the Church*.

symbolizing the union in the Holy Spirit between people. The sacraments are our living contact with the humanity of Christ through which alone we share in divine life.[27] To speak of the *body of Christ,* as does the apostle Paul and following him, Aquinas, is to speak of a body like no other, whose life is sourced in the resurrected and glorified body of Christ by the power of the Holy Spirit and in union with God the Father. The sacraments make that body present to us and make us present as that body.

In this book, I am exploring the connection between physicalism and managerialism through an analysis of how managerialist organizational theory accepts as fundamental a particular materialist vision of the body as functional, organized as bits and pieces, and lacking the complex unity and purposefulness true of human bodies. Securing the connection will not conclusively collapse physicalism and management theory into a homogeneous account. The point is to show how the logic of physicalism enlivens a managerial approach to leadership, strategies, and techniques in the church. With this connection in mind, I will argue such an account falls short of providing a description of the human body, and in turn, the social body of the church as an essential *unity* whose material life cannot be extricated from a proper account of what is logically involved in the church's identity as the "body of Christ." The writings and logic of Thomas Aquinas provide a resource for how to account for the church as the *mystical body of Christ* rather than a mere organization of religious adherents. The significance of Aquinas's position is that the church is treated as the site of membership and union with the living God, an ecclesial body unified by the love and grace of the Holy Spirit.

Method

This book takes a number of areas of inquiry and periods of thought into account in order to analyze one kind of contemporary ecclesiology and suggest an alternative. The challenge is to retrieve a logic and analysis that draws on the anthropology and sacramental theology of the thirteenth century theologian, Thomas Aquinas, and use them to analyze and critique the theory and practice of managerialism and managerial-oriented accounts of the church from the past century. The methodology deployed for this kind of work requires attending to a number of questions: first,

27. As Aquinas states in *ST* 3a.26.1.*ad*.1, "The sacraments mediate the divine power, but only by virtue of the perfect mediation of the assumed humanity of the Word."

under what conditions can the theology of Thomas Aquinas from the thirteenth century be retrieved to serve questions and analysis for the twenty-first century? Second, what about Aquinas's theological outlook is prescient to the stated concerns of this book around organizational and managerial theory and practice as adopted by certain forms of contemporary ecclesiology?

To the first methodological question, the response is that this book makes use of a form of theological reasoning most commonly referred to as a "theology of retrieval."[28] Though not formally a school of thought or a movement, theologies of retrieval tend to employ the theological judgments of pre-modern thinkers in order to interpret, and in some measure transcend, the constraints of modern theology by unearthing a neglected teaching or rationale in order to address a perceived disorder in contemporary analysis or practice. Such an approach *de-centers* the contemporary analysis by trying to stand with the Christian past, which, precisely because it is foreign to contemporary conventions, can function as an instrument for the enlargement of a theological vision. "Retrieval," then, is a mode of theology, an attitude of mind, and a way of approaching the theological task.[29]

As a "theology of retrieval," this book seeks to give close attention to significant contributions of Aquinas in matters of anthropology and ecclesiology in order to call into question and reframe the contemporary theological discussion about the nature and purpose of the church. The point is not to repristinate Aquinas's thought, but to read present theological conditions in a way that opens up a path of inquiry that takes the development of thought from the time of Aquinas to include misdirections and errors of analysis and judgment that have contributed to a number of incoherent positions, most notably, the technique and missional approaches in ecclesiology.

What retrieving Aquinas makes possible is a renewal of a thoroughly argued and articulate account of the church against which the deficits of a managerial-inspired ecclesiology are made clear. In particular, Aquinas's doctrines of God and creation represent a theologically rigorous and

28. See note 3 above.

29. Webster, "Theologies of Retrieval," 590. The school of thought held under the title of Radical Orthodoxy is a recent and persuasive example of a theology of retrieval that contravenes the dominance of modernity by attending to modes of thought and judgment that question the premises of modernity and provide an alternative theological account.

metaphysically sophisticated account of human nature, salvation, and our relation to God. Whilst there is no explicit ecclesiology in Aquinas's work, it can be derived from his wider theology in such a way that the church is understood in relation to Christology, pneumatology, the sacraments, and the threefold order of ministry. By contrast, the application of management theory to the contemporary organization of the church allegedly has no metaphysical foundations or implications; it is simply an organizational and bureaucratic tool that enables a sustainable management of the church and its resources in the context of twenty-first-century capitalist democracies. Competition for resources within a complex economic culture allegedly makes the application of such techniques imperative. Under these conditions, the implicit metaphysical assumptions of these techniques remain masked behind their pragmatic usefulness.

The form of managerialism under scrutiny in these pages is most clearly evidenced in the contemporary business sector and increasingly so in the education sector.[30] In recent years, such managerial forms have simply been layered on top of the church's explicitly theological self-understanding as expressed in the theory and practices associated with worship and official teachings. At first glance, comparing the "metaphysical ecclesiology" of Thomas Aquinas with the "managerial functionalism" of the twenty-first-century church seems methodologically reckless and unnecessary. However, this book will make a two-fold contention that draws these very different discourses into critical relation. First, Aquinas's theology of the church, derived from his doctrines of God and creation, has significant practical implications for the daily life of the body of Christ, the church. It is not simply a theory, but an instance of speculative and practical reason. Second, the functional managerialism that is so often seen in today's church is not metaphysically or theologically innocent; it masks a latent ecclesiology that is wholly inadequate to the biblical witness and the church's traditional self-understanding. Moreover, it can be unmasked as supremely *im*practical when examined in the light of the church's fundamental orientation to the kingdom of God.

In retrieving the theological vision of Aquinas, this book brings to the foreground a theological heritage that is expansive enough to address

---

30. Hoyle and Wallace, *Educational Leadership*. Hoyle and Wallace reference the "continuous flow of policies" in UK schools that serve to empower policy-makers to deploy managerial strategies of control that inevitably contribute to the need for more policies and more control. What starts out as a *means* to improve education becomes in the case of managerialism an imposed *end*.

contemporary human and ecclesial conditions with a significant level of subtlety and precision. What is more, Aquinas's comprehensive attention to matters of human wellbeing and divine life and activity provides the basis for this book to attend to the implicit metaphysical assumptions of managerial-inspired approaches to the church, in particular, the physicalist assumptions of the purpose and meaning of the human body and by analogy the social body of the church. To make use of Aquinas for such a task is an exercise in thinking *with* Aquinas through applying his outlook and principles to judge particular matters that are concerned with questions of ultimate importance.[31]

To summarize, a theology of retrieval, as evidenced in this book, does not advocate a simple return from modern theology to what might be considered a more authentic Christian teaching from the past. The purpose is to respond adequately to the present situation while maintaining continuity with the Christian tradition within which both Aquinas and contemporary ecclesiology are firmly located.[32] To draw on Aquinas as an authority in present matters is to make the explicit claim that his thinking continues to offer a resource and measure for the larger Christian tradition. To put a finer point on it, Aquinas's descriptive method of engaging questions of human life with and towards God displays an internal consistency that avails his work to ongoing consideration and use. His is the work of a thirteenth-century theologian that has shown remarkable buoyancy for contemporary retrieval and application.[33]

31. Vann, *Morals Makyth Man*, 15.

32. Henri de Lubac's, *Surnaturel* (1946), provides one of the clearest deployments of a theology of retrieval in the last century. In this work, de Lubac sought to excavate what he regarded as a primary Christian insight, namely that "natural" being is ordered to participation in God. As John Webster notes, "what made the retrieval necessary was the notion of 'pure nature' which had lodged itself in nineteenth-century neoscholasticism but which could be traced back through Cajetan to strands of late medieval and early modern scholastic thought." Webster, "Theologies of Retrieval," 588. The resultant separation of nature from grace made the patristic and earlier medieval tradition virtually inaccessible. In *Surnaturel,* De Lubac explicates modernity by placing it at the end of a long defection of Christian theology from its native vision of the end of created being in participation in God.

33. The range and variety of uses of Thomas is wide and ever-growing. For instance, theologians (e.g., Stanley Hauerwas and Matthew Levering), philosophers (e.g., David Braine and David Burrell), and moral theologians (e.g., Paul Wadell and Charles Pinches) regularly deploy Thomistic notions and logic to recent trends in politics, medical ethics, and philosophical psychology.

Outline

The particular questions addressed in this book emerge from the actual practices and methodologies employed by churches that fit within the general category of "mainline," particularly denominations like Anglicanism, Methodism, and Lutheranism in the United States and the United Kingdom. Such practices and methods have not emerged in a vacuum. In fact, the use of managerial and organizational theories in the church emerge, I contend, as a result of the decline in the participation and membership in these denominations, and an overall receding influence of the church in the greater society. As will be argued, this decline has fueled church leaders to adopt strategies from corporate and business life.

The basic structure of the book is chiastic in form. The opening chapters are concerned with the church and its particular shape and focus when managerialist logic is uncritically adopted. An analysis of the rise and supremacy of managerialism in organizational theory and practices follows. This analysis reveals an implicit account of the social body that rests on the assumptions of the reductive and mechanistic heritage of Francis Bacon, René Descartes, and Julien Offray de la Mettrie that contributed to a contemporary physicalist metaphysic of the human body. The anthropology of Thomas Aquinas in then surveyed for a more robust and holistic vision of the human body, which provides the basis for a more constructive and unifying account of the church as the body of Christ, where humanity is ordered and oriented to its proper goal, the beatitude of God. The final chapter returns to the shape and form of the contemporary church, and contends that the ecclesial vision of Aquinas equips church thinkers and practitioners with an alternative basis to a managerial-inspired logic.

To elaborate, the opening chapter summarizes the historical and sociological accounts for the decline in the church, and outlines the two major responses to this decline. The work of sociologists Rodney Stark and Mark Chaves, and historians Randall Balmer and Lauren Winner are used to identify the social factors that have contributed to the decline. The two responses, the technique-oriented and the mission-focused, are detailed through attention to a representative work of church practitioners and consultants. Both responses, it will be argued, assume characteristics of managerialism, particularly in the importance given to deploying the criterion of effectiveness and predictability when determining what goals are essential for the church.

In recent years, there has been an increase in philosophical and theological critiques of the organizational and managerial practices in the church. These critiques fall into several categories. Chapter 2 begins with Alasdair MacIntyre's critical account of managerial logic through his analysis of the character of the "Manager" in the modern social imaginary. MacIntyre is particularly concerned with particular forms of bureaucratic rationality, and the stress within this rationality upon the market as the mechanism for sorting out human relations through purely instrumental reasons that place value on the achievement of the managerial goals of effectiveness, efficiency, predictability, and control.

The criterion for managerialism critiqued by MacIntyre is followed by a brief genealogy of managerialism in context of the evolving world of organizational theory and practice. Clare Watkins and Stephen Pattison link this emergence of managerialism with a growing assimilation of a managerial logic within the church. In their estimation, the church ought to engage the tools of management with caution, using only those tools deemed appropriate to the teaching of the church.

Richard Roberts, Michael Budde, and John Milbank see the privileging of managerial theory and practice in the church as requiring something more than caution. They decry the methods and logic of managerialism as a corrupting invasion into the very fabric of Christian life and practice. Working through related arguments, these theologians give precedence to the church as a special body within the world that operates by means of divine gift manifest in the unique proclamation of the gospel, and made material in the sacraments. Despite their suspicions of organizational thinking, they are careful to separate what it means for a church to function well, and what it means for a church to adopt the implicit rationality of organizational theory. All the same, the analysis in the second chapter will demonstrate how the current theological critiques of managerialism in the church do not express adequately an understanding of the individual human body as the basis for understanding the church as a particular social body.

The third chapter turns to the subject of managerialism as a particular form of organizational theory. Having argued that managerialism when imported into accounts of the church is problematic, this chapter will trace the conceptual history from the Thomistic-Aristotelian metaphysics of the scholastic period, to the Cartesian shift of the sixteenth century out of which a reductive understanding of the human body became the normative model for later centuries. Such a legacy, I contend, became the basis for the reductive metaphysic of the social body as exemplified in the emergence of managerialism in the late nineteenth century through the organizational theories of Henri Comte de Saint-Simon and Max Weber.

The implicit anthropology of managerialism is addressed in the third chapter through the work of Chris Shilling and Karen Dale. The significance of their analysis is their identification of a materialist account of the human body in the organizational theory that undergirds managerialism. Collectively, they address the question: what kind of body is an organization? In attempting to create a more scientific and, therefore, more rational approach to organizations, the proponents of managerialism rely on a close analogy between a well-functioning organization and a vision of the body as functional, organized as bits and pieces, and lacking the complex unity and purposefulness true of bodies, both individual and social. The result is the prevalence and precedence of an individual and corporate rationality that uses efficiency, calculability, predictability, and control as the guiding principles for business, industry, and, later, to all organizations and institutions.

Drawing on the Cartesian legacy, managerialism, it will be argued, rests on a number of physicalist assumptions. First, the human body can only be properly understood through a process of rationalization, that is, a process that reduces the operations and states of the body to that of its constituent parts. Second, a human body requires the coordination of efficient causation. Third, the human body is primarily purposed for biological survival and growth. These assumptions are then examined in light of managerial logic and practices, and aligned with the emphasis in technique and missional-based ecclesiologies on the role of programs, leadership, and strategic planning.

The fourth and fifth chapters retrieve the theological anthropology and sacramental theology of Thomas Aquinas and argue that the vision of the church that develops from Aquinas's work is a robust and viable alternative to the managerial vision that is evident in sectors of the contemporary church. Chapter 5 focuses on questions of human nature in the *Summa Theologiae* and Aquinas's commentary on Aristotle's *De Anima*. The work of Robert Pasnau, Eleonore Stump, and the hitherto unpublished scholarship of Fabian Radcliffe will guide this analysis. The benefit of Aquinas's anthropology in a study on ecclesiology is that he accounts for the human body as something more than simply one material organic being among other material organic beings. Human beings are living, rational animals with capacities that extend beyond our material existence into complex and immaterial human activities like culture, language, and friendship.

When the focus turns to Aquinas's sacramental theology in chapter 5, Radcliffe's work will assist, as will the work of Stump and Herbert McCabe. The analysis of sacramental theology will include Aquinas's commentaries on the Pauline Epistles, as well as the principal passages in the *Summa* (i.e., 3a, 7–15, 60–65, and 73–78). Central to Aquinas's sacramental theology is the contention that although we form one human race because our bodies are linked with those of our common ancestors, our destiny and proper end is to belong to the new human race through our bodies being linked with the risen body of Christ. In the sacraments, specifically, the Eucharist, humans share a life, the life of Christ, who is the source of human unity. Such an account differs sharply from the managerial ecclesiologies that seek to organize religious communities along the lines of a well-managed institution with particular attention to a shared vision of each particular community. In sum, managerial ecclesiologies lack substantive attention to how unity and purpose of the church is realized; that is, they lack a sufficient account of how bodily human life is oriented and ordered to the ultimate end of divine beatitude.

The final chapter focuses the preceding analysis on the question of the social character of the church. Implied in the use of "body" on analogy of the human body, the church, as a visible social body, is more than simply a loose fellowship of like-minded people. Unlike the modern organization and the managerial logic contained therein, the ultimate reason for the church's visibility is not reducible to the mechanisms of corporate-style leadership, strategies, and techniques. What is necessary are forms of leadership and organization that match the implicit identity and purpose of the church as Christ's body. Such forms are evident in the exercise of *prudentia* as "right practical reason," the vision of the church as a unifying social body, and the understanding of the church as formed and ordered to divine *beatitude*. These forms and the allied ecclesial vision, this book concludes, provides a constructive alternative to the social categorization that would define the church by its organizational character rather than its eschatological destiny.

1

The Problem of Decline

IN 1972 DEAN M. Kelley, an executive of the National Council of Churches in the United States, provoked a storm of controversy, especially among Christians within the denominations that identify as "mainline," with his book *Why Conservative Churches Are Growing*. His first sentence declared, "In the latter years of the 1960s something remarkable happened in the United States: for the first time in the nation's history most of the major church groups stopped growing and began to shrink."[1] By "major church groups," Kelley had in mind the collection of Protestant church denominations categorized as "mainline." Such groups include the Methodist, Episcopal, Lutheran, and Presbyterian churches. These Protestant denominations represent a *mainstream* in the religious landscape: the dominant, culturally established, and theologically progressive[2] churches that the majority of self-confessed Protestant Christians would identify through membership and participation.[3] In general, the mainline churches in the twentieth century invested heavily in the ecumenical movement and in social causes, including civil rights,

1. Kelley, *Why Conservative Churches Are Growing*, 1.
2. The qualifier "progressive" is related to the more commonly used, "liberal," especially with regard the particular theological vision of the church, Scripture, and the place of engagement of both with modern culture and scholarship. In general, "liberalism" is understood to be "a loose term to designate systems of political organizations that stress the liberty of individuals in a state of nature, their rights in society, and their freedoms over against coercive authority." Noll, *America's God*, 547. In the context of the church in America, a progressive or liberal represents "a Christian perspective based on reason and experience, not external authority." Dorrien, *The Making of American Liberal Theology*, 2.
3. Roof, *America Mainline Religion*, 8.

opposition to the Vietnam War, and the pursuit of equal rights for women.[4] According to Kelly, the time of cultural dominance by the mainstream was over; a new era was emerging, the era of independent and religiously conservative churches who observed organizational "strictness" in matters of belief and practice.[5]

By the latter half of the twentieth century, sociologists and historians were beginning to recognize what Kelley announced in his book: the sudden rise of the conservative faiths and the rapid decline of the more liberal "mainline" denominations.[6] Some sociologists suggest that this decline extends back to 1776, at the very moment the colonies of North America sought independence from English sovereignty.[7] Although the prevalence of religious belief remains high within the American public,[8] this has not resulted in stable participation in organized religious traditions, like that of Protestant denominations. Research data demonstrates the decline of attendance in mainline churches from 40 percent in 1965, to 26 percent in 1997,[9] to a further drop to 15 percent by 2009.[10]

The data of the decline in attendance is underscored by the simultaneous decline in the cultural influence of mainline Christians. Historians Randall Balmer and Lauren Winner quote George A. Campbell Jr., publisher of the periodical *The Christian Oracle*, declaring on the

4. Balmer and Winner, *Protestantism in America*, 29.

5. Kelley, *Why Conservative Churches Are Growing*, 78–81.

6. Stark and Finke, *The Churching of America, 1776–1990*, 3. The data on the growth of American Protestants who identify as "evangelical" seems to support Kelley's claim. "While the percentage of American Protestants claiming mainline affiliation decreased from 57 percent in the early 1970s to 47 percent in the late 1990s, conservative Protestant denominations grew from 43 percent of all Protestants to 53 percent in the same period." Chaves, *Congregations in America*, 33.

7. Stark and Finke, *The Churching of America, 1776–1990*, 234.

8. Sociologist Mark Chaves records the percentage of Americans who claim "some belief in a higher power" to be consistently in the 85–90 percentile of the adult U.S. population. See Chaves, *Congregations in America*, 29.

9. Ibid., 31.

10 "The Barna Group—Report Examines the State of Mainline Protestant Churches." A comparison with decline in the churches of the United Kingdom demonstrates a similar trend. According to Michael Moynagh, the institutional church is in serious if not terminal decline. Between 1980 and 2005, church attendance in England declined from 10.1 percent of the population to 5.7 percent. In Scotland, the figure was 17.1 percent of the population declining to 10.3 percent. The proportion of decline was greatest in Wales, where in 1980 14.1 percent of the population attended church. By 2005, this had reduced to 6.4 percent. See Moynagh et al., *Emergingchurch. intro*, 16, and Barrow, "From Management to Vision," 8.

eve of the twentieth century, "We believe that the coming century is to witness greater triumphs in Christianity than any previous century has ever witnessed and that it is to be more truly Christian than any of its predecessors."[11] Despite the self-confident predictions, mainline Protestantism suffered the greatest decline in the very century its influence was to extend into every aspect of American social, political, and economic life. This trajectory, according to historian Martin Marty, was partly the result of the particular nature of churches thought to be mainstream. "Mainline churches always have the advantage," Marty argues, when,

> the official culture is secure and expansive . . . [but they] suffer
> in times of cultural crisis and disintegration, when they receive
> blame for what goes wrong in society but are bypassed when
> people look for new ways to achieve social identity and loca-
> tion. So they looked good in the 1950s as they looked bad in
> the 1970s.[12]

Balmer and Winner support Marty's conclusion. They end their analysis by noting, "even though mainline Protestantism continued to embody the aspirations of middle-class Americans, as it had in the 1950s, Americans' allegiance to its denominations dropped precipitously in the final decades of the twentieth century."[13]

The factors of decline notwithstanding, there remain disagreements as to the degree of the decline in mainline churches.[14] The counter argument states that while the data used to measure the decline is accurate, it does not tell the full story. In other words, the analysis is missing essential elements not taken into account when calculating the data. According to historian E. Brooks Holifield, participation in congregations in the U.S.

11. Balmer and Winner, *Protestantism in America*, 194.

12 Marty, *A Nation of Behavers*, 71. It is worth noting, as summarized by Theo Hobson, that in parallel to the cultural shift is the theological shift taking place under the influence of Karl Barth, Dietrich Bonhoeffer, and others and that of their admirers who openly challenged the primacy of the liberal schools of thought. See Hobson, *Reinventing Liberal Christianity*.

13. Balmer and Winner, *Protestantism in America*, 195.

14. Michael Jinkins notes with a sense of irony, "the literature on the church's decline seems to be the only thing growing in North American Protestantism." Jinkins, *The Church Faces Death*, 12. In contrast to the estimation of Jinkins, Martyn Percy and Ian Markham see the "fact" of mainline church decline as insufficient to the "more nuanced" appreciation of how "some congregations which would designate themselves as liberal are spiritually vital and growing." Percy and Markham, *Why Liberal Churches Are Growing*, 3.

has remained relatively constant from the latter half of the eighteenth century to the present. During the 300 years of European settlement, from 35 to 40 percent of the population has actively participated in American congregations.[15] Sociologists Roger Finke and Rodney Stark concur with Holifield's general argument about the lack of decline in church participation, but go further in suggesting that religious adherence in mainline churches has actually increased over the years from 1776–2000. In their study of census records, denominational reports, and yearbooks of churches throughout the U.S. and Canada, Finke and Stark place the rate of religious adherence in the year 2000 as 40 percent higher than in 1776.[16] The decline noted by other scholars, Finke and Stark argue, is more representative of the measurement of religious *attitudes* than it is with an actual portrayal of the percentages of people who claim membership in a congregation or denomination.[17]

The results of this analysis have been challenged as simply another form of misreading data. For instance, Mark Chaves argues that what Finke and Stark fail to reveal is the shift in church practices relating to the measurement of congregational membership. Based upon the more restrictive practices of limiting church membership to those who meet specific criteria, practices that are more recent allow membership to a wider population and with fewer restrictions. Chaves notes, "Today, fewer people attend religious services than claim formal membership in religious congregations, but that situation was reversed earlier in our history".[18] Drawing on the scholarship of Robert Putnam,[19] Chaves argues

15. Holifield, "Toward a History of American Congregations," 24.

16. Stark and Finke, *The Churching of America, 1776–1990*, 22–23. Nancy Ammerman concurs with Holifield, Stark and Finke. She begins her analysis of American congregations by noting, "at the close of the twentieth century, the United States was, by all accounts, among the most religious of modern Western nations. In spite of high levels of education, technology, and mobility—long assumed to be harbingers of religious decline—almost all Americans said they believed in God, the vast majority identified with a particular religious tradition, well over half actually belonged to a local congregation, and somewhere between 25 and 40 percent of the population . . . showed up for services on any given weekend." See Ammerman, *Pillars of Faith*, 1.

17. Stark and Finke, *The Churching of America, 1776–1990*, 236.

18. Chaves, *Congregations in America*, 30.

19. In particular, Putnam, *Bowling Alone*. In his 2010 work, *American Grace*, Putnum confirms his earlier thesis about the decline in civic engagement, and in particular, religious observance. "Americans who came of age in the twenty-first century," Putnam notes, "are much more likely than Americans who came of age in the twentieth century to report lower church attendance than was true of their families

that when it comes to a whole range of civic and voluntary associations (including churches), "virtually every indicator of civic engagement currently available shows decline in the last third of the twentieth century".[20] In light of the conclusions of sociologists like Finke and Stark, Chaves continues that those wishing to maintain that religious participation has been stable over the last three or four decades "must explain how it could be that religious trends are so different from trends affecting virtually every other type of voluntary association".[21]

The question of the degree of decline remains active in scholarly debate. What remains uncontroversial, however, is that the data indicates a general shrinking of mainline denominational bodies. In light of decline, the pressing question has become, what can be done, and by whom? This and like questions have seen the increase of appeals to church growth and renewal within mainline traditions. A significant part of this appeal is the reliance by the leadership of these traditions on research and strategies that reflect the rationalized ends of the contemporary corporate culture, in particular: efficiency, calculability, predictability, and control.[22]

Responding to Decline with Organizational Strategies

The sociological and historical research that traces the declining trends within mainline churches details the *fact* of decline, but not responses to the decline. The corollary to this research is the work within the church by practitioners and researches who, almost since the advent of the decline, sought to appropriate resources, particularly from the social sciences (e.g., psychology, sociology, or organizational theory), in order to

---

when they were growing up, a pattern that confirms our conclusion that generational replacement is producing a slow but steady decline in religious observance." Putnam and Campbell, *American Grace*, 78–79.

20. Chaves, *Congregations in America*, 31.

21. Ibid., 32.

22. See Ritzer, *The McDonaldization of Society*. In this seminal work, Ritzer argues that the organizational methodology of companies like the fast-food chain McDonalds has become normative in most areas of human enterprise. Such practices, according to Ritzer, parallel Max Weber's thesis on bureaucracy as a form of the rationalization process. Efficiency, calculability, predictability, and control are the four dimensions of McDonaldization, which shape not only business practices, but also education, work, health care, politics, and the family. John Drane argues that Ritzer's thesis is also applicable to how the church organizes its life. See Drane, *The McDonaldization of the Church*; Drane, *After McDonaldization*.

provide specific advice or strategies for what steps a church or denomination should take to address the worrisome trend of decreasing church membership. Operating "on the ground," as it were, these practitioners and researchers focused on the particulars of congregational life often under the premise that sociological categories inherent to a congregation produce more accurate assessments of church life than theological categories alone.[23]

This new attention to congregational life has given rise to responses that seek to identify problems and solutions for the church that correspond to the logic and analysis of the social sciences. Writers such as Gilbert Rendle, Alice Mann, and Christopher Duraisingh, for example, come to the question of decline with conceptual and practical tools designed to assist individual congregations and entire denominations to find a new path for growth. For Rendle and Mann, the best hope for the church is the technique-based approach of formulating vision statements and exploring parish uniqueness;[24] for Duraisingh, hope is found through realigning the priorities of the church to reflect a more *missional* understanding of what the church is, and who the church is for.[25] Their contributions are part of the emerging field of Congregational Studies and will be examined in the remainder of this chapter.

Congregational Studies cannot be reduced to one single idea or practice; rather, it is a blanket term for a host of theories, practices and consultations that include leadership studies, parish evaluation, conflict management, planning and visioning, transitions, and vitality.[26] Books, videos, seminars, and a myriad of consultants form part of a growing field that has become the new standard for everything from theological training programs to parish retreats. The jargon and logic of leadership studies, the practices of management consultants, and the research of cultural studies at Diocesan conventions and around church "board meetings" is a sign of how prevalent the field of Congregational Studies has become.

---

23. Roberts, "Theology and the Social Sciences," 373.

24. Rendle and Mann, *Holy Conversations*.

25. Duraisingh, "From Church-Shaped Mission to Mission-Shaped Church."

26. James R. Nieman provides a working definition of congregational studies as, "the disciplined process for examining a congregation holistically that uses multiple research methods. . . . Fundamental to this approach is that the centrality and integrity of a congregation are preserved rather than the congregation being reduced to an illustration of a scholarly theory or an object for academic scrutiny." Nieman, "Congregational Studies," 133.

Proponents of Congregational Studies argue that this rise in popularity of more "practical" tools to address social and cultural changes facing the church is simply the counter-balance to what is considered the *academic* study of ecclesiology. There is a need, proponents suggest, for the church to adapt to new historical situations. As such, normative concepts of the church must interact with the "inculturated life" of its members.[27]

Theorists and practitioners within Congregational Studies agree that the historical situation of the contemporary church has given rise to the need for church practice and structures to be reexamined. According to Fredric Roberts, churches in the United States, "are suffering from a collective anxiety attack."[28] In his work, *Be not Afraid!*, Roberts diagnoses this "anxiety attack" of the church, specifically mainline churches, to be the result of the growing generation gap in church attendance, the cultural irrelevance of parish life and practice, and the rise of non-denominational "megachurches" that are attracting people due to their ability to "contemporize" worship forms, gathering space, and program offerings. Daniel Smith and Mary Sellon concur with Roberts's assessment and add that such declines in congregations are a sign that church members in mainline church settings have learned only to "share their church rather than their faith."[29] The authors continue: the decline is a sign of a people-led church, and not a "Spirit-led church."[30]

From Roberts's notion of a "collective anxiety attack" and the kind of concern voiced by Smith and Sellon emerges a response to decline that includes attention to congregational uniqueness and identity, communal-shaped planning that is effective, and a renewal of church leaders who think strategically about the management of time, resources, and people. These responses form a kind of practical "tool-kit" that can be applied to a church regardless of location, size, or denominational identification. To understand how that "tool-kit" can be deployed under such various conditions, it is worth examining how each piece is meant to operate.

First, uniqueness as the goal for a parish is a notion well accepted by proponents of a Congregational Studies approach to the church. Roberts,

27. Haight and Nieman, "On the Dynamic Relation between Ecclesiology and Congregational Studies," 578. For Haight and Nieman, Congregational Studies, as a specific and concrete historical approach to the church, "provides the antidote to the theological reductionism" explicit in more formal theological accounts of the church.

28. Roberts, *Be Not Afraid!*, 1.

29 Smith and Sellon, *Pathway to Renewal*, 21.

30. Ibid., 22.

for instance, argues that an individual church in search of a revitalized future must take the following points to heart. Honoring uniqueness means knowing who you are (as a congregation and denomination); knowing what you believe and why you believe it; and integrating your shared history and beliefs into all dimensions of the collective life of the parish: organizational, liturgical, pastoral, and outreach.[31]

The process of identifying the unique character of a particular parish is, according to Janet Cawley, the necessary first step towards change. Congregational identity, Cawley notes, is like personal identity: in order for a person to change, they must learn the skills of self-knowledge. Cawley maintains that:

> The search for a comprehensive statement of identity that the whole congregation can understand and buy into continues because a congregation that knows its identity, like a person who knows himself or herself, can be flexible, open to considering change, and open to responding to the promptings of the Holy Spirit with new initiatives.[32]

Whereas some congregations are satisfied with a false identity—a mistaken understanding of whom they are and the conditions under which they live—the sign of a healthy church is an openness to what makes a congregation unique and distinct from all others.[33] Gilbert Rendle and Alice Mann go as far as associating openness to parish identity with the genealogies of Jesus in Matthew's and Luke's Gospels. There Jesus's genealogy is aired for all to see, thereby clarifying who Jesus is. Rendle and Mann note: "to be authentic is to know and accept the self, to use our identified strengths and to acknowledge those parts of us that are limited and incomplete".[34] If the Gospels are clear about Jesus's identity and his uniqueness, Rendle and Mann suggest, surely the church would want the same?

A constituent element of defining a parish identity is the practice of creating a mission and/or vision statement. "Faith communities," asserts Lynne Baab, "have particular values and emphases."[35] According to Baab, these values function like the DNA of a congregation. The task of

31 Roberts, *Be Not Afraid!*, 2.

32 Cawley, *Who Is Our Church?* 8.

33. Ibid., 5.

34. Rendle and Mann, *Holy Conversations*, 18.

35. Baab, "Myths."

identifying the values and emphases of a congregation is something in which the entire congregation participates. Gilbert and Mann speak of the "vision process" as a "holy conversation." Visioning, they contend, is "a structured conversation by a group of people about what they believe God is calling them to be or to do."[36] The emphasis on structured conversation is important, for the methodology behind creating a vision statement follows a set pattern of collecting demographic data from the parishioners and the immediate community, asking questions about the context of the parish in relation to other local faith and non-faith organizations, and identifying measurable areas of strength within the programs and interests of the parish community.[37] Baab summarizes the methodology of visioning as asking of a congregation: who are we and what are we about?[38]

The actual makeup of a mission and/or vision statement helps expound the process that precedes its final writing and adoption by a congregation. Mission and vision statements are common ingredients in organizational identity, from the transnational shoe manufacturer Nike[39] to Dillanos Coffee Roaster[40] in the small town of Sumner, Washington State. The adoption of mission statements for individual churches has followed the general trend set by corporations and companies worldwide. Mission statements are meant to reflect the very substance and hopes of the organization in question. Gilbert and Mann list two components to a mission statement that help make the statement more than just a loose definition of corporate identity. When it comes to congregational identity, a mission statement is ideally *axiomatic* and *unique*. It is axiomatic in that it states little more than a general description or definition of what can be expected from a congregation in a particular tradition. For example, church traditions that give precedence to the inerrancy of Scripture or the full inclusion of gay and lesbian parishioners will include language that communicates such a general position. The point is to present characteristics that represent where the congregations fit within the ecclesial landscape.

36. Rendle and Mann, *Holy Conversations*, xviii.
37. Roberts, *Be Not Afraid!*, 23–25.
38. Baab, "Myths."
39. "To bring inspiration and innovation to every athlete in the world."
40. "Help people, make friends, have fun."

Next, having noted a general description, the second component of a mission statement is the description of what makes a particular congregation unique from other churches, even churches within its own tradition or denomination. Descriptions of the historic character of a church or a focus on ministry with youth are examples of the uniqueness that a specific parish might choose to emphasize. According to Gilbert and Mann, the mission statement "states what is important to the particular congregation because of who it is, where it is located, and the historical moment it is in—what separates it from others."[41]

In the process of delineating the uniqueness of the congregation, the "holy conversation" within the congregation is designed so that specific objectives and goals for the current and future life of the parish will emerge. Focusing on established objectives and goals by the entire congregation is how a declining church can incorporate a strategy towards effective communal-shaped planning. Objectives, note Gilbert and Mann, state what the congregation and its leaders must commit themselves to do or to be in order to address the unique future being shaped. Goals, then, state how the congregation will accomplish those objectives.[42] For the goals to prove helpful, they must be specific, measurable, attainable, relevant, and time-bound. In other words, the objectives and goals must flow out of the uniqueness of the parish and establish in clear and unambiguous terms the direction that parish will take in the future. It is critical for congregations to have a clear and realistic sense of their identity with appropriate goals, argues Janet Cawley, if they are ever to engage in effective planning.[43]

Loren Mead and Billie Alban agree with Crawley, but they add that clarity of vision is not enough. A new direction for a congregation, Mead and Alban argue, is insufficient, "unless the processes and procedures of the organization itself are realigned toward the new direction".[44] In their

41. Rendle and Mann, *Holy Conversations*, 85. Moreover, the entire practice of creating mission statements is seen to bolster the legitimacy of the church to people familiar with contemporary corporate practices.

42 Ibid., 86.

43. Cawley, *Who Is Our Church?* 95. Kennon Callahan captures Cawley's emphasis on planning, and links it to a theology of providence, when he states, "God's promise draws us toward our future with compassion and certainty. The diagnostic, strategic, and responsibly hopeful dynamics of the approach here to long-range planning make it most effective in helping local congregations to move decisively forward." Callahan, *Twelve Keys to an Effective Church*, xi.

44. Mead and Alban, *Creating the Future Together*, 39.

work in Congregational Studies, Smith and Sellon attempt to provide a plan for the kind of congregational realignment that Mead and Alban suggest. Taking the agreed-upon process of establishing a vision with objectives and goals, Smith and Sellon broaden it into a strategy for congregational renewal. Effective planning is more than the follow-up step to defining a mission; it is fundamental to addressing the kind of change that a community experiences as a result of establishing a vision and declaring a unique identity. The acceptance of renewal, the authors note, is crucial for a congregation open to revitalization in the face of the "collective anxiety attack" of churches living in the current cultural milieu. Drawing on the insights of appreciative inquiry,[45] Smith and Sellon list five steps for effective planning that ought to be used regularly in the organizational life of a parish: develop a clear sense of what you want to achieve and a commitment to achieve it, honestly assess where you're starting from, design steps that will move you from where you are to where you want to be; take those steps, and assess whether your actions are getting you where you want to go and then make adjustments as needed.[46]

The sequencing of these steps makes good organizational sense, but according to the authors, it also makes good theological sense. "God is always inviting a congregation to step into a new future," Smith and Sellon state. "God also invites people to discover and design anew the processes for getting there."[47] This idea is deepened a few pages later: "renewal planning is an intentional joining with God in God's continuing process of creation to bring new hope and healing to the world."[48] The linking of effective planning with God's work of creating solidifies the priority the local congregation has as the principle site of God's work. A well-organized church with a clear mission and measurable goals is, according to the rationale of Smith and Sellon, a witness to the manner of God's creating and a foretaste to a God-ordained future.

45. A method of organizational analysis originating in the work of David Cooperrider and Suresh Srivastva. Appreciative Inquiry (AI), "involves systematic discovery of what gives 'life' to a living system when it is most alive, most effective, and most constructively capable in economic, ecological, and human." Cooperrider and Whitney, *Appreciative Inquiry a Positive Revolution in Change*, 319.

46. Smith and Sellon, *Pathway to Renewal*, 141.

47. Ibid., 136.

48. Ibid., 40.

The task of guiding a congregation through visioning and planning is something that involves the entire parish; it is designed to be a "holy conversation," according to Rendle and Mann. Yet even a *holy* conversation requires specific people in the organization who are tasked with leading. What kind of leadership does the congregation need in order for renewal to take place? Congregational Studies writers and practitioners offer several suggestions.

In the estimation of Thomas Bandy, "old Christendom" with its generalized tasks to preach, administer the sacraments, and pander to rich people is over, as he has it. The only appropriate form of leadership for the contemporary congregation is, Bandy maintains, that of *entrepreneur.*[49] The entrepreneur, Bandy argues, takes responsibility for customizing their learning track for their own life-context and goals. Entrepreneurs occupy a "world of story, mentoring, irrational experience and risk-taking,"[50] a world that is now thoroughly "post-Christian," which realigns the focus of training for church leaders from ecclesial concerns to "missional" practices.[51] Bandy goes as far as to suggest that the traditional model of seminary training is inadequate for the task of training leaders for post-Christendom. "You need knowledge and skills that simply are not recognized, taught, or even on the 'radar screen' of any single denomination or seminary."[52] Congregational context, or what Bandy refers to as the specific 'micro-culture' of a parish, is the single greatest concern for the entrepreneur minister.[53] Hiring and developing such leaders, Jim Lundholm-Eades notes, is key to "best practices" for church management and the continual mission of the church.[54]

49. Bandy, *Mission Mover*, 34. In recent years, Michael Jinkins contends, the interest in entrepreneurship has provided many churches with "the most persuasive interpretive filter through which matters of evangelism are understood. Thus the church's growth or decline is frequently understood in terms of market forces and product appeal." Jinkins, *The Church Faces Death*, 13.

50. Bandy, *Mission Mover*, 47.

51. Ibid., 99.

52. Ibid., 73.

53. In a similar vein, Stephanie Spellers refers to the need for "Relational Evangelists" in the church: those who shape an entire culture of leadership through attention to the context and incarnational reality of each church. Such a "Relational Evangelist" embraces transformation and organizes action around people's passions and gifts. See Spellers, "The Church Awake," 38–40.

54. Lundholm-Eades, "Best Practices in Church Management," 16. Also, Frank, "Leadership and Administration," 117–20. Frank refers to "church leadership" as an

The re-development of church leadership along entrepreneurial lines is linked to the call for more attention to be placed on how church leaders are ultimately church *managers*. As John Wimberly Jr., writes, "The church IS a business, make no mistake about it."[55] Wimberly continues: "If we want to maximize our ministry, we need to increase our efficiency as managers."[56] This is echoed in the influential work of Robert White, who was part of a larger effort to advocate for church pastors to embrace their role as managers. "Any textbook on organizational effectiveness will tell you," White states, "that a clear definition of executive authority and responsibility within an organizational framework is essential."[57] White's central argument is that a church without a pastor-manager is one doomed to collapse under a lack of appropriate leadership.[58] Towards the end of the twentieth century, this "executive" ministry model made a deep impact on ecclesial imagination with the emergence of the previously noted "megachurches." Willow Creek, situated in the suburbs of Chicago, serves as an example of a church that early on implemented the role of management and corporate practices in their operation as a congregation, and identified such implementation as a source of their growth and success.[59]

The adoption of managerial practices by proponents of a congregational study approach to the church is not generally as explicit as the example of Willow Creek. Smith and Sellon, for instance, distance themselves from overt use of business practices in congregational settings, yet they nevertheless stress the role of business-like strategies, decision-making processes, and evaluative schematics in their formulation of parish regeneration.[60] John Wimberly identifies these practices, along with limiting risk and maximizing personal and financial resources, as key to effective church management. "To fully maximize the vision and allow the peace of Christ to manifest itself in the lives of congregations," Wimberly notes, "managers need to pay close attention to the systemic inputs of people, facilities, and money that generate the ministry outputs

---

"enormous industry" that reflects, particularly in the U.S., the "success story" narrative of the likes of "experts" such as Rick Warren, Bill Hybels, and Ken Blanchard.

55. Wimberly, Jr., "The Challenges of Incarnational Life."

56. Ibid.

57. White, *Managing Today's Church*, 11.

58. Ibid., 13.

59. "Churches as Businesses"; Chaves, "Supersized," 23.

60. Smith and Sellon, *Pathway to Renewal*, 11.

God calls on congregations to produce."[61] Elsewhere, Wimberly refers to management in the church as "rooted in the incarnational aspect of our life"; it is a "holy calling."[62] To deny the place of management in the life of the congregation is, following Wimberly, to deny that money, logistics, people and power are part of being human; the same humanity that Jesus embraced in coming amongst us as God in the flesh.[63]

In summary, what Roberts, Smith and Sellon, and Wimberly announce in their work is that the best hope for a declining church is exercised through deploying the "tool-kit" of practices related to *congregational uniqueness, entrepreneurial leadership*, and *management-inspired techniques*. Such values draw on the "best practices" of modern organizations and are, in the estimation of these and like-minded practitioners, appropriate and necessary for churches who wish to adapt to the emerging social imaginary that constitutes the modern West. The church needs to respond, Roberts concludes, to recognize the unique place of the church in cities, towns, and suburbs, and the productive and realistic ways the local congregation can be renewed.[64]

Responding to Decline through Appeals to Mission

The technique and business-like method is one of the leading approaches put forward by proponents within Congregational Studies. The other comes to the question of decline by way of privileging certain features of the life of the church. This approach, exemplified in a number of writers and practitioners within mainline denominations, seeks to emphasize the general direction the church should take through giving attention to the organizing principle of *mission*.

---

61. Wimberly, Jr., *The Business of the Church*, 143.

62. Ibid., 144.

63. Ibid., 145. William Hoyt refers to effective church management as knowing "the story in the stats," a story, Hoyt contends, that is ultimately the story of what God is doing through a particular church. Hoyt argues, accurately counting the right things can profoundly impact ministry effectiveness. "Knowing 'the story in the stats' can help inform ministry decisions and lead us to do the most important things that produce the results that most please our Lord. Gathering and studying the right numbers can help us wisely invest our church's resources of time, effort, people, money, and facilities." Hoyt, *Effectiveness by the Numbers*, xvi.

64. Roberts, *Be Not Afraid!*, 179.

In an address to the 2009 General Convention of the Episcopal Church in the United States, the Presiding Bishop, Katharine Jefferts Schori, spoke directly to the challenge of being in a dwindling denomination. "The heart of this church will slowly turn to stone if we think our primary mission work is to those already in the pews inside our beautiful churches, or to those at other altars," Jefferts Schori declared,

> We are in cardiac crisis if we think we can close the doors, swing our incense and sing our hymns, and all will be right with the world. The heart of this body is mission. . . . Every time we gather, the Spirit offers a pacemaker jolt to tweak the rhythm of this heart. The challenge is whether or not . . . the muscle will respond with a strengthened beat, sending more life out into the world. . . . Can you hear the heartbeat? Mission, Mission, Mission.[65]

The emphasis on "mission" offers an apparent corrective to a focus of energy on the inner life of the church, what Fred Hiltz calls a shift in perspective from a culture of institutional *membership* to a culture of radical *discipleship*.[66] Such a shift in culture begins with a reevaluation of what constitutes the primary work of the church. If, as Jefferts Schori suggests, the work of the church is in mission, what might this work look like?

According to Christopher Duraisingh, a "mission-shaped" church is attentive first to where the Spirit of God is leading the church, as opposed to what the Spirit of God has contributed in the past. This shift is also designed to move the concept of mission out from the colonializing history that church mission is often attached, to a broader vision of mission that recognizes the world of the church to include the local community as much as the foreign country. In a time of an accelerating suspicion of institutional religion in a post-Christendom culture, the church needs to be a diversity of structures and modes. A renewed sense of what and where the "mission field" is occupies the heart of the *Mission-Shaped*

65. Quoted in Duraisingh, "From Church-Shaped Mission to Mission-Shaped Church," 8.

66. Hiltz, "Go to the World! Go Struggle, Bless, and Pray," 307. The shift that Hiltz refers is a particular challenge within mainline Christian traditions where the task of recruiting is less urgent in light of a more inclusive understanding of God's salvation. As Martyn Percy notes, if a less urgent understanding of salvation "is also coupled with a sense that the tradition is hesitant about articulating ultimate truths, and must also allow for individual freedom, then the missionary task becomes more complex." Percy, *Shaping the Church*, 97.

Church Report and "Fresh Expressions" movement in the UK. "The essential aspect of church is its missionary nature," a recent report from the Church of England contends, "a fresh movement of the Spirit [as expressed in its] prayer, outgoing love, and evangelism in obedience to our Lord's command. . . . If the Church is not missionary, it has denied itself and its calling, for it has departed from the very nature of God."[67] Consequently, the identity of the church is inseparable from its mission: a mission of praying, practicing, and going forth in love to heal, reconcile, and make known the "always-breaking-in" reign of God.

Duraisingh identifies the second task for the "mission-shaped" church to be developing habits of awareness for where the "reign of God" is present in the community of the church, rather than expending energy and time in the kind of activities associated with "mission projects" to other countries. Such projects, suggests Duraisingh, consume extraordinary resources of the church that could be better invested in identifying training for congregations to further their involvement in the immediate community. In place of projects, Stephanie Spellers suggests, the church should invest in the building of habits around "radical welcome." "We pursue God's mission," Spellers argues, "whenever we move toward justice and mutuality in Christian community . . . bringing new life to the margins, [through] radically welcoming each other to bring our whole selves before God."[68] The place of radical welcome shifts the focus from the work of mission being an external event in the life of the church, to mission being what happens when the church offers hospitality to its neighbors.

Finally, new forms and practices of the church ought to be explored in light of shifting values within the context where the church is situated. This, Duraisingh suggests, is the most challenging of the directives in that it asks clergy and congregations to emphasize the perceived needs outside the church over the maintenance of the community that already identifies with the church.[69] No longer does one size fit all. The market, the *Mission-Shaped Church* report emphasizes, requires diverse forms of church, including cell church, in which committed relationships can develop outside the established walls of the church.[70] To forfeit this mis-

67. *Mission-Shaped Church*, 41.

68. Spellers, "The Church Awake," 33.

69. Duraisingh, "From Church-Shaped Mission to Mission-Shaped Church," 12–13.

70. *Mission-Shaped Church*, 54.

sional approach is, for Duraisingh, to risk losing the ecclesial character that most defines the purpose and orientation of the church.[71]

A central tenet to the missional understanding of the church derives from what Martyn Percy refers to as the "ecclesial *terroir*" for each individual parish. *Terroir*, a term usually reserved for the wine industry, refers to the combination of factors (e.g., soil variety, altitude, microclimate) that make one wine from one region different from other wines from other regions. When applied to the church, the *terroir* defines the history and ethos of a church, its stories, buildings, forms of organization, and ecclesial and theological accents. "The 'ecclesial *terroir*,'" Percy notes, "is something that a minister needs to be able to read sensitively and deeply if they are to cultivate congregational life and offer connected parochial ministry."[72] Referencing what this sensitivity means for clergy, Percy argues for a shift in education for ministers that provides

> deeper forms of discernment that enable ministers to move beyond the surface or presenting task of demand-led organization, and make time and space to read each congregation and parish as a semi-discrete but related locally distinctive expression of Christian faith.[73]

Percy's construal of an ecclesial *terroir* reflects, at one level, the notion of the missional-focused approach to the church wherein a fundamental shift is required in the face of decline away from large-scale denominational plans and towards renewing the distinctive characteristics of the local congregation. In similar vein to the concept of congregational uniqueness and effective communal-shaped planning explored in the previous section, proponents of the missional approach hold that each church has its own unique setting and surrounding community in which practices such as "radical welcome" and community-focused ministry can be applied. The idea is that these practices are universal in their applicability, and when taken up by a parish as an organizing principle,

71. Duraisingh, "From Church-Shaped Mission to Mission-Shaped Church," 28. In a similar vein to Duraisingh, church historian, Diana Butler Bass, refers to the likes of Dietrich Bonhoeffer, Howard Thurman, Oscar Romero, and Henri Nouwen as those who, "pushed away obstacles that constricted the flow of faith, creating wide channels for God's spirit." These figures, Bass contends, are the exemplar's for a church that commits to the kind of missional work that Duraisingh suggests as vital. See Bass, *A People's History of Christianity*, 293.

72. Percy, *Shaping the Church*, 103.

73. Ibid.

will shape the identity and purpose of that parish to reflect the unique "mission field" of the parish. What is required is that the church realign its priorities and common life to meet the criterion of mission, and in doing so, become a unique missional community.[74]

The two approaches of response to church decline explored in this chapter—one more technique-oriented, the other demographic and sociological—represent two general trends by practitioners and researchers to develop tools and trajectories for the church to address the fact of decline. In both cases, the question of decline is answered through reconfiguring the means and structures of how the contemporary church operates. In addition, in both cases, following the prescribed outline of thinking and strategies is essential for a sustainable future for the church. The differences in how these responses move towards this future are not insignificant, yet there exists a unifying thread that binds the two. The central questions of these approaches are these: *what is the most efficient and sustainable mode for a growing and thriving church? And what tools are necessary for this end?*[75]

The desire for a sustainable church *is* crucial for any account that takes seriously the pressures and fears that often accompany shrinking communities. Tools to attend the pressures and fears *are*, therefore, an important part of a response to decline. Likewise, attending to the shape mission takes in how the church both negotiates a complicated world and practices Christian hospitality and discipleship is critical to how the church remains faithful to the tenets of the gospel.[76] Yet, it is precisely

74. David Roozen and Kirk Hadaway align the move to a more contextualized understanding of the church with the growth in some mainline churches around particular demographics. Using the title, "niche churches," Roozen and Hadaway mention the growth in congregations that focus primarily on the gay/lesbian community, the deaf community, or particular racial/ethnic groups. See Hadaway and Roozen, *Rerouting the Protestant Mainstream*, 81.

75. The emphasis on *effectiveness* in the work of congregational studies parallels the logic of contemporary organizational theory, and in turn, the shift to forms of Weberian rationality that act as justification for how an organization measures its purpose and identity. Theorist, John Ladd, summarizes this logic well: "the sole standard for the evaluation of an organization, its activities and its decisions, is its effectiveness in achieving its objectives[;] . . . this kind of effectiveness is called rationality." Ladd, "Morality and the Ideal of Rationality in Formal Organizations," 504. This logic will be explored in chapter 3.

76 See, Wells, *A Nazareth Manifesto*. Wells argues that the mission of the church ought to reflect the mission of God as revealed in Jesus, that is, to be "God with us" (Emmanuel). In contrast to the modes of mission that have sought practicing "working

in the midst of fears and pressures that Christians need to employ caution before accepting too quickly programs and approaches that stipulate a successful way forward through the adoption of methodologies and practices oriented to particular goals that may, under analysis, prove to be at odds with the goals of the church. As such, how the church responds under declining conditions warrants a conceptual analysis of precisely how sustainability is imagined, and what assumptions are "taken on" in the process. If, as these approaches contend, the best way forward for the church is through the realignment of priorities, or the adoption of new strategies for growth, then a number of questions arise: what are the assumptions that these priorities and strategies employ, and how do these methods contribute to an understanding of what the church is, and what the church is for? It is to this analysis that we now turn.

---

with," "working for," and "being for" when it comes to the church engagement with the world, the mode of engagement most evident in scripture is "being with," as companions and friends who together benefit from God being with us in Jesus. The mode of "being with," according to Wells, transforms the social actions and evangelism of the church from solving problems to imitating the primary way God interacts with humanity and the creation. "Being with," Wells concludes, is always the default of any social initiative, which may then be modified as circumstances and opportunities dictate.

2

"We are All Managers Now": The Church and Management

THE TECHNIQUE-ORIENTED AND MISSIONAL-FOCUSED responses to church decline are constructive attempts to discover and articulate a path to a more sustainable and growing church. In the context of what Thomas Franks calls the "rhetoric of crises," such responses can be viewed as entirely beneficial to the ecclesial enterprise. In language familiar to a church framework, and with conceptual tools sourced from the latest managerial manual, the work performed by those who employ technique-based and missional-focused approaches to the church allies with the concerns around church decline with a promise of a more effective and sustainable church if the proper techniques or organizational realignments are deployed.

Notwithstanding the practical efforts of the technique and missional approaches, questions arise when such work is placed under theological scrutiny. In particular, the logic of both the technique and missional approaches privileges the pragmatic question of what *works* to make the church grow or be more sustainable. Whereas a more theologically oriented question asks: *is the technique or approach true to the nature and character of the church?* The attention of recent approaches to church sustainability is to questions relating to effectiveness, predictability, and control. Such attention to generic goals demonstrates a set of assumptions concerning an understanding of the church, assumptions that correlate with the emergence of a bureaucratic or instrumentalized managerial rationality through the increase and proliferation of training and manuals that maps means to predetermined ends (e.g., growth,

38

survival, or influence) through the implementation of particular ratio-nalized strategies.[1] This emergence of an instrumentalized managerial rationality that privileges the organizational character of the church is a form of what Willard Enteman refers to as the *ideology of managerialism.*[2]

The notion of "managerialism" derives from the function of people fulfilling the role of manager (i.e., those within corporations who "man-age" or provide leadership to marketing, strategy, and finance) by employ-ing practices related to the coordination of knowledge and relationships toward the common goals of efficiency, effectiveness, predictability, and control. Management becomes managerialism when the job function, and the coordination of knowledge and relationships, become a form of col-lective social control that shapes the thought and action within any sector of society, including business, but extending into education, government, and not-for-profits.[3] As a form of collective social control, managerialism is exercised explicitly by treating all social bodies as requiring the nec-essary management in order to grow, survive, or exert social influence. Managerialism assumes that in all societies all productive processes that constitute society are in need of coordination and management.

In the estimation of Martin Parker, managerialism maintains an influence by offering tools and techniques that are designed to protect people and organizations against chaos and inefficiencies through the civilizing process of ordering. Parker identifies the three coordinating assumptions of managerialism as the need to control nature, the need to

1. Instrumental reasoning (or rationality) is a phrase usually associated with Max Weber and the critical theory of the first generation of the Frankfurt School. Charles Taylor defines "instrumental reason" as "the kind of rationality we draw on when we calculate the most economical application of means to a given end. Maximum efficiency, the best cost-output ratio, is its measure of success." Taylor, *The Ethics of Authenticity*, 5. Weber's use of such rationality and its implications for managerialism is explored in chapter 4.

2. See Enteman, *Managerialism*, 154; Diefenbach, *Management and the Domi-nance of Managers*, 124; Anthony, "Management Ideology"; Klikauer, *Managerialism*. For the purposes of this study, an ideology is defined as a comprehensive vision, a way of looking at things. It provides a worldview phrased as a set of ideas that are proposed by a dominant class or group. As Rahel Jaeggi outlined, "ideologies are the means by which the predominant situation is instilled in the hearts and minds of the individual." Jaeggi, "Rethinking Ideology," 64.

3. Parker, *Against Management*, 9. In the estimation of Thomas Diefenbach, "Man-agement is everywhere; managerial bureaucracies are now to be found in government, in the City, the Church, the multinationals, the armed forces, the universities, the busi-ness corporations and every sector of public life" (p. 1). See Diefenbach, *Management and the Dominance of Managers*.

control human beings, and an increasing need to control organizational abilities.[4]

Control over nature names the belief that social progress is equivalent to the ability of humans to place increasingly tighter limits on the natural world, which, in the logic of managerialism, is defined by disorder and chance. The story of the natural order is one of a long struggle against adversity, of the attempts to survive in the face of crop failures, floods, and diseases.[5] In light of technological advancements, so the story goes, humans are now capable of understanding and organizing the world to the point of making "nature" subject to the management of human beings. Management is the key element to a progressive attitude that allows for an increase in the sum total of control that humans employ over the world and its resources.[6]

A second assumption of managerialism is that human beings themselves are a source of disorder in a world that is already assumed to lean towards chaos. Whereas the first assumption addressed the external world, the second is concerned to order the "internal" nature of humans, which is thought to have a propensity towards irrationalism. The goal of ordering human nature is to make it more amenable to the world of objective facts and calculable futures. The rise of industrial psychology and organizational sociology, Parker maintains, has provided theories of motivation and accounts of "best practices" that are deployed within institutions in order to harmonize individual natures with collective betterment.[7]

Parker's third assumption is that modern forms of management provide an alternative to the social organization of earlier societies where it is thought that autocracy and primitivism kept people in general, and workers in particular, in various forms of social and economic bondage.

4. Parker, *Against Management*, 2.

5. Such control is evident, economist E. F. Schumacher notes, in the way contemporary society sets itself apart from the natural world, seeking instead to dominate and conquer it. See Schumacher, *Small Is Beautiful*, 14–21.

6. Parker, *Against Management*, 3. Thomas Klikauer notes that "the mantra of management studies is not critical thinking or historical hermeneutics but the control of nature, markets, corporations, and humans now termed human resources" Klikauer, *Managerialism*, 14. Parker and Klikauers' assumptions sound a particularly Hobbesian tone, in that the role of management echoes the role of the sovereign political body over the people, what Hobbes refers to as "a common power to keep them all in awe." Hobbes, *Leviathan*, 84.

7. Parker, *Against Management*, 4.

Managerialism, on the other hand, is thought to be democratic and transparent, premised on the notion that an efficient ordering of people and things is what makes the achievement of collective goals possible. Under the "new order" of managerialism, accountability is maintained, human energy reserved, and economic progress is made available to all. "When the cruel autocrat becomes the responsible manager," Parker notes, "the greatest good of the greatest number will be achieved."[8]

Managerialism stipulates that there is no social body that should not be managed, and assumes that there is no purpose for social bodies other than increased functionality and survival. Inherent is the belief that management provides a solution to the social, political, and economic challenges in society, and further, it operates with knowledge and expertise disguised as impartial and objective.[9] Where managerialism is dominant, its ideology is made to appear as common sense and requires no further explanation. Moreover, managerialism maintains that as long as there is *dis*organization in society, there will need to be greater amounts of organizational analysis and structures.[10] At its basis, managerialism is primarily concerned with offering a set of methods, rationales, and activities to solve problems.[11]

The assumptions of managerialism have come under mounting critique from Parker, Enteman, and others as part of a growing concern with the increasing privilege managerial strategies have in business and non-business spheres. Such critique extends to scholars concerned to name the implicit authority given to managerialism in the church, and the further concern with how such authority orders ecclesiology towards rationalizing practices that have the potential of aligning the identity and purpose of the church with the implicit ends of a managerial logic.

What follows is a survey of three critical approaches to managerialism that seek to elucidate the rationale and impact of a managerial logic, particularly in light of the commitments of the church. Alasdair MacIntyre, while not directly addressing the church, provides an influential appraisal of managerialism through an analysis of what he refers to as the "character" of the "Manager." Next, the work of Stephen Pattison

8. Ibid.

9. Christopher Grey notes that, "the activities classically thought of as 'managerial' are in fact performed by all sorts of people in all sorts of contexts, both in and outside the workplace." Grey, "'We Are All Managers Now'; 'We Always Were,'" 562.

10. Parker, *Against Management*, 62.

11. Diefenbach, *Management and the Dominance of Managers*, 11.

and Claire Watkins represents an attempt to reconcile the kind of critique offered by MacIntyre with an analysis of the constituent practices within the modern managed organization. Pattison, in particular, recognizes the implicit claims of managerialism proving potentially corrupting to how the church understands her mission. Yet, he goes on to recognize the fact of management as being too solid to dismantle either in society or in the church. He notes, "the rise of managerialism in the Churches is inevitable, unstoppable and, in many ways, desirable."[12] The third approach belongs to thinkers who evaluate the rise of managerialism in the church as something like a betrayal to a more theologically coherent mission and identity.[13] Richard Roberts, Michael Budde, and John Milbank are representative of those who give such an account of managerialism's systemic hold on contemporary Western ecclesiology. It is to an exposition of these three approaches that we now turn.

The Manager as Modern Identity

In *After Virtue*, Alasdair MacIntyre provides a penetrating critique of managerialism through his analysis of managerial values. These values have emerged in the context of a "declining moral landscape" in the West, a context where social relations have become uprooted from the more solidaristic and harmonious relations of previous ages. Thick, premodern forms of social identity are now dislocated by morally thinner understandings of social order that reflect the atomistic individualism of modernity. As a result, normative consensus about the meaning and purpose of social identity and social good have been supplanted by the normalizing of disagreements about such identity and good to the point where no such consensus is deemed possible. Instead of a morally rich environment of shared conceptions of societal good and individual purpose, the modern West has settled for an *emotivist* doctrine whereby claims for what constitutes human good and societal benefit are a matter of choosing between rival moral claims all of which are grounded in personal preference.[14]

12. Pattison, *The Faith of the Managers*, 159.

13. Roberts, *Religion, Theology and the Human Sciences*, 164.

14. MacIntyre, *After Virtue*, 11. Emotivism, according to MacIntyre, "is the doctrine that all evaluative judgments and more specifically all moral judgments are *nothing but* expressions of preference, expressions of attitude or feeling, insofar as they are moral or evaluative in character" (p. 12, emphasis in original). For the emotivist,

MacIntyre acknowledges that these debates and disagreements are often informed by logic; the conclusions do indeed follow from the premises. But, he claims, modernity operates out of rival premises and society possesses no rational way of weighing the claims of one premise against another, and it is precisely because there is in society no established way of deciding between these claims that moral debate is unremitting. Hence, "all moral, indeed all evaluative, argument is and always must be rationally interminable".[15] Because moral discourse has therefore become the expression of individual preferences, incapable of rational consensus, practical reason has come to be equated with the instrumental reason of bureaucratic institutions, the choice of efficient means to arbitrarily chosen ends. Whatever the mutual antagonism between individualism and bureaucratic impersonality, MacIntyre argues, they are dialectical opposites that thrive off one another.[16] Moreover, they do so to most telling effect in, what MacIntyre refers to as, the "character" of the "Manager."

The question of what constitutes emotivism, and what such a doctrine actually looks like in the character of the Manager, is addressed by MacIntyre in relation to his discussion on the conception and practice of social relations. MacIntyre argues that emotivism's primary requirement is "the obliteration of any genuine distinction between manipulative and non-manipulative social relations."[17] According to him, emotivist moral philosophy regards moral discussion as nothing more than an attempt by one party to alter the preferences and opinions of another party so that they accord with their own, regardless of the means deployed to effect this change.

By collapsing the distinction between personal and impersonal reasons, emotivism undermines the possibility of treating persons as ends in themselves. MacIntyre notes, "To treat someone as an end is to offer them what I take to be good reasons for acting in one way rather than another, but to leave it to them to evaluate those reasons."[18] For emotivism, how-

---

saying that an act is right or wrong was thus supposed to be rather like saying "Boo!" or "Hooray!" For a classic exposition of emotivism, see chapter 6 of Ayer, *Language, Truth and Logic.* For a critical account of MacIntyre's argument against emotivism, in particular, MacIntyre's conflation of the words *use* and *meaning* in reference to emotivism, see, Mulhall, "Liberalism, Morality and Rationality."

15. MacIntyre, *After Virtue*, 11.

16. Ibid., 35.

17. Ibid., 23.

18. Ibid.

ever, no moral debate can be anything other than an attempt by one party to make another party an instrument of their own purposes "by adducing whatever influences will in fact be effective on this or that occasion."[19]

In order to show what the world looks like through emotivist eyes, MacIntyre proceeds to describe three central "characters" of modern culture, each of whom embodies the obliteration of the distinction between manipulative and non-manipulative relations in a particular way. MacIntyre uses the term "character" to refer to the fusion of a specific role with a specific personality type that he takes to be emblematic of modernity. Characters are not to be confused with social roles in general. As MacIntyre sees it, "they are a very special type of social role which places a certain kind of moral constraint on the personality of those who inhabit them in a way in which many other social roles do not."[20] The three central characters of the emotivist culture are the Aesthete, the Therapist, and the Manager.[21]

The Aesthete regards the social world as an arena for the satisfaction of his or her own desires, and social relations as occasions for contriving behavior in others that will be responsive to his or her wishes. The Therapist is similarly disinclined to treat people as ends in themselves, concentrating rather on techniques through which neurotic symptoms can be effectively transformed into "directed energy" and "maladjusted individuals into well-adjusted ones." The Manager represents the obliteration of the distinction between manipulative and non-manipulative relations in the socioeconomic field in much the same way as the Therapist represents the same obliteration in the sphere of personal life. The Manager treats ends as given, as outside his or her scope; his or her concern is also with technique, with directing human and non-human resources in order to achieve these pre-determined goals with maximum efficiency and effectiveness. According to MacIntyre, "among the central moral fictions of the age we have to place the peculiarly managerial fiction embodied in the claim to possess systematic effectiveness in controlling certain aspects of social reality."[22] In the midst of competing value claims, the Manager as

19. Ibid., 24.
20. Ibid., 27.
21. Ibid., 23–35.
22. Ibid., 74.

arbitrator of change and the coordination of social goods has become the central character of the modern social imaginary.[23]

A principal claim of the Manager's is that techniques for efficiency and effectiveness are value-free despite the explicit claim to authority the Manager takes in reference to the exercise of the techniques. In addition, Managers justify their claim to authority and the requisite organizational power by maintaining expertise in effecting and controlling change, and doing so with law-like generalizations that possess strong predictive powers. For MacIntyre, these claims of the Manager are morally loaded because they are inseparable from a mode of human existence in which "the contrivance of means is in central part the manipulation of human beings into compliant patterns of behavior; and it is by appeal to his own effectiveness in this respect that the manager claims authority within the manipulative mode."[24] In other words, the claims are morally questionable, and even a "theatre of illusions."

In order to vindicate claims of expertise and organizational authority, the work of the Manager requires a stock of law-like generalizations that enable "the Manager to predict that, if an event or state of affairs of a certain type were to occur or to be brought about, some other event or state of affairs of some specific kind would result."[25] This claim, MacIntyre argues, and its related presumption concerning the existence of a domain of morally neutral "fact" about which the manager can be "expert," parallels the claims made by natural scientists. Civil servants and managers alike, contends MacIntyre,

> Justify themselves and their claims to authority, power and money by invoking their own competence as scientific managers

23. Enteman, *Managerialism*, 161. The language of "social imaginary" is that of Charles Taylor, who defined such an imaginary as, "something much broader and deeper than the intellectual schemes people may entertain when they think about social reality in a disengaged mode. I am thinking, rather, of the ways people imagine their social existence, how they fit together with others, how things go on between them and their fellows, the expectations that are normally met, and the deeper normative notions and images that underlie these expectations." Taylor, *Modern Social Imaginaries*, 23. Taylor's "social imaginary" and MacIntyre's Characters are related in the way that both represent a form of existence, a way of seeing the world, which goes beyond the limits of a strict intellectual scheme or concept, and the particulars of any individual person or character.

24. MacIntyre, *After Virtue*, 74. Also, Diefenbach, *Management and the Dominance of Managers*, 30.

25. MacIntyre, *After Virtue*, 77.

of social change. Thus, there emerges an ideology which finds its classical form in a pre-existing sociological theory, Weber's theory of bureaucracy. . . . [I]n his insistence that the rationality of adjusting means to ends in the most economical and efficient way is the central task of the bureaucrat and that therefore the appropriate mode of justification of his activity by the bureaucrat lies in the appeal to his (or later her) ability to deploy a body of scientific and above all social scientific knowledge organized and understood as comprising a set of universal law-like generalizations, Weber provided the key to much of the modern age.[26]

MacIntyre regards modern social science as lacking the teleological basis that guarded pre-modern moral thinking and practice from the arbitrary character of modern moral theory. This is in large part due to the role of social science in displacing theism, in discrediting those religious worldviews on which, he claims, morality itself depends. A society where science, whether natural or social, is uncritically revered, he argues, is a society adrift. The crux of his argument against the Manager therefore is how this character derives its claims to legitimacy from an uncritical reliance on social sciences that have displaced questions about the good of human living with concerns about controlling human behavior.

In the estimation of MacIntyre, the logic of what counts in modernity as scientific knowledge is faulty because it ignores the reality of chance. It does so by claiming that the human species can flourish without either grounding in a thick moral description of human good, or a teleological basis for how human good is reached. Social science, in particular, hubristically denies "the permanence of Fortuna, Machiavelli's bitch goddess of unpredictability."[27] This pervasive unpredictability, which for MacIntyre is at the heart of human existence, rendering "all our plans and projects permanently vulnerable and fragile," prevents the social sciences from patterning themselves after the physical sciences, prevents them from gathering law-like generalizations about social behavior, and

26. Ibid., 86.

27. Ibid., 93. The emergence of "Enterprise Risk Management" is an example of the kind of control over chance that MacIntyre finds troubling. In current business practices, "Risk Management" as a dominant mode of managing corporate risk and reputation has given rise to organizational prestige and influence of the bearers of new risk ideologies such as "Chief Risk Officers." What Michael Power's terms "the moral vocabulary of governance," which is deployed by such "Risk Officers, seeks to overcome risk, and therefore, chance, through organizational control by means of corporate social responsibility (CSR) that places shared responsibility for the risk on a wide range of stakeholders. See Power, *Organized Uncertainty*, 66–103.

finally prevents managerial planning and prediction from being effective instruments of social control. It was, and remains, he argues, dangerously naive for Enlightenment thinkers and their heirs to assume that "fragility and vulnerability could be overcome in some progressive future." Yet that is what modern science and those—such as the Manager—who act in its name continue to claim.[28]

MacIntyre's rebuttal of the primacy of modern scientific expertise in general, and social science in particular, leads him to conclude that the claims of "bureaucratic managerial expertise" are illusory. The Manager's claim to authority, he asserts,

> is fatally undermined when we recognize that he possesses no sound stock of law-like generalizations and when we realize how weak the predictive power available to him is. . . . The dominance of the manipulative mode in our culture is not and cannot be accompanied by very much actual success in manipulation. . . . [T]he notion of social control embodied in the notion of expertise is indeed a masquerade. Our social order is in a very literal sense out of our, and indeed, anyone's, control. No one is or could be in charge.[29]

In other words, the self-promotion of Managers and their expertise is thus placed under question. The Manager as character, MacIntyre maintains, is other than he or she at first sight seems to be. The social world of everyday hardheaded, practical, pragmatic, no-nonsense realism, which is the environment of management, is one that depends for its sustained existence on the systematic perpetuation of misunderstanding and of belief in fictions.[30]

According to MacIntyre, the Manager's "objectively grounded" claims are in essence nothing more than expressions of his or her own arbitrary, but disguised, will and preference. The effects of Enlightenment scientific prophesy, MacIntyre claims, have been to produce not scientifically managed social control, but a skillful dramatic *imitation* of such control. Previous success gives the *impression* of power and authority, and

---

28. MacIntyre, *After Virtue*, 103. Attending to the power of predictability in the church, John Drane cautions, "creates a constant pressure to homogenize all our understandings of discipleship and lifestyle. There is inevitably a temptation to process people so that they all turn out like clones of one another." Drane, "The Church and the Iron Cage," 155.

29. MacIntyre, *After Virtue*, 106–7.

30. Ibid., 107.

therefore, the most effective bureaucrat is nothing more than modernity's best actor.[31]

MacIntyre's arguments about management have commanded considerable support within critical organizational analysis keen to unmask the implicit assumptions at the heart of contemporary managerialism.[32] His analysis has its detractors,[33] yet the aligning of the character of the Manager, the role of effectiveness and efficiencies in the social relations of organizations, schools, hospitals, and churches, and finally, the promise of predictive power based on a scientific methodology, coalesce to form a description of the power managerialism wields in the modern social imaginary, and subsequently, the depth of influence managerialism has in all aspects of social relations.

MacIntye's analysis of the Manager has implications for how the church is understood in organizational terms. If, as MacIntyre maintains, thick pre-modern forms of social identity are now dislocated by more morally thin understandings of social order that reflect the atomistic individualism of modernity, then it is reasonable to expect that forms of social dislocation and the rise of the Manager become part of the social imaginary of the church. But to what degree, and what are the arguments against such an advent, particularly in light of the face of church decline? And are there any benefits to an ecclesiology that allows managerialism to play some part in the church's self-understanding? The remainder of this chapter seeks to addresses these questions through providing historical context to the rise of managerialism and analyzing two general approaches that attend to the role of managerialism in the life of the church.

31. Ibid.

32. Examples include, Alvesson and Willmott, *Making Sense of Management*; Mangham, "Macintyre and the Manager"; Jackson and Carter, *Rethinking Organisational Behavior*; Grey, "'We Are All Managers Now'; 'We Always Were.'"

33. Paul du Gay is a notable example of a critic of MacIntyre within organizational studies. Through the work of several publications, du Gay has attempted to restore the character of the Manager to a more balanced social actor, one who contributes to the ordering and success of businesses and other institutions without succumbing to the illusions MacIntyre accuses the Manager of representing. See Gay, *In Praise of Bureaucracy*; Gay, "Alasdair MacIntyre and the Christian Genealogy of Management Critique."

The Path to Managerialism

According to Stephen Pattison, a key symbolic moment for the advent of managerialism in a mainline denomination was the accession of George Carey to the Archbishopric of Canterbury in the Anglican Communion. In a pre-enthronement interview in 1991 with the *Reader's Digest*, the new Archbishop stated that he believed that the church should be run more like a business, arguing that, after all, Jesus himself was a management expert. Such an appeal to business practices, Pattison notes, is more than a desire for a better-organized church. Behind the acceptance of manage-ment by the Archbishop of Canterbury lays a complex of factors that have made management language and practices appear indispensable.[34]

Pattison comes to questions of managerialism in the church with a particular emphasis on the shift in the practice of leadership that accom-panies the adoption of management aims and objectives. Like MacIntyre, Pattison sees the role of manager as shaping what constitutes the theory and practice of management. While he does not employ MacIntyre's so-cially defining "character" description, Pattison recognizes that the role of the manager has grown over the decades to have significance beyond the pragmatic organizational functions of a business leader.[35] How is it, Pattison asks, that such a development has occurred in the understand-ing of management and the manager, that leads one management writer to be able to proclaim that the manager is the "keeper of society's con-science and the solver of society's problems"?[36] In response, Pattison maps four historical phases of management development that contribute to the ascendency of "management" in most organizational structures in the UK and the US. A brief overview of these phases is needed in order to provide the background for how managerialism develops into an ideol-ogy that is eventually adopted into modern ecclesiologies.

The development of the modern manager begins, for Pattison, with the advent of the industrial society. The period between 1890 and 1930 was an era of intensive industrialization, the growth of large-scale cor-porations, and the introduction of mass production and distribution, particularly in the United States. An influential theorist of this period was Frederick W. Taylor, who believed that all human activities were

34. Pattison, *The Faith of the Managers*, 159.

35. Pattison, *The Challenge of Practical Theology*, 73.

36. Pattison is quoting from the work of noted management writer Peter Drucker. See ibid.

susceptible to organization along rational lines. Universal, precise, impersonal laws of organization could be discerned, Talyor argued, and deployed across the spectrum of industries and organizations of the time. Taylor referred to these laws of organization as "scientific management." Underlying this scientific approach, which was designed to increase industrial efficiency and to eliminate conflicts between managers and manual workers, lay three principles: the development of a science of work to replace the old rule-of-thumb methods by which workers operated; a scientific selection and progressive development of the worker that brings together the science of work and the scientifically selected and trained workers for best results; and, the equal division of work and responsibility between workers and management, cooperating in close interdependence.[37]

What has come to be known as "Taylorism," according to Pattison, continues to be an influential way of thinking about management, particularly in deploying an objective basis for the designation of jobs within organizations to fulfill specific tasks that are quantifiable.[38] Adherence of the methods of Taylorism is designed to eliminate any subjective bias from the process of management.[39] As such, the manager within Taylorism operates with a strict sense of tasks and priorities that are measured against the management objectives of the organization. In this period, the manager is one part of an entire organizational mechanism.

The second phase of managerial development is characterized by Pattison as the "social period" and includes the years between 1920 and 1950.[40] In organizational theory, this period is most readily associated with theorist Elton Mayo's emphasis on the informal work group as the center for managerial concern and attention. In response to the more objective and "scientific" claims of Taylorism, Mayo suggested that management is successful when people, rather than mechanics or economics, are privileged. As such, this period saw the elevation of personal motiva-

37. Pattison, *The Faith of the Managers*, 16.

38. Peter Drucker claims that Scientific Management may well be the most powerful as well as the most lasting contribution to Western thought since the Federalist Papers. See Jackson and Carter, "The 'fact' of Management," 199.

39. Ibid., 198.

40. Several writers collapse Pattison's second and third phases (i.e., social and psychological) into one under the title, Human Relations School. This combined phase is defined by the shift in focus from process to interpersonal relations. See ibid., 199; Dale, *Anatomising Embodiment and Organization Theory*, 21.

tion techniques, a turn from individual work to teamwork that is coordinated and requires the willing co-operation of the individuals involved, and a desire for institutional efficiency that is shared by both individual workers and the organizational leadership.[41] This more egalitarian and informal shift gave rise to a period of psychologically oriented organizational development.

The social period was succeeded by a psychological period that ran from the 1940s until the 1970s. It included the development of techniques of Organizational Development. The application of psychology, notes P. D. Anthony,

> extended from an initial concern to improve methods of selection and training to a much more general concern with the individual's motivation in which, finally, the business organization and the tasks which it requires to be performed are both changed in order to make work become the satisfier of fundamental human need.[42]

Many significant managerial techniques that form part of the modern organization were developed in this period. For instance, staff appraisal and counseling, supervisory training and job design emerged as the technical organizational prescriptions of previous periods gave way to personal development. In addition, Organizational Development stressed the involvement of subordinates in the shaping of their own job descriptions and in some cases, defining their role without reference to the larger organizational mission.[43]

At the beginning of the 1980s, a new confidence was found particularly in American industry and managerial techniques. This was articulated through the central contention that the only object of business is to compete with others for the favors of the customer as "king." In order to compete, it was argued, a slow and unresponsive bureaucratic culture had to give way to new approaches that require people to exercise discretion, take initiating, and assume a much greater responsibility for their own organization and management.[44] This approach came to be known

41. Pattison, *The Faith of the Managers*, 17.

42. Anthony, "Management Ideology," 21.

43. Pattison, *The Faith of the Managers*, 17.

44. Morgan, *Images of Organization*, 69. A classic text of TQM is Peters and Waterman, *In Search of Excellence: Lessons from America's Best-Run Companies*.

as "new wave" or, as it was more commonly called, "total quality management" (TQM).

The indicators for this phase include a further shift from a scientific to a more emotivist attitude towards the employee whereby how the employee *feels* about their work begins to weigh in the management process. This shift extends from the organization itself to the customers it serves, so that the customer receives empowerment to shape what products an organization should produce and determines the level of engagement the organization should have in the marketplace. The rise of the "customer as king" approach helps create what Don Slater calls, the "consumer culture."[45] In this new approach, an organization is effectively coordinated through its value system and culture, rather than through the rules and commands of Tayorlism.

"New wave" management also includes a number of other prescriptions such as decentralization, small flexible working units, and management by contract rather than by hierarchical control. The blurring of boundaries between employer and employee, and organization and the marketplace, gives rise in this period to the importance of innovation and flexibility, the centrality of creative teamwork, empowerment of the individual, employee participation, and flattened organizational hierarchies through the reduction of formal bureaucracy.[46]

The effect of "new wave" management was a new logic: productivity and profitability, efficiency and effectiveness are increasingly dependent upon a new cultural economy of subjectivity at work. Put simply, human subjects are exhorted to expand and intensify their contribution as "human resources" in order to enhance production, maximize value, thus leading the organization to success. The slogan "people are our most important asset" became a statement about the depth of involvement the worker was expected to have in the fabric of the organization.[47]

What emerged from the "new wave" shift is a seemingly contradictory set of definitions for the manager: first, the manger as the leader who sets priorities and helps move an organization using their charismatic

45. Slater defines consumer culture as, "a social arrangement in which the relation between lived culture and social resources, between meaningful ways of life and the symbolic and material resources on which they depend, is mediated through markets." Slater, *Consumer Culture and Modernity*, 8.

46. Pattison, *The Faith of the Managers*, 18.

47. Costea, Crump, and Amiridis, "Managerialism, the Therapeutic Habitus and the Self in Contemporary Organizing," 666.

authority, and second, the manager as the source of empowerment for employees who individually exercise their own leadership to steer an organization towards the goals of quality management and profit.[48] While the domain of the manager may appear in a state of flux, the task of management to engender organizational productivity through increased efficiencies and improved technical strategies that maintain an effective competitive advantage for the organization remain the animating principles for managerialism. As Pattison argues, couched in the language of organizational flexibility, innovation, and empowerment, is the instrumental rationality of techniques and technologies all designed to act like implicit religious-like values within the organization that over time have extended into the social imaginary of the surrounding culture.[49]

In the current phase of "new wave" management, the techniques and technologies that Pattison refers to embody a number of assumptions about the nature of management and the role of the manager. One fundamental assumption argues that people, as long as they are equipped with the right strategies, can largely control the world and effectively "colonize" the future. According to Clare Watkins, the approach of group dynamics and social behavior adopted by major organizations has contributed to a renewed optimism in the power of people to overcome the uncertainties implicit in shifting social dynamics.[50] Such optimism, Pattison notes, supports the claim of modern management to be an infallible instrument for controlling and manipulating the future for the better.[51]

A corresponding assumption combines the optimism of technique deployment with the belief that the true worth of any activity is demonstrated through forms of objective measurement, what George Ritzer refers to as the rational process of *calculability*.[52] An approach to management that privileges quantifiable outcomes is a particularly attractive

48. Grey, "'We Are All Managers Now'; 'We Always Were,'" 570.

49. Pattison, *The Faith of the Managers*, 38. Slater contends that "soft" management language of "new wave" organizational practices exhibit the evidence of an "ideological miracle" whereby the consumer culture of the 1980s was tied to the "most profound, deep structural values and promises of modernity: personal freedom, economic progress, civic dynamism and political democracy." Slater, *Consumer Culture and Modernity*, 11.

50. Watkins, "The Church as a 'Special' Case," 378.

51. Pattison, *The Challenge of Practical Theology*, 87. This aligns with MacIntyre's argument on the power of prediction that the character of the Manager is said to deploy. See MacIntyre, *After Virtue*, 103.

52. Ritzer, *The McDonaldization of Society*, 72.

assumption when organizational resources are limited.[53] Pattison notes that public sector or non-profit organizations operate with such thin financial margins that optimal effectiveness with minimum resource can become the dominant criteria to determine the organization's overall worth.[54] Many business leaders, Pattison continues, appeal to the specification of standards and outcome measures in organizations as ensuring that individually and corporately businesses continue to move towards the organization's ultimate purpose. For example, the emergence of TQM within "new wave" organizational thinking promotes building quality into every aspect of the process of production, such as ensuring that all members of the organization feel responsible for quality.[55] How can an organization grow, TQM proponents ask, if there are no benchmarks to measure success or failure?

A final assumption of the nature of management belongs to the rise of symbolic significance of the role of the manager as a "maker of worlds by the use of words." According to Iain Mangham, "Language is the currency of interaction at all levels of encounter and its manipulation is a key feature of persuasion. . . . Organizations are created, maintained and changed through talk."[56] Pattison contends that one outgrowth from "new wave" management theories is an interest in the power of language to legitimate managerialism as a proper exercise of organizational authority. Managers,

> create and perpetuate verbal symbols, myths and narratives that locate and give meaning to their own work and that of others in their organizations. That is why communication skills are so highly prized in almost all management job descriptions. That is perhaps why managers spend most of their time in oral communication with others.[57]

53. On this matter, Pattison references the quip by Charles Hanby, "If you can't count it, it doesn't count" as an overt example of privileging the quantifying of human activity in organizations. See Hanby, *Beyond Certainty*, 137.

54. Pattison, *The Challenge of Practical Theology*, 77.

55. Pattison, *The Faith of the Managers*, 76.

56. Mangham, *Power and Performance in Organizations*, 82. In like manner, Klikauer speaks of the political and ideological character of managerial speech that "shows forth most clearly when conceptual thoughts have been methodically confined to the service of controlling and improving existing managerial conditions." Klikauer, *Managerialism*, 146.

57. Pattison, *The Faith of the Managers*, 59.

Characteristically and ideally, words and concepts that become successful within the ambit of management follow a set of grammatical rules. Successful words and concepts, according to Pattison, need to be low in definition and direct reference, vague and mysterious in terms of precise content, easy to say, vivid and radical sounding in metaphorical and imagistic terms, radically action-oriented ("doing words"), and polysyllabic, so they sound complicated, technical, and difficult to understand.[58]

Two of the most prominent uses of this grammar are deployed through the development of organizational "mission" and "vision."[59] As was addressed in the previous chapter in relation to church identity, the organizational vision is what is supposed to motivate an organization—to give it a sense of ultimate direction and even ultimate meaning. The organizational mission, often embodied in a short mission statement, points to what the organization intends to do in order to realize its vision. In managerial activity, mission is the way that vision becomes a clear statement about where an organization is going and what it conceives its main purpose and aims to be. Often the mission of an organization is expressed in a short mission statement that tries to set out using the grammatical rules just mentioned, what the organization aims to do and become.[60]

The benefit of the deployment of "world making words" through the grammar of managerial activity is often associated with a basic appeal to an organization's purpose, particularly in a season of transition. The concepts that form the vision and mission of the organization are designed to provide symbolic value to the activity of the organization as well as provide a sense of direction by means of the attainment of measurable corporate goals. Presented as such, the assumption is that any and all organizations benefit from a deployment of a managerial grammar and purpose-driven logic, for the mechanisms implicit are viewed as value-free in as much as each individual organization develops its own "world" through this grammar and logic. Under such conditions, Philip Selznick contends, the effective manager can shape an organization's "character" by transforming a neutral body of people into a committed polity.[61] Managerial activity, therefore, relies principally on infusing day-to-day

58. Ibid., 61.

59. As is evidenced in the previously detailed work of Congregational Studies, the role of managerial activity defined through "mission" and "vision" is an essential component to the implicit ecclesiology of Congregational Studies.

60. Pattison, *The Challenge of Practical Theology*, 79.

61. Selznick, *Leadership in Administration*, 9.

behavior with long-run meaning and purpose through the elaboration of socially integrating myths by means of the language of "uplift" and "idealism." "The assignment of a high value to certain activities will itself," argues Selznick, "help to create a myth, especially if buttressed by occasional explicit statements."[62]

These assumptions of "new wave" management contribute, Thomas Diefenbach argues, to the ideological justification of the prime objectives, social structures, and processes of the modern, managed organization.[63] As a kind of organization that often mirrors the theoretical and practical justifications of other organizations, the church, Pattison and Watkins caution, must be careful in exactly what it adopts and how it justifies its own organizational life. If the task of the church is to live out of the complex truth of Scripture, it can never be content, they argue, with a setting out of sub-goals, which almost inevitably distract from the dynamic concern of the eschatological goal, which is proper to the church.[64] If the ecclesial organization is to use some kind of management by objective, or setting of sub-goals, it must accompany its action with some kind of critical corrective that makes plain the provisional nature of such objectives, and the infinite possibility of equally valid other sub-goals.[65] As Watkins notes, in the case of the church the essential ambiguity of the task, "the sheer diversity implied by the vocation to be the proclaiming of God's Word, makes such a managerial setting of objectives extremely difficult. Not only is this task difficult, it also is questionable in itself."[66]

Whereas Pattison and Watkins call for caution in light of the ascendency of managerialism in the church, there remain a number of scholars who believe that the assumptions of managerialism are not only thriving in the church, but are fundamentally corrupting the church and her mission. In general, these thinkers are concerned to show that the contemporary church has incorporated the logic of rationalized processes such as efficiency, calculability, and predictability that are not basic to the Christian faith. This incorporation has established controlling criteria for the church so that the characteristics of church mission and identity

62. Ibid., 151.

63. Diefenbach, *Management and the Dominance of Managers*, 156.

64. Pattison, *The Faith of the Managers*, 91–92.

65. Watkins, "The Church as a 'Special' Case," 381.

66. Ibid.

demonstrate an "organizational drift."[67] This means that the genuine identity of the Christian church is pushed into the background by influences
of financial, cultural, political, or other natures. The response from the
church, critics suggest, is to bring theological judgments to bear upon
these organizational constructions.[68]

Managerialism as Rationalizing Commodification

Imagine sitting next to someone on a train who has her laptop open
and her mobile phone pressed to their ear. As the train runs smoothly
through the countryside, the person next to you issues instructions about
hiring, firing, expanding here and reducing there, letting so and so in
on the latest developments, and making cautious inquires about closing
down an unprofitable program before it uses any more resources. Is this
person sitting next to you a business manager, or perhaps, a Christian
minister? What is going on here? John Milbank asks.[69]

The encounter on the train is, for Milbank, a fictive image of a very
real impulse within the church, particularly the Protestant denominations, in modernity. During the nineteenth century, Milbank contends,
the impulse to shape ecclesiology on organizational trends resulted in
efforts to define the point of Christianity to be the production of more
Christians. In this period,

> Christianity is reduced to a readily graspable product: the
> promise of a mysterious relationship with Jesus, the absolute au-
> thority of a printed book, the reduction of complex doctrine to
> formulas about atonement, a single punctual act of faith which
> is like an absolute banknote, redeemable in eternity. The point
> is that as many people as possible should buy this product—the

67. Brodd, "Church, Organisation, and Church Organisation," 259.

68. Kenneson, "Selling [Out] the Church in the Marketplace of Desire," 319. Also,
Meeks, "Hope and the Ministry of Planning and Management." Meeks questions the
legitimacy of any "ministry as management" model that is insufficiently Christological. As Meeks attests, modern managerial practices in the church artificially separate
theology and polity thereby creating two criterion with independent rationales and
judgments, one pertaining to "life in Christ," the other to "organizing people." Church
planning and management ought to have no other goal, Meeks concludes, "than helping to create mature, active ministers in the congregation who are free and disciplined
to participate in God's liberating history with God's creation" (p. 160).

69. Milbank, "Stale Expressions," 117–18.

interrelations, the social practices of these people are more or less beside the point.[70]

The consumerist language of "product" in Milbank's description is intentional. The *ethos* of much of Protestant Christianity follows a capitalist logic, where the business of the church is aligned with practices ordered around the commodity of the "redeemed soul." The shape this ethos has taken in contemporary ecclesiology, Milbank argues, is the promotion of ecclesial "brands" wherein the gathered group who are organized as (particularly in the UK) a "Fresh Expression" or "mission-shaped church" reflect a homogenous social order of personal taste.[71] The growth of these "brands" is a reflection of what Milbank calls, the "barbarism of instrumentalizing reason": for such commodification of Christian thought and practice cannot avoid the reduction of such thought and practice to an expression of effective self-fulfillment that ignores the physical and social manifestation of the church.[72]

Milbank's argument against ecclesial "barbarism" can be summarized as, first, the challenge of a rationalized commodification of the mission and identity of the church, and second, the reduction of ecclesiology to a "religious inwardness" that privileges private belief (i.e., "corporate" values) over the social manifestation of the church.[73] These twin concerns provide a framework for critique that is particularly interested in addressing these two points as they are manifest in the contemporary church so that an alternative account can be provided that attends to the spiritual ecology of embodied human contact through more genuine expressions of political activity by members of the church.

"It is tempting," notes Richard Roberts, "to liken the present state of some mainline Christian denominations . . . to that of religious 'outlets' sharing the fate of well-established multinational stores which suddenly find themselves with a range of products which do not relate to a rapidly changing 'designer' market."[74] What develops within this state of church decline has been addressed in the previous chapter through an introduc-

70. Ibid., 120.

71. Ibid., 124.

72. Ibid., 128.

73. The term, "religious inwardness" belongs to Bernd Wannenwetsch, but the notion of a privatized form of religious commitment is part of Milbank's critique. See Wannenwetsch, "Inwardness and Commodification."

74. Roberts, *Religion, Theology and the Human Sciences*, 40.

tion to forms of Congregational Studies that privilege both the adoption of techniques and a market-like focus on disseminating the message of the church by means of more "mission" activity. In line with the earlier critiques of MacIntyre and Pattison, Roberts argues that the implementation in the church of managerial practices and schemes of market appraisal that promotes an enhancement of performance amounts to a loss, rather than a gain, to the church's mission and identity. Where Roberts and others, including Michael Budde and Bernd Wannenwetsch, focus their argument is on the corruption in patterns of thought and action in the church that has allowed the encroachment of a rationalized commodification to transform ecclesial life to better suit the managerialism of contemporary society. This managerialism, states Budde, is detrimental to the gospel and the way of life it establishes in the world.[75]

According to Roberts, modern management involves the loss of relative autonomy within social, economic, and political spheres through the assimilation of all social arrangements into "provider-receiver" or "provider-customer" relationships. Under such an arrangement, all ends-means relationships are thereby transformed to serve as various forms of transactions.[76] In this context, strategic objectives that determine the shape of the transaction become the prerogative of executive management. Operating at a distance from the customer, the executive management relies on market research and corporate consultants who provide the necessary rationale for proceeding by means of one set of objectives as opposed to another.[77] In this sense, management always has a dual

75. Budde, "The Rational Shepherd," 99.

76. Roberts, *Religion, Theology and the Human Sciences*, 162. In like manner, Kenneson contends that "in a social/political/economic sphere like the United States . . . everyday life is thoroughly shaped and governed by management and market relationships, [and] tends to transform everything (and everyone) into manageable objects and marketable commodities." Kenneson, "Selling [Out] the Church in the Marketplace of Desire," 319. Such an arrangement is what financial guru George Soros calls the "Transactional Society." According to Soros, "The replacement of *relationships* by *transactions* is an ongoing, historical process that will never be carried to its logical conclusion, but it is well advanced—far more advanced than in earlier periods of capitalism." Soros, *Open Society*, 113.

77. Enteman argues that management often operates remotely from the actual functions of the organization. For example, school administrators usually have little to do with educating students, hospital administrators usually have little to do with providing health care, and administrators of government agencies usually have little to do with delivery of the agencies' primary services. This common remoteness from the territory of operations gives support to the popular notion that there is such a thing as

task: managing the internal conditions of the organization and managing the external opportunities and constraints for the organization.

Deriving from the strategic objectives, the implementation of blanket "mission statements" informs the aims and objectives in terms through which managers secure the conformity of front-line workers through a top-down deployment of techniques and strategies that are advertised to increase efficiencies and improve production. These workers then encounter the "receivers," consumers, or "customers" in relationally pre-determined and supervised modes of transaction through carefully crafted "store fronts" (concrete and virtual) where an equally well-crafted "message" is communicated by means of regulated greetings, customer service focused on personal fulfillment, and the enhancement of the "shopping experience" through the results of market-research in matters of the variety of music, images, and in some cases, video, that is used. In this management scenario, nothing is left to chance.[78]

Under these managerialized conditions, which Roberts believes have successfully imposed uniformity across many apparently diverse sectors of society and culture, anything distinctive in the message or significance to a local culture or community is captured, rationalized, regularized, and then redirected by managers, who then present their reconstruction of reality to be accepted and owned by the very consumer whose social imaginary is entwined with this reality. This process, Roberts concludes, is adaptable to new social conditions and changes in cultural values since it immediately sets about homogenizing the changes into new forms of production using the already established mode of transactional relationships.[79] In other words, even when faced with the latest trend in organizational practice or entire new industries, managerialism is capable of assuming them into the pattern of regulation and manipulation by means of a managerial logic. As Grey notes, when it comes to the extent of managerial control, the issue is not whether management will continue

---

professional management. See Enteman, *Managerialism*, 162.

78. Wannenwetsch notes that such an arrangement is an example of the "Hobbesean cosmological-anthropological revolution" that has shifted attention onto the supposed insatiable needs of every human. This revolution, Wannenwetsch maintains, has given rise to what he calls the *animal desiderans*, the needy animal. See Wannenwetsch, "Inwardness and Commodification," 33.

79. Roberts, *Religion, Theology and the Human Sciences*, 63.

to exist as an activity. Rather the critical issue is the kind of management there will be.[80]

The managerialized conditions that maintain the mode of transactional relationships privileges an emphasis on productivity, which translates into increased profit margins. This affects how the workers relate to the organization. In brief, it means greater demands made on fewer employees, who in turn must become more, not less, devoted to "their" firm in order to maintain employment. As Michael Budde and Robert Brimlow argue, "firms must cultivate bonds of affection, common purpose, and mutual support between themselves and employees."[81] Yet, Budde and Brimlow continue, this is no easy task, "given the alienation and distrust among employees produced by wave after wave of corporate downsizing, layoffs, and movement toward temporary, part-time (and underpaid) employees."[82] All of this inclines corporations to seek to provide a sense of "vocation" and "spiritual fulfillment" among the ranks of their employees, thus making secularized religious concepts part of the corporate human resources arsenal.[83]

In sum, modern management combines the confluence of a "provider-customer" transactional relationship within a prescribed supply-side organizational structure, with a crytpo-religious "vocation" that orders employees towards the "values" of efficiency and effectiveness that are masked by appeals to a corporate culture of affection and common purpose. Roberts calls this management scenario a "remythologization of the effective and affective self in the religiosity of the enterprise culture" that is conducted around the quest for greater productivity through greater efficiency.[84] For Roberts, this "remythologization" is manifest in three aspects of managerialism. First, the pragmatic and immanentist ethos of the maximization of self-awareness and performance operates as a form of dependence by employees on the "mission" of the corporation. Second, the central notion of charismatic leadership overshadows

80. Grey, "'We Are All Managers Now'; 'We Always Were,'" 576.

81. Budde and Brimlow, *Christianity, Incorporated*, 9.

82. Ibid., 13.

83. Pattison speaks of "hidden religio-ethical assumptions" in the practices of management, in particular, the building by managers of "corporate cultures" that include rituals, practices, and ideas that play an almost cultic role in maintaining allegiance to the organization. See Pattison, *The Faith of the Managers*, 1–7.

84. Roberts, *Religion, Theology and the Human Sciences*, 54.

all corporate operations. Third, the rise and ascendency of emotivism undergirds the primacy of choice in corporate deliberation.

To the first aspect of "remythologization," Roberts warns that the dependence born from managerial manipulation sits ill with the traditional Christian cultivation of sacrifice, dependence, and passivity in the face of divine transcendence manifest in divine immanence.[85] As Arne Rasmussen makes clear, Christian thought and practice is shaped by formation and discernment through participation in the cultic life of the church, a life marked by sacrificial-love and receptivity that displays the divine gifts of grace and love. Christian discernment, Rasmussen continues, is a communal process that refuses the kind of manipulation implicit in the organizational dependence of the modern management context.[86]

Second, "remythologization" is evident in the self-conscious search in management culture for the charismatic persona, the super-performer, who can correct the unproductive and inefficient life within a corporation by means of the organizational *charisms* of motivation and communication. The charismatic leader, equipped with the entrepreneurial talent mentioned in the previous chapter, is, in the estimation of Alan Roxburgh and Fred Romanuk, the leader who can cultivate effective, lasting *missional* transformation in an organization.[87] Moreover, as Peter Drucker contends, the charismatic leader integrates motivation and communication to build up teams of people and use decisions on pay, placement, and promotion to ensure that those teams work well.[88] Despite the promise of such leadership, Roberts counters that such individual *charisms* are not fundamentally ordered to the benefit of the organization. Managerialism, Roberts argues, is about power, obedience, and conformity in a low-trust environment that is often masked by appeals to reflexivity and empowerment. As such, the exercise of a kind of personal asceticism by the charismatic leader carries an implicit commitment to maintaining power, obedience, and conformity that takes precedence over other demands and relationships.[89]

Martyn Percy's work on religious charismatic figures is helpful in elucidating the connections between the religious figure and the

85. Ibid.

86. Rasmusson, "Ecclesiology and Ethics," 184.

87. Roxburgh and Romanuk, *The Missional Leader*, 112.

88. In Pattison, *The Faith of the Managers*, 11.

89. Roberts, *Religion, Theology and the Human Sciences*, 71.

charismatic, entrepreneurial leader in modern management. In the first place, Percy contends, charismatic leaders have a charismatic message. This is usually revolutionary in character. It promises "salvation," and requires a rejection of ties to the external order so that the message itself becomes the only route of escape from a perceived crisis.[90] This is particularly apposite at times of social anxiety, when the fundamental aims and methods of an organization are in question. Into this scenario, the leader who manifests the power to direct the entire mission of an organization can enter with dynamic self-defining authority that dictates reality for and on behalf of others.[91]

Second, charismatic leaders tend to have certain personality elements. These may include the ability to communicate their indispensability in times of change. This indispensable status is gained, for example, from the ability to demonstrate almost miraculous powers in taking an organization or a community from the brink of failure to the pinnacle of success. Percy notes that such power does not necessarily translate into an identification of the leader with the people who are deemed, "followers." Charismatic leaders often display the ability to remain aloof, distant and mysterious; a personality set that only further contributes to the high status of the leader to perform "miracles."[92]

Such leadership aligns with what Bruno Dyck and Elden Wiebe call the practice of "social salvation" within organizational practice. "Social salvationists," Dyck and Wiebe argue, demonstrate power to transform social structures by means of prophetic language and action.[93] The example of the American business Amway is provided by Dyck and Wiebe as one organization that operates with an implicit understanding of salvation through the activities of individual "salvationists" who are trained to use Amway products as tools to create a "better America." Amway, Dyck and Wiebe contend, sees itself as a purveyor of a prophetic message that is designed to transform (i.e., save) the "ordinary person" by means of economic success through the application of specific managerial practices, and a highly defined course in personal charismatic leadership. In Amway, as in other similar organizations, the understanding of what constitutes salvation may change as circumstances change, but the role of

90. Percy, *Words, Wonders and Power*, 53.

91. Roberts, *Religion, Theology and the Human Sciences*, 168.

92. Percy, *Words, Wonders and Power*, 53.

93. Dyck and Wiebe, "Salvation, Theology and Organizational Practices across the Centuries," 316.

the entrepreneurial and charismatic leader remains constant within the organization.[94]

The third aspect of Robert's account of "remythologization" within managerialism echoes the rise and ascendency of emotivism from the fragments of tradition-bound society. As was noted earlier, emotivism for MacIntyre signals the devolution of social discourse to an expression of individual preferences that is incapable of rational consensus. In such a climate, practical reason has come to be equated with the instrumental reason of bureaucratic institutions, the choice of efficient means to arbitrarily-chosen ends.[95] For Roberts, the bureaucratic culture is in part an attempt to redirect the obsolescent rationality of late or advanced capitalist society through the imposition of a new order in the name of "choice" and "freedom."[96] This new order of choice and freedom renders possible the exploitation of the human experience of ultimacy and identity-creation to a kind of "spirituality" that serves as a resource and tool to be used in promoting organizational promotion and change.

An example of Roberts's "new order of choice and freedom," which has a spiritual quality, is found in the work of management writer, Henry Mintzberg. Referring to what he calls "controlling inside the unit," Mintzberg concludes that, "the job of managing is significantly one of information processing, especially through a great deal of listening, seeing, and feeling, as well as a good deal of talking".[97] Careful framing of the distribution of information around the *feeling* of workers, will, Minztberg continues, better direct the behavior of the workers to the stated organizational goals while maintaining a climate of "empowerment."[98] In this process, the manager helps "bond" people into "cooperative groups" where identity-creation is promoted and through which the manager maintains influence as a "gatekeeper" of the overall identity and power within the organizational structure.[99] In such a context, the manger helps create and support important rituals and ceremonies that contribute to

---

94. Ibid., 315.

95. MacIntyre, *After Virtue*, 35.

96. Roberts, *Religion, Theology and the Human Sciences*, 55.

97. Mintzberg, *Managing*, 56.

98. Ibid., 66.

99. Ibid., 79. On this point, Enteman argues the fundamental social unit within a managerial ideology is neither individuals nor the state, but organizations. See Enteman, *Managerialism*, 154.

the bonds within the cooperative groups.[100] The benefit of this model of management, notes Mintzberg, is that it promotes a level of freedom and choice among workers while allowing consistent control of information, identity, and power to remain localized in the role of the manager and across the bureaucratic chain of manager-like positions (e.g., consultants) that supports the manager.[101]

The vision of management promoted by Mintzberg privileges the internal status of workers (e.g., their thoughts and feelings) as the site for organizational promotion and change. Through shaping the institutional strategy for success by means of creating "bonds" within the organization where religious-like rituals and ceremonies contribute to the emotional state of the worker, modern management creates the illusion of an internally consistent, empirically verifiable, and relationally based social arrangement (i.e., as a "gatekeeper"). Such an arrangement seeks to provide a total worldview and way of life that binds individuals and organizations together and shapes people, purposes, and actions in a fundamental way.[102] In sum, what is endorsed is a dominant or exclusive organizational identity that seeks to generate an emotional (i.e., "internal") investment by workers to the more "public" activity of the organization itself.[103]

MacIntyre and Roberts warn that the arrangement promoted by Mintzberg inevitably appeals to choice and personal preference. In privileging the *internal* life of motivation and feeling, managerialism

> constructs and participates in a metaphysics of naïve realism, of modernity's relegation of religion to the internal and disembodied, and a specious fact/value distinction that empowers those capable of defining the factual, the real, and the objective.[104]

The relationship between efficiency and internal worker motivation (i.e., how to increase corporate efficiency through an increased desire on the part of workers to be productive) has been a major concern for the producers of management knowledge *ab initio*. From a Taylorist concern to link job design with material benefits, to the "new wave" approach that links efficiency with the enrichment of work routines, the mechanisms of managerialism to manipulate the *inwardness* of the worker, in order to

---

100. Mintzberg, *Mintzberg on Management*, 12.

101. Mintzberg, *Managing*, 91.

102. Pattison, *The Faith of the Managers*, 2.

103. Parker, "Organisation, Community and Utopia," 73.

104. Budde, "The Rational Shepherd," 104.

promote the effective running of organizations, displays a "remythologi-zation" of modern corporations from mere generators of products to an entire ideology that has the capacity to shape attitudes, dispositions, and ways of inhabiting the world.[105]

The process of "remythologization" through pragmatic appeals to effectiveness, the rule of charismatic leaders, and the implicit religios-ity of the enterprise culture is, Roberts contends, a critical issue for the identity and purpose of the church. Can a managerialized church serve the wider religious and spiritual needs of humankind, Roberts asks, or should it simply acquiesce in its reconfiguration as a "quality"-bound, "supply-side" organization dedicated to a well-marketed and efficient de-livery of what amounts to a pre-determined product in limited (because privileged) competition with other outlets in the spiritual marketplace?[106]

Any managerial normalization of the church, Roberts contends, is a form of ecclesial betrayal, for in adopting the methods implicit to mana-gerialism, the church surrenders its imagination, thought, and agency.[107] Yet such normalization is already identifiable in the contemporary church through appeals to ecclesial restoration by means of a culture of perfor-mativity and appraisal, and through what Roberts calls, managerialism's "rule of the body."

The suggestion that ecclesial restoration comes by means of a cul-ture of performativity and appraisal echoes the argument of the previ-ous chapters with regard to the reality of church decline, and the rise of technique and missional-based responses. What is evident in the growth of methods-based approaches to securing the identity and purpose of the church is the perspective that allows this identity and purpose to be evaluated in terms that are instrumental and functional in orientation.[108]

According to a rationalized and instrumentalized account of the church, managerial modernity has given to the church the means of re-gaining real *power*; church leaders have but to grasp this power as means

105. Jackson and Carter, "The 'fact' of Management," 199; Budde, "The Rational Shepherd," 99.

106. Roberts, *Religion, Theology and the Human Sciences*, 161.

107. Roberts, "Order and Organization," 84.

108. Williams, *Faith in the Public Square*, 13. Michael Jinkins contends that the anxiety of decline, particularly in how it is expressed in North America, reveals an implicit rationalism that looks for simple cause-effect relationships to explain phe-nomena and an assumed primacy of entrepreneurship that meshes well with the North American proclivity for the "bourgeois myths of self-improvement" and of the inde-pendent "self-made" individual. See Jinkins, *The Church Faces Death*, 13.

and dedicate it to the end, the gospel itself. The power in question is the implementation of accountability within the leadership of the church, and a more aggressive resource allocation to sectors within the church that fit within the defined strategies of church hierarchy.[109] An example of this methodology can be found in the work of Robin Gill and Derek Burke, who apply this managerial logic to the accounting of church worship. The implementation of strategic resource allocation and planning, argues Gill and Burke,

> would treat the fostering of communal worship of God in Christ through the Spirit as the chief priorities of the churches. The extent to which the churches lead more rather than fewer people to take part in such worship could clearly be monitored. Naturally it would be important to keep a careful qualitative check on this worship and particularly on the (sometimes fairly elusive) ways in which worship might teach and mold both individual lives and structures.[110]

What Gill and Burke suggest for the church is a combination of fidelity and expertise of various kinds in the formulation of its current objectives. The setting of such objectives is the responsibility of leaders. According to Gill and Burke, the setting of objectives is made complicated by the need for leaders to negotiate an ever-changing society. In this new context, contends Gill and Burke, a new style of church leadership is emerging that exercises power through providing the necessary vision for the church to adjust to the shifting contours of the culture. The new leadership,

---

109. Roberts, *Religion, Theology and the Human Sciences*, 168. Mark Haugaard refers to this kind of "power creating" as "social order power" that stems from "social structures which lend order to an action through the reproduction of meaning" (p. 158). Haugaard identifies "social order power" in the work of organizational theorist Stewart Clegg. This variety of power creating is most evident in organizations that self-identify as "communities" or even "families." In the context of Roberts's critique, "social order power" is constituted and maintained through combining the spread of the gospel with the practices of efficient management. The "reproduction of meaning" that takes place in such a context refers to the advertised neutrality of the management practices that become the implicit foundation of ecclesial understanding even as the gospel is maintained explicitly as the guiding principle behind the purpose of the church. See Haugaard, "Reflections on Seven Ways of Creating Power."

110. Gill and Burke, *Strategic Church Leadership*, 69, quoted in Roberts, "Order and Organization," 83.

foster vision—theological, moral and strategic—and enable this vision to be realized by the whole church. It would be their job as strategic leaders to think, plan prayerfully, to coax, to monitor, to help others to learn, and above all, to identify and enhance opportunities for qualitative and quantitative growth and to be firm about subsidized projects that do not promote growth. Only by carefully monitoring outcomes, both quantitatively and qualitatively, would they be able to do their job effectively.[111]

Moreover, the task spelled out in managing outcomes through fostering vision in the pursuit of institutional and organizational efficiency, is, according to Roberts, an exercise that disempowers the church of prophetic engagement with the normative commitments of society, and disengages the church from the central task of worship.[112] Both prophetic engagement and worship require a degree of professional relative autonomy and the exercise of a *traditioned* discernment made possible through a common life modeled on the action and suffering revealed in Jesus Christ; a life exercised through the sacramental ministrations of the church.

Managerialism and the Rule of the Body

Milbank's second point against the ecclesial "barbarism" of managerialism addresses the normalization of managerialism in the church, and the emphasis it gives to the coordinating power employed to control *how* the church fulfills its identity and purpose. The concern with managed conditions is how they contribute to the reduction of ecclesiology to a "religious inwardness" that privileges private belief (i.e., "corporate" values) over the social manifestation of the church. Roberts calls this the "rule of the body," since the promotion and execution of managerial coordination is designed to efficiently restructure the "body" of the church

111. Gill and Burke, *Strategic Church Leadership*, 86, quoted in, Roberts, "Order and Organization," 84.

112. Roberts, "Order and Organization," 85. In a similar vein, Justin Lewis-Anthony notes that a "managerial-leadership" model that stresses effectiveness, particularly in light of organizational challenges, assumes that such leadership is *coherent, systematic, and justifiable.* Echoing the critique of MacIntyre, Lewis-Anthony contends that the "managerial-leadership" model betrays an implicit emotivism on behalf of organizational managers who are seeking through effective leadership a means to secure power. See Lewis-Anthony, *You Are the Messiah, and I Should Know*, 36–56.

to resemble more closely the values of managerialism. The restructuring to which Roberts alludes includes a shift in description with regards to the church as a "service agency," and the institution of new forms of the church that seek to make the content of the church more acceptable to the Western social imaginary.[113]

The description of the church as a "service agency" follows from the positioning of the church within the larger organizational world that coincided with the growth of mainline denominations and of organizational theory and practice in the first half of the twentieth century. The periods detailed above, from Taylorism to "new-wave" management, give particular warrant to a description of an organization in terms of the kind of *product* produced, and the manner of this production. Concerned to place the church within other social bodies, church leaders were inclined to describe the church using a functional and organizational rationale. Craig Van Gelder argues that this inclination developed out of the inherent logic of this period where it was accepted that all organizations are organized to *do* something. In other words, an organization when it is formed must seek to accomplish some identifiable goal that serves to legitimate the organization's existence.[114]

One influential response to the question of an "organizational church goal" came from a church leader who articulated this goal through the lens of business marketing. George Barna, for instance, argues that churches need to recognize their work as the producer of a certain project, namely, the product of the "gospel." As in the business world, Barna writes, "every church must be managed with purpose and efficiency, moving toward its goals and objectives. Our goal as a church, like any secular business, is to turn a profit. For us, however, profit means saving souls and nurturing believers."[115] With such a goal in mind, Barna contends that churches should then consider their purpose to be the meeting of people's needs, in similar fashion to a company creating products to meet the demands of the buying public. Think of the church not as a religious meeting place, Barna notes,

113. Roberts, *Religion, Theology and the Human Sciences*, 162.

114. Van Gelder, "Rethinking Denominations and Denominationalism in Light of a Missional Ecclesiology," 26.

115. Barna, *Marketing the Church*, 26.

but as a service agency—an entity that exists to satisfy people's needs. We believe that, in the Person of Jesus Christ and the fellowship of the Body of believers, we have the perfect solution to people's needs. We are well prepared to fulfill those needs—not the needs that we claim people have, but the needs that people themselves recognize and express. Using the same resources, the Church already has—time, talent, money, facilities—how can we squeeze the greatest possible results from those resources and achieve our goals as a service agency in the employ of the God of all creation?[116]

Barna's marketing approach for the church echoes Peter Drucker's understanding of nonprofits (including churches) as purveyors of a "changed human life." Drucker writes, "the 'non-profit' institution neither supplies goods nor controls. . . . Its 'product' is neither a pair of shoes nor an effective regulation. Its product is a changed human being. The nonprofit institutions are human-change agents."[117]

The presupposition of Barna and Drucker on the question of ecclesial identity and purpose is that the church is a service agency that exists to satisfy "felt needs" through serving its constituency by providing services (i.e., "ministry") that address the problem of "human change" through an ever-expanding variety of programs and responses. In short, the ministry of the church is transformed into need-fulfillment. If the church's goal is to meet felt needs, then the whole enterprise is ultimately shaped by those needs that the consumer desires to have satisfied. This consumer orientation in the church echoes the retailing industry's maxim: the customer is always right. The result is the transformation of the church's "body" into a market-oriented institution that privileges the instrumental rationality of "supply/demand" economics through devaluing the transformative and reorienting of thinking and acting that comes by membership in the body of Christ. Instead, the logic of Barna and Drucker assume that, at least in principle, the church can be made relevant and desirable to almost anyone if it simply knows how to market itself more effectively.[118]

116. Ibid., 37. According to Don Slater, the culture represented in the argument of writers like Barna is the culture of a "market society" where central to the exercise of the culture is the act of choosing between a range of produced goods and services. See Slater, *Consumer Culture and Modernity*, 24.

117 Drucker, *Managing the Non-Profit Organization*, xiv.

118. Kenneson, "Selling [Out] the Church in the Marketplace of Desire," 339. Brodd refers to the "inner secularization" that occurs within the church when means (e.g., marketing) are used that confuse the "genuine" identity of the church as the

The kind of instrumental reasoning that animates church market-ing finds a renewed appearance in more recent attempts to articulate the shape of the church by means of new *forms* of how the church is orga-nized and where the church operates. The basic premise for these new forms or expressions is one of uniformity of membership and decentral-ized power structures.[119]

A notable example of a reimagined form of the church is the "Fresh Expressions" program that arose following the 2004 Church of Eng-land report, *Mission-Shaped Church*. "Fresh Expressions of Church" are church initiatives that operate as extra-parochial congregations focused on particular interests or activities, what *Mission-Shaped Church* calls a "particular network of people." An example of such a network is a "work-place church" or a "school-based church" that is organized around these contexts and the communities represented in these contexts.[120] Such "Ex-pressions" are designed to have little formal connection to an established congregation. They are to be "alternative worship communities" that seek to respond to "post-modern culture" through engaging in "post-modern instincts in the preferences for a multi-media approach."[121] The goal is to have a "mixed economy" of ecclesial forms that operate through specific "rhythm and style" depending on the target audience and the particulars of the location of the Expression.[122] For each ecclesial form there are spe-cific mission goals (e.g., growth within certain demographics), and the structure of the Expression is designed to meet these goals.[123] As such, there are endless varieties of ecclesial forms for the Expression to take.

One of the ways this is discussed in through the notion of a "mixed economy" of ecclesial forms, which, according to Stuart Burns, is simply another way of stating that human response to God changes from one

visible body of Christ. See Brodd, "Church, Organisation, and Church Organisation," 259. The critique of marketing in the church, particularly in the US, is taken up more fully in Moore, *Selling God*, and Miller, *Consuming Religion*.

119. The "imposed uniformity" that Roberts fears as the result of increased mana-gerialized conditions in the church is challenged by these renewed church expressions. As will be argued, however, such diversity is derived from the same logic that animates church marketing, and therefore, an instrumentized managerial rationality.

120. *Mission-Shaped Church*, 43.

121. Ibid., 45.

122. Croft, Mobsby, and Spellers, *Ancient Faith, Future Mission*, xiv.

123. The merging of particular demographics and consumer logic in Fresh Expres-sions displays the kind managed coordination described by advocates of "new wave" management. See Grey, "'We Are All Managers Now'; 'We Always Were,'" 559.

generation and culture to another. "We need to be free to explore fresh ways of hearing the gospel . . . new ways of hearing the radical thing Jesus was trying to say in his day . . . and applying them now, where we are."[124] Yet, as Andrew Davison and Alison Milbank argue, being "free to explore fresh ways of hearing the gospel" masks an implicit privileging of novelty and consumer choice over established practices and traditions that form stable congregations that are committed to a particular place with the accompanying challenges of a true diversity of people.[125] Furthermore, the impetus behind the novelty of Fresh Expressions displays "middle-class" values, where "money makes choice possible, and where money grants security that prevents 'the new' from being too destabilizing or confusing."[126] If Fresh Expressions advocate a "mixed economy," it is an economy that potentially leaves out those whose ability to choose is hindered by poverty, sickness, or age.

In parallel to the consumerism of Fresh Expressions is the notion that new church communities are best operated as more decentralized and "virtual" spaces than that of the established congregation. An operating assumption of the *Mission-Shaped Church* report is that the emergence of globalization and internet technologies have shifted what constitutes a "community" away from descriptions of locality and geography to the realm of "networks" of people that exist across localities.[127] The response of the church, the report contends, is full engagement in a network-model of ministry through a whole range of diverse expressions that seek to "facilitate encounter with God and God's people" wherever people may be, and by whatever means it makes sense to reach such people.[128] The *means* for this network-model of ministry matter only in so much as they lead to the desired *end*.

124 Stuart Burns, "Concluding Thoughts," in Croft and Mobsby (eds.), *Ancient Faith, Future Mission*, 173.

125. Davison and Milbank, *For the Parish*, 100–103.

126 Ibid., 101.

127. *Mission-Shaped Church*, 5.

128. Ibid., 13. Helen Cameron contends that the kind of network-model attended to in projects like Fresh Expressions deploy the "dominant means of social coordination" that implicitly enables "transactions to take place in the most advantageous location, rather than close to actors in time and space." Cameron, "Networks—The Blurring of Institution and Networks," 77. Such transactions are part of the rationale of a market-oriented rationality.

The means-to-ends rationality has already been critiqued in the analysis of the work of MacIntyre, Pattison, and Roberts, yet Davison and Milbank add that the network-model also displays a *dis*incarnated theology. "If the Church is truly to be incarnational," they argue, "then she must be local, for there is no universality before complete immersion in the particularities of our own corporeality."[129] Davison and Milbank continue later, "both time and space have become shaped by the fullness and the humanity of divine revelation."[130] The network-model, while striving to be inclusive of cultures and dominant social norms, risks disconnecting from the Christian heritage of patient enduring within cultures where norms shift without reference to the concrete existence of communities like the church. As such, the church has a mission of abiding, which is, to be a *material* presence, mediating the treasures of the gospel and calling others to the "mission of mediation and reconciliation in their turn. To abide has . . . the sense of serve: to abide in Christ's love is to wash the feet, to love others in the sense that God loves us."[131]

The example of Fresh Expressions fits within Richard Roberts's concern with the normalization of managerialism, particularly as the logic of the Fresh Expressions project seeks to privilege consumer choice and means-to-ends rationality in an attempt to shape the "body" of the church to be more welcoming to the modern social imaginary. As a "quality-bound," "supply-side" approach to church mission, Fresh Expressions, like the earlier manifestation of church marketing, risks reducing the identity and purpose of the church to a product that is formed and reformed depending on the felt-needs of the religious consumer. As Davison and Milbank caution, such a reduction risks distorting the

---

129. Davison and Milbank, *For the Parish*, 154. In like manner, Ben Quash notes that the risk of some Fresh Expressions is that they are "communities which people have opted into rather than found themselves present to. Place is not their starting point, and if you take *place* out of the equation it is prone to being replaced by a more naked sort of *choice*." Quash, *Abiding*, 20. The importance of place in Christian theology is, John Inge contends, part of "God's rationality" in which he interacts with the world. As Inge notes, "places are the seat of relations or the place of meeting and activity in the interaction between God and the world". Inge, "Towards a Theology of Place," 46.

130. Davison and Milbank, *For the Parish*, 190.

131. Ibid., 139. In a similar vein, Roland Riem advocates for initiatives like Fresh Expressions to be coordinated and nurtured within an established "public body" rather than staking a claim in a form of anti-institutionalism. See Riem, "Mission-Shaped Church," 136–39.

theological vision of the church, and likewise, the actual disciplines and practices that have maintained the vibrancy and faithfulness of the church over the centuries. To shape "Christ's body" purely on contemporary social conditions and by means of an implicit managerial logic is to distort the "body" and render it almost unrecognizable. It is to acquiesce to the "barbarism of instrumentalizing reason" that John Milbank warns is a powerfully corrupting force on the church.

The Shape of the Organized Church

The analysis of MacIntyre, Pattison, and Roberts contribute to a significant critique of managerialism as the dominant ideology within organizational theory, and by extension, the managed church. For MacIntyre, the influential and "objectively grounded" status of the Manager in social, political, and economic arrangements masks claims that are in essence nothing more than expressions of the Manager's arbitrary, but disguised, will and preference. Instead of a morally rich environment of shared conceptions of societal good and individual purpose, the modern West has settled for an emotivist doctrine whereby claims for what constitutes human good and societal benefit are a matter of choosing between rival moral claims, all of which are grounded in personal preference.[132] Furthermore, the character of the Manager represents an attempt from within the logic of organizational theory to provide predictive power and control to the fragmented state of social and political relations.

In the work of Roberts, Budde, and Milbank the critique of the ethos of managerialism receives particular focus as to the distortion created when such an ethos is applied to the purpose and identity of the church. This distortion comes because of the ascendency of means-ends rationality through the purposive goals of efficiency, effectiveness, and control: goals generated from the last century of organizational theory. The privileging of these ends by practitioners of technique-based and missional-focused approaches distracts the church from her principle purpose to be the site of membership and union with the living God, an ecclesial body unified by the love and grace of the Holy Spirit. In place of a theological vision of the church as a visible social body incorporated by the divine humanity of Christ, managerialism provides habits of thought and practice that display the kind instrumentalizing reason that seeks to

132. MacIntyre, *After Virtue*, 11.

organize all social, political, and economic spaces into managed units that serve pragmatic ends.

These critiques, significant as they might be, gesture towards an additional layer of analysis that singles out the metaphysical assumptions of managerialism as it pertains to a theological account of the church. Whereas the preceding analysis identifies and clarifies the logic of managerial conditions in sectors of the contemporary society and in particular, the church, there remains room for questions pertaining to the specific way managerialism represents a certain metaphysical understanding of organizations as a kind of social body.

The contention of this book is that the particular definition and description of the social body that emerges from organizational and management theory displays an account of the human body that fits within the general theories of physicalism. In brief, a physicalist understanding of the body provides the metaphysics for an understanding of organizational life as the privileging of the managerial practices of efficiency, calculability, predictability, and control. When applied to the church, such an account proves erosive to a more holistic and unifying understanding of the church as the body of Christ, where sacramental participation by individuals entails connection and membership in the glorified humanity of Christ.

In sum, the reality of church decline and the rise of managerial-inspired thought and action has come in recent years under scrutiny in terms of what the church takes on when adopting the logic of managerialism. What may look like the use of value-free techniques that inspire a scientific-like certainty are actually practices heavy in assumptions that can erode the life of the church through *re-orienting* the purpose of the church to the values of efficiency, effectiveness, control, and predictability. What is missing from the preceding analysis is the significance of the "body": socially, anthropologically, and theologically understood. Such an account requires attention to how the social body is understood through the ideology of managerialism, and following, how such an ideology rests on an account of the physical body addressed by a physicalist metaphysic.[133] The next step of analysis, therefore, is to explore the

133. Graham Ward refers to the "managed body" as the "depoliticized body" wherein the body is understood primarily as "mere flesh," that is, a body void of living "embodiment." Under such conditions, the "depoliticized body is a body waiting to be controlled, coerced, and manipulated by the political, economic, and cultural powers that play with it." Ward, *The Politics of Discipleship*, 222.

methodological and conceptual framework of managerialism that has given rise to a managerial logic that when adopted, shapes any social body into a managed social body.

3

The Shape of Management or What Kind of Body Is a Managed Organization?

I T IS THE CONTENTION of this study that the current normalization and domination of a certain kind of managerial-inspired organizing in the church rests upon the application of a logic that operates by means of an instrumentalizing rationality. This logic and rationality is sourced in the assumptions of a certain metaphysical understanding of the body that privileges physical operations and states. The resulting "body" requires coordination if it is to have a purpose beyond growth other than survival. When applied to the social body of an organization, the physicalist account implicitly supports the emergence of the coordinating scheme of managerialism, which organizes and orders the purpose and identity of the organization to meet the generic pre-determined ends of efficiency, effectiveness, predictability, and control.

In order to trace the conceptual bridge between managerialism and the metaphysics of the body upon which it rests, this chapter will address how the rationalized "body" of organizational theory inhabits the legacy of mechanical and reductive accounts of the body that emerged in the early modern period through the conceptualization of the body as a kind of integrated machine with special purpose subsystems.[1] This conceptual heritage was founded and furthered through the work of Francis Bacon, René Descartes, Julian Offray de La Mettrie, and others through to the eighteenth and nineteenth century when this heritage became the

---

1. Wheeler, "God's Machines: Descartes on the Mechanization of Mind," 310.

groundwork for the likes of Henri de Saint-Simon and Max Weber to impose analogous mechanized and rationalized conditions to an understanding of social bodies. From this conceptual heritage, management and a managerial logic has emerged over the past century with the stated purpose of shaping the social body through mechanisms and techniques designed to create an arrangement that suits the ends of management.

The path that leads to the dominance of this "managed body" is the topic to which we now turn.

The Rise of the Rational Body

Organizations are constructed entities made out of the arrangement of people, buildings, equipment, and the like. As constructed entities, organizations represent a kind of conceptually understood social body, a body that can be analyzed as to its movement, growth, and purpose. In the estimation of Karen Dale and Gibson Burrell, there is a clear link between how a human body is perceived and understood, and how an organization operating as an analogous body is perceived and understood.[2] The organization, particularly the modern managed organization, Dale and Burrell maintain, received its "limbs" from the combination of the pre-modern guilds and businesses with the rise of a rationalized theoretical framework in new organizational theories, and its "soul" from the Cartesian shift that countered the established Aristotelian-Thomistic system that was concerned with *what things are* (i.e., natures) and *how things are* with the science of mechanism that gave precedence to the question of *how things work* and *how can things be improved.*[3]

This Cartesian shift bears the name of Descartes, though its history and development includes a range of theorists who added to, or even exaggerated or ignored, particular aspects of Descartes's project. In general, the shift defines the gradual assimilation of core doctrines and understandings of the natural world to the scientific method that promotes quantitative and empirical investigation.[4] What was in the sixteenth century called natural philosophy became through the developments of the seventeenth and eighteenth centuries, natural *science.* And this natural

2. Dale and Burrell, "What Shape Are We In?" 15.

3. Ibid., 16.

4. Gaukroger, *Descartes' System of Natural Philosophy*, 19.

science was concerned to defend and promote the usefulness of its methods and discoveries for improving the human condition.[5]

The history of thought from scholastic natural philosophy to Total Quality Management is far too expansive to attend here with all its conceptual plots and sub-plots. In order to establish a genealogy between physicalist notions of the human body and managerial conceptions of the social body, we will attend to core doctrines in this history by means of examining briefly the interplay of method, motion, and purpose in Bacon, Descartes, and La Mettrie.

The shift from scholasticism to mechanism in the methodology of Bacon, Descartes, and their followers is defined by Stephen Gaukroger as the move from *demonstrating* the truth of the natural world that is received through the senses and conceptualized syllogistically, to *discovering* how the natural world operates through impartial experimentation. So when Bacon advocated the purging of "idols" from the mind, Gaukroger argues,

> when Galileo presented his arguments in the context of a patronage system that was disinterested, when Descartes argued that scholastics should be replaced by men of the world as natural philosophers, when Boyle and the members of the Royal Society attempted to present their findings in the closest way to bare "facts," what they were all seeking, in their different fashions, was a way of securing objectivity, not a means of securing truth.[6]

For the Thomistic-Aristotelian tradition of thought that dominated the intellectual sphere of Europe for the three centuries prior to Bacon and Descartes, the purpose of natural philosophy was to understand the various kinds of things in the world, and the kinds of knowledge appropriate to them.[7] For this tradition, existing things are explained and understood by understanding their natures (*esse*), and to grasp the nature of something is to grasp the source of all its natural properties. For instance, to ask why a stone falls, the answer is that stones have the property of being heavy, and heavy things fall.

5. Gaukroger, *The Emergence of a Scientific Culture*, 39. Gaukroger attributes the promotion of scientific utility particularly to the work of Francis Bacon.

6. Ibid., 244.

7. Like Cartesianism, the Thomistic-Aristotelian tradition is named after the two central figures who gave prominence to many of its positions, yet the tradition itself encompasses a wide range of figures and derivative positions, some of which were exaggerations or distortions of the central positions of Aristotle and Aquinas.

Furthermore, knowing something scientifically (*scientia*) requires knowing its *propter quid*, its *on account of what*, and knowing the *propter quid* means knowing the cause. Things can and do have multiple causes, so complete or perfect knowledge necessitates knowing all the causes accounting for something. In pursuing *scientia*, one works from underlying principles related to what kind of thing or phenomena it is in itself in order to provide an account of whether the thing or phenomena is something that changes or is unchanging, and whether its existence is dependent or independent.[8] From this general position, everything from human form to planetary movements was studied.

When it comes to existing things, a central tenet of this tradition is the distinction between naturally existing things (e.g., cows) and artifacts (e.g., a knife). A biological entity, like a cow, is an example of a living organism that has a particular substantial form (*ens per se*), whereas a knife is an artifact or synthetic entity that the Thomistic-Aristotelian tradition understood as having a coincidental existence, what the tradition referred to as "accidental form" (*ens per accidens*).[9]

From this doctrine of substances emerged an understanding of naturally existing things as possessing *intrinsic* principles of motion and rest, while artifacts were considered to possess merely *extrinsic* principles of motion and rest insofar as they are artifacts. This point is easily illustrated. Iron possesses an innate or intrinsic principle of downward motion. An iron knife moves downward not by virtue of being a knife but by virtue of being iron. The knife's downward motion is extrinsic to its being a knife but intrinsic to its being iron. The principle of motion or rest can be specified as an orientation toward a determinate end. Iron's intrinsic principle of motion or rest is its innate orientation toward the earth's center as the lowest point (in Aristotle's and Aquinas's conception of the cosmos). A knife receives from its artist or craftsman its artificial form according to which its specific use (i.e., cutting) is its determinate end. On account of what does a knife have its particular form? On account of cutting. Using a knife to cut is the determinate end of a knife insofar as it is a knife.[10] To weigh this distinction and its consequences was to get at the nature and truth of what makes iron, iron, and a knife, a knife.

8. Gaukroger, *The Emergence of a Scientific Culture*, 79.

9. A more substantive account of Thomistic metaphysics is provided in chapter 4.

10. Barnes, "Natural Final Causality and Providence in Aquinas," 353.

By the late sixteenth century, this way of approaching the world in terms of natures, substances, and a principle of motion or rest that relies on both was increasingly coming to be thought of as a form of sterile investigation. The problem was diagnosed as methodological: Thomistic-Aristotelian natural philosophy was committed to a mode of enquiry that could not possibly constitute a method of discovery.

Francis Bacon, as an early proponent of discovery as the principal task of natural philosophy, distinguished between understanding, on the one hand, how things are made up and what they consist of—an exercise he associates with the scholastic method—and, on the other, by what force and in what manner they come together, and how they are transformed. We should pursue understanding of latter, he thought, for this is what leads to the augmentation and amplification of human powers. The goal, Bacon argued, is no longer the discovery of truth conceived as the outcome of reviewing existing things, but the discovery of relevant, informative truth, where the criteria of relevance and informativeness derive from the ability of that truth to take people beyond their present state of engagement with natural processes to one in which their degree of control over those processes is increased, enabling them to change and transform the processes.[11]

In order to arrive at a true interpretation of the world, Bacon insisted, what is needed to begin is an understanding of human faculties and their limitations. In the *Novum Organum*, then, Bacon identifies the senses, memory, and reason as the faculties involved in knowledge, and seeks specific "ministrations" or "helps" to heal their inherent limits. These infirmities, which for Bacon "have their foundation in human nature itself," are referred to as "the idols of the tribe," the first category of four "idols of the mind" to which Bacon attributes the errors of human knowledge.[12]

For Bacon, the deficiencies of the senses provide the first occasion for error: "By far the greatest hindrance and aberration of the human understanding proceeds from the dullness, incompetency, and deceptions of the senses."[13] The senses, which are "infirm and erring," fail us in two ways. Sometimes they provide no information; sometimes they provide false information.

11. Gaukroger, "The Unity of Natural Philosophy and the End of Scientia," 29.

12. Harrison, *The Fall of Man and the Foundations of Science*, 174.

13. Bacon, *The New Organon*, 45.

In the first case, of things that lie beyond the threshold of visibility, nothing can be known. Given this, Bacon reasoned, it "is better to dissect nature than to abstract." We should therefore be more concerned to "study matter, and its structure (*schematismus*), and structural change (*meta-schematismus*), and pure act, and the law of act or motion."[14]

Bacon's primary criticism of the Thomistic-Aristotelian natural philosophy was that it was directed towards understanding of the wrong kinds of processes. What we should be concerning ourselves with are "artificial" processes, those like motion and structures by which natural phenomena might be constrained and controlled.[15] To meet this demand, what is needed is not a system that excludes natural processes, since these still need to be understood if they are to be controlled, but rather a system that includes both natural and unnatural processes.

Bacon's promoted method was taken up with great consequence by Descartes, among others. His biology, for instance, offered novel explanations of traditional biological problems (such as natural finality, biological function, and the types of causation at work in living processes) in terms of new and emerging technologies of the period, especially the mechanism and engineering of clocks and the early forms of farm and industrial machines. In his *Treatise on Man*, Descartes specifically invoked these technologies in the course of working through an analogy between the structure of the body (nerves, muscles, tendons) and mechanical operations (tubes, springs, and motors).[16] Describing such artificial and natural processes in the same terms, Descartes blurred the unity and boundaries of living bodies by integrating them into an imminent, monistic plane of matter that reduced both natural and artificial structure and motion to the laws of power, control, and force. Under this description, *life* itself ceased to have any special ontological status; it became a mechanical illusion, something metaphysically indistinguishable from matter.[17]

It is in Descartes's theorizing about the materiality of the human body where the mechanism associated with the Cartesian tradition emerges with some clarity. In his *Synopsis of the Following Six Meditations*, Descartes argues that,

14. Ibid.
15. Gaukroger, "The Unity of Natural Philosophy and the End of *Scientia*," 25.
16. Wheeler, "God's Machines: Descartes on the Mechanization of Mind," 313.
17. Vaccari, "Dissolving Nature," 142.

We need to recognize that body, taken in the general sense (*in genera sumptum*), is a substance, so that it too never perishes. But the human body, in so far as it differs from other bodies, is simply made up of a certain configuration of limbs and other accidents of this sort; whereas the human mind is not made up of any accidents in this way, but is a pure substance.[18]

Descartes postulated that all operations that the Thomistic-Aristotelian tradition ascribed to the human soul, other than those of thought, could be accounted for mechanistically. For him, there is no *a priori* ground (i.e., no notion of substantial form or intrinsic purpose) to establish how any arrangement of matter can be distinguished from a living thing. There are no souls of any kind animating matter, the human mind being purely rational and having no part whatsoever in the workings of the body. Consequently, in *The Passions of the Soul*, Descartes can define human bodily life with reference to a machine:

And let us recognize that the difference between the body of a living man and that of a dead man is just like the difference between, on the one hand, a watch or other automaton (that is, a self-moving machine) when it is wound up and contains in itself the corporeal principle of the movements for which it is designed, together with everything else required for its operation; and, on the other hand, the same watch or machine when it is broken and the principle of its movement ceases to be active.[19]

Descartes understood the status of the human body as a comprehensive mechanism of efficient causes, wherein the operations of the body are explainable as a succession that instantiates some law-like regularity in the production of some movement.[20] All natural phenomena (again, other than human thought) were to be explained in terms of the mechanical laws of matter in motion. Descartes clearly articulated the role of the "mind" in humans in terms of "consciousness," narrowly conceived as the awareness of "thoughts" or experiences "within us."[21]

18. Descartes, "Synopsis of the Following Six Meditations," 10.

19. Descartes, "Passions of the Soul," 219.

20. As Simon Oliver notes, for the Cartesian tradition, the nature of something is fundamentally material and its matter is inert. "Whatever order and goal-orientation we find in nature is not internal or intrinsic to nature; it is imposed from without" (p. 160). Under this description, only efficient causation was thought necessary to account for human activity and purpose. Oliver, "Teleology Revived?"

21. Hacker, *Human Nature*, 24. As such, Descartes does not refer to humans as

However, in establishing the body as an autonomous object of processes and structures from the internal operations of the mind, the focus on natural philosophy would become primarily on what could be examined and manipulated.[22] Consequently, Descartes's notion of the body as "matter in motion" becomes, for the tradition that develops in his name, a core doctrine that moves Bacon's desired methods of empirical experimentation and beneficial manipulation of processes to the forefront of investigation.[23] In light of Descartes's contribution, natural philosophy became a systematic enterprise and the natural world of bodies largely an independent and autonomous field of inquiry as far as the mechanical explanations of its fundamental processes are concerned.

Stephen Gaukroger notes that for the two centuries following Descartes, empirical research shaped by a mechanistic understanding served as the basis for how studies of the natural world, in particular the human body, proceeded.[24] The Cartesian system, Gaukroger continues, was astonishingly comprehensive, offering novel and often detailed mechanist accounts of everything from cosmology, optics, the formation of the earth, the tides, magnetism, the circulation of the blood, reflex action, and the development of the foetus, to animal and human psychophysiology.[25] Yet at the heart of this system was the notion of the mechanized body that on analogy with developing technology in automation, continued to inspire a vision of the human body as a machine, a *bodily machine*.

---

rational animals, but as a "thing that thinks," a thing "that doubts, understands, affirms, denies, is willing, is unwilling, and also imagines and has sensory perceptions." See Descartes, *Meditations on First Philosophy*, 316.

22. See Rozemond, *Descartes's Dualism*. In recent years, what Justin Skirry calls the "traditional" interpretation of an "independence" between body and mind in Descartes, has come under scholarly scrutiny. As Skirry reads Descartes, mind and body are united *per se* so as to form one, whole scholastic substance. This position, Skirry notes, is much closer to the hylomorphism of Aquinas than is traditionally argued. See Skirry, *Descartes and the Metaphysics of Human Nature*.

23. According to David Braine, after three and a half centuries of success in scientific and technological advancement, the Cartesian idea of a mental substance has been discarded, but the Cartesian idea of matter has remained. Dualist and physicalists alike, argues Braine, are committed to an inner/outer divide of mind/body (in the case of dualists) and mental "events," "states," and "processes"/bodily operations (in the case of physicalists). This divide, Braine contends, contributes to the "mythology" that the "inner" domain (i.e., mind or mental state) is always the source of causal relations, "thus reducing agent-causation to event causation." Braine, *The Human Person*, 60.

24. Gaukroger, *The Emergence of a Scientific Culture*, 254.

25. Ibid., 257.

Through theorists such as La Mettrie, the human body became almost indistinguishable from the automata of industrial eighteenth-century Europe and England.

The contribution of La Mettrie builds on the empirical methodology of Bacon and the mechanistic physics of Descartes. In brief, his work furthered Bacon's desire for an improvement of the human condition through forms of process manipulation, and Descartes's mechanistic thesis. For La Mettrie, this thesis outlined an engineering approach to the human body that sought a detailed understanding of function: the mechanisms by which each part in the body carries out its predetermined end.

Through his philosophical writing, most notably *Man-Machine* (*L'Homme-machine*, 1748), La Mettrie applied his medical knowledge to questions such as the nature of matter and human beings and the relationship of human beings to nature and society. La Mettrie investigated with an eye to humanitarian reform, especially to the alleviation of human suffering, and he did so as a medical doctor committed to a materialist metaphysic.[26] Though his general approach draws on the Cartesian heritage, he rejected any need for Descartes's account of the immaterial mind, noting in favor of a materialization of the mind "since the excellence of reason does not depend on a meaningless word (immateriality) but on its force, its extent or its acuteness."[27] For La Mettrie, the privileging of materiality combined with the notion of the human body as a "living picture of perpetual motion" contributes to an approach to the human subject as a machine capable of re-engineering without fear of crossing into the *un*natural. This is so, given that there are no organizational structures (i.e., like the Thomistic substantial form) other than the biological structures of the body itself. "Let us then conclude boldly that man is a machine, and that there is in the whole universe only one diversely modified substance,"[28] he writes.

---

26. Materialism, or physicalism, is the general theory that every real, concrete phenomenon in the universe is physical and *only* physical. Moreover, as David Braine notes, "materialism proposes that the physical behavior which exhibits life or consciousness can ultimately be explained without bringing in non-physical principles" Braine, *The Human Person*, 1.

27. La Mettrie, *La Mettrie*, 4.

28. Ibid., 39. La Mettrie included non-human animals in his understanding of mechanism and materialism, arguing against notions of human uniqueness in reference to other animals.

La Mettrie is one of the early Cartesian theorists to expand the mechanical analogy that Descartes used in reference to the body, and use it as a way of describing all of what constitutes a human being. Operations associated with conscious feeling, thought, and even moral reflection, are redescribed by La Mettrie within the logic of the machine. All human functions, ranging from sensation to thought, are mechanically derived and coordinated functions internally regulated by the principle of efficient causation. His is a rational ordering of human form and function wherein "the cold skeleton of reason takes on rosy, living flesh" by means of a mechanical system of a self-moving organism.[29] In light of this, La Mettrie is able to state that the way advancements in human wellbeing move ahead is not through speculation about the nature of the mind, but through the manipulating of the bodily systems, and the body itself, through medical and other physiological sciences that attend directly to the organization and coordination of the human form.[30]

The conceptual shifts evident in the work of Bacon, Descartes, and La Mettrie contributed to normalizing of a rational and materialist approach to the natural world. In particular, the organization, function, and purpose of human bodily life went through a transformation that was inspired by the centrality of technological metaphors for the human person. As a kind of machine, the visible structures of the body, its physical systems and operations, were reconceptualized in instrumental-mechanical terms, thereby contributing to an increasing dissolution of the human body as the bearer of either a unique substantial form (and therefore, a specific essence and purpose), or for that matter, any uniqueness in comparison to other biological organisms.[31] As living organisms and machines became subsets of physical systems, the range of possibilities for controlling or even mastering bodily operations became increasingly the focus of scientific advancement.

Following the trends in naturalistic biology by the likes of La Mettrie, the trope of the coordinated mechanized body entered into multiple realms of knowledge as bodies and machines underwent a conceptual parallel development. By the nineteenth century, machines, persons, and societies as a whole were all being considered as subject to the laws of

29. Judovitz, *The Culture of the Body*, 140.

30. Gaukroger, *The Collapse of Mechanism and the Rise of Sensibility*, 399.

31. Vaccari, "Dissolving Nature," 169.

power, control, and force, and all by a controlling scientific rationality.[32] As the Scottish philosopher Thomas Carlyle would write in reference to the expansion of the Cartesian shift in the eighteenth century,

> Were we required to characterise this age of ours by any single epithet, we should be tempted to call it, not an Heroical, Devotional, Philosophical, or Moral Age, but, above all others, the Mechanical Age . . . which, with its whole undivided might, forwards, teaches and practises the great art of adapting means to ends. . . . Our true Deity is Mechanism. It has subdued external Nature for us, and we think it will do all other things.[33]

In the period after Carlyle wrote his essay, the conceptual distance between the notion of the human body and that of the social body entered a new phase of reconceptualization as the rational and materialist approach to the natural world became the basis for understanding, organizing, and manipulating, social bodies. La Mettrie had written at the end of eighteenth century that organization was sufficient to explain everything.[34] This proved to be most apposite as theorists, living in the age of revolution and industrial growth, sought ways to understand and improve the status of the body politic through mechanisms of order.

Organization Is Everything

One of the central proponents of early organizational theory was the nineteenth-century philosopher Henri de Saint-Simon.[35] Sheldon Wolin notes how Saint-Simon conceived the notion of "organization" in response to the troubled aftermath of the French Revolution. "In Saint-Simon's vocabulary 'organization' connoted far more than a simple condition of

32. Snider, "Cartesian Bodies," 310. In the background of Descartes, Bacon, and La Mettrie, are Thomas Hobbes, David Hume, and John Locke, whose arguments on perception, causality, and politics contributed to the conceptual dominance of a materialist metaphysic that extended from the human body to the body politic.

33. Thomas Carlyle, "Signs of the Times." *Edinburgh Review* 49 (1829) 439–59, quoted in, Porter, *Flesh in the Age of Reason*, 374.

34. La Mettrie, *La Mettrie*, 28.

35. Starbuck, "The Origins of Organizational Theory," 156. Saint-Simon is an exemplar in the development of organization theory, but it would have been possible to draw on John Stuart Mill or Auguste Comte as other examples of theorists seeking to use "scientific" or "rational" conceptions to the organization of business and society. Saint-Simon's mature thinking on organizational theory can be found in, Saint-Simon, *Social Organization, the Science of Man and Other Writings*.

social harmony and political stability," Wolin maintains; "organization promised the creation of a new structure of power, a functioning whole superior to the sum of the tiny physical, intellectual, and moral contributions of the parts."[36] In terms drawn from the Cartesian tradition, Saint-Simon himself argued, "Men shall henceforth do consciously, and with better directed and more useful effort, what they have hitherto done unconsciously, slowly, indecisively, and too ineffectively."[37] The man-machine who could be manipulated through attending to the functional parts emerged in Saint-Simon as the new order for social organization.

Saint-Simon envisioned the notion of organization to be a system of power, enabling business and political actors to exploit nature in a systematic fashion and thereby bring society to an unprecedented plateau of material prosperity. This required the rational arrangement of the functioning parts, the subordination of some tasks to others, the direction of work by those who possessed the relevant knowledge of industrial processes. Industrial organization required a new social hierarchy in order to create "a scientifically optimal division of labor that would produce social harmony, productivity, efficiency, and technological innovation."[38]

The new social hierarchy would represent an ascending scale of contributions, from the workers at the bottom to the industrialists, scientists, and artists at the top. The *industriels*, as Saint-Simon labeled the scientists, artists, and industrialists, symbolized the essential skills needed to maintain an industrial civilization. Just as the public interest was inevitably furthered by the unhampered pursuit of private gain by those in the business sector, so a Saint-Simonian society was to benefit from allowing the *industriels* to develop their special skills to the fullest and to pursue their own ends without restriction.[39]

A Saint-Simonian society was envisioned as a counter to the democratic ideals of his time. Among the most significant of Saint-Simon's contributions to organization theory was his recognition that the logic of

---

36. Wolin, *Politics and Vision*, 337.

37. Saint-Simon, *Henri Comte De Saint-Simon 1760–1825*, 85, quoted in, Wolin, *Politics and Vision*, 337. It is worth noting that whereas Saint-Simon begins with a premise of an organization functioning as a "whole superior to the sum," the later emergence of managerialism, under the influence of Weber and Taylor, reverse the emphasis to one of parts (i.e., workers and their particular tasks) being primary to the overall functioning of the organization.

38. Starbuck, "The Origins of Organizational Theory," 156.

39. Wolin, *Politics and Vision*, 338.

organization was at loggerheads with the claims of equality popularized by eighteenth-century revolutionary theories. As Wolin notes, "organization and equality were antithetical ideas in that the former demanded hierarchy, subordination, and authority, while the latter denied all three."[40]

Saint-Simon understood, however, that it was possible, even necessary, for a modern industrial society to strike a bargain with appeals to democratic ideals: necessary because no order could be maintained except on a mass basis; possible because the material needs of the masses could be satisfied by the application of scientific principles to production.[41] The masses, in Saint-Simon's estimation, desired neither freedom nor equality, only the alleviation of their material lot. If this were accomplished, they would give generous loyalty to the organization and, as an extra dividend, produce more efficiently. The industrial order, by providing a new structure for society, a new principle of authority, a new form of integration, was to be the counter-revolutionary antidote to the agitation of the masses, a radical remedy for the social ills in the wake of so much revolution.

In his vision of an organized society, Saint-Simon privileged the rule of scientific laws over the commonly held convictions about the necessity of centralized government. Government would be reduced to nothing, or almost nothing. Political action "will be reduced to what is necessary for establishing a hierarchy of functions in the general action of man on nature"[42] and to clearing away obstacles to useful work. The direction of society was to take the form of administration; that is, the control over things rather than people. Human energies would be redirected, away from the attempt to dominate each other, to the goal of dominating nature. Wealth, power, plenty, and knowledge would arise through a kind of social alchemy that derived from transcending individual limits by means of a coordinated deployment of productive and efficient control of social, political, and economic processes. Such efforts, Saint-Simon surmised, would give rise to a properly rational humanity that could counter human limitations by means of higher goals and purposes than the ferment of revolution and chaos.[43]

40. Ibid.

41. Ibid.

42. Saint-Simon, *Henri Comte De Saint-Simon 1760–1825*, 89, in Wolin, *Politics and Vision*, 338.

43. Wolin, *Politics and Vision*, 339–40.

The desire of Saint-Simon for the transformation of the human ir-rationalities of economic and social serfdom into the rational and coor-dinated behavior of a properly ordered and controlling humanity proved influential in the latter half of the nineteenth century, and well into the twentieth and current centuries. Saint-Simon's work, for example, lies at the foundation of Max Weber's notion of *zweckrationalität*, or instrumen-tal rationality. For Weber, an action is instrumental when

> the end, the means, and the secondary results are all rationally taken into account and weighed. This involves rational consid-eration of alternative means to the end, of the relations of the end to the secondary consequences, and finally of the relative importance of different possible ends.[44]

From the basis of instrumental rationality, Weber sets his discussion of work organization in the context of a rationalizing drive to replace traditional methods of organizing productive activity with a carefully designed "scientifically optimal division of labor" reminiscent of Saint-Simon. And like Saint-Simon, such design begins with advancing an anthropology for the rational individual.

In the estimation of Weber, the building block of rationality is the purposeful individual: human action as purposeful or intentional. Pur-posive action is conscious, anticipatory action guided by intent, aimed at the achievement of ends. The rational individual is a rational pursuer of self-interest. He or she also calculates the most efficient means to a goal. Having goals and alternative means to achieve these ends, the actor must weigh probable costs and benefits in choosing actions. Furthermore, "ra-tional choice," Barbara Townley argues, "elaborates the original premise of rational action. Choice arises from preferences (desires) and expecta-tions (beliefs) and is guided by a calculation of the costs and benefits accruing to alternative actions and their likely outcomes."[45]

At the heart of rational choice is action. To explain an action, there must first be verification that it stands in an optimizing relationship to the desires and beliefs of the agent. The action should be the best way of satisfying the agent's desires, given his or her beliefs. Moreover, it is nec-essary that these desires and beliefs be themselves rational. At the very least, they must be internally consistent. With respect to beliefs they must also impose a more substantive requirement of rationality: they should be

44. Weber, *Economy and Society*, 153.

45. Townley, *Reason's Neglect*, 28.

optimally related to the evidence available to the agent. In forming their beliefs, the agents should consider all and only the relevant evidence, with no element being unduly weighted. As a logical extension of this requirement, it is important that the collection of evidence itself be subject to the norms of rationality. The efficacy of action may be undermined both by gathering too little evidence and by gathering too much. The optimal amount of evidence is partly determined by the agent's desires. More important decisions make it rational to collect more evidence.

It follows that rational choice elaborates the individual who engages in it. It presumes self-interest and a calculating individual, and a self with a number of stable preferences. Rational choice aims to maximize these preferences. This requires that preferences are ranked and that these preference rankings fulfill a range of conditions with regard to their completeness and consistency. Human progress, then, is understood as the application of technical conceptions to forms of human cooperation towards greater performance and productivity. Hence the belief assumed with a managerial logic that "numbers are important" and in the rational act of allocating resources (material and humans). This sort of rationalization converts managerial decisions into depersonalized actions that serve "accounting demands" and "market needs."[46]

From a premise of deliberate intent and cooperation, the focus then becomes the mechanisms and techniques through which this can be secured. As one of the defining features of formal organization is that they are purposeful, oriented to the pursuit of relatively specific goals, which are presumed to be rational, clearly defined, and explicit. Organizations must be centrally coordinated for the pursuit of these, and there must be unambiguous criteria for selecting among activities to achieve predetermined goals with maximum efficiency.[47] Organizations become presented as a single, unified rational decision-maker, purposive and intentional, with clear goals and identifiable preferences for outcomes.

Moreover, organizations employ a variety of devices designed to imbue individual and corporate behavior with rationality. What is desired of rational organizations is a proper balance between efficient formal approximations that can have a reliable social effect, and substantive good sense to know their limits and to improve them.[48] To accomplish

46. Klikauer, *Managerialism*, 107.

47. Townley, *Reason's Neglect*, 32.

48. Stinchcombe, "Reason and Rationality," 286.

this, the organization, notes Wolin, pursues a course of action thought to maximize rational choice and effectiveness. This course of action includes the specification of the individual's duties and functions, the assignment of authority within the structure so that the member will know where to look for commands, and the establishment of limits to his or her choices. The result sought is the shaping of the worker's attitudes so that the individual comes to feel a sense of identity with the whole and consequently reflects the stability and order of the organization.[49] By these arrangements an environment is established where a "correct" or rational choice by the individual is possible; that is, a choice adapted to the organization's objectives. In such an environment, individual choice towards the goals of the organization operates as an investment that is used by management to further the stability and profitability of the organization.[50]

The kind of authority exercised through a rationalized organization comes by way of bureaucratic rationality, whereby the highest degree of efficiency is sought at every level of production. The notion of bureaucracy is not unique to Weber, but he is seen as melding rational choice and efficient productivity in imitation of lessons learned from Otto von Bismarck's deployment of a military-like hierarchy within social, political, and economic institutions in pre-war Germany. For Weber, just as a well-run and efficient army is designed to survive defeats on the battlefield, a well-run and efficient business had to be designed to survive market booms and busts.[51] In the estimation of Townley, the most serious consequence of the association of bureaucracy with rational choice is that bureaucracy is taken to be a mode of organization regardless of function, applicable, for example, to state, political parties, church, sect, and firm.[52] In this way, the common properties of organizations, irrespective of function, may be highlighted. Any organization can be compared to any other. The substantive qualities of specific organizations become of less conceptual importance. An efficient army, an efficient church, and an efficient government are, in the employment of a bureaucratic rationality, simply expressions of a single overriding description.

From the understanding that bureaucratic organization is the embodiment of rationality, offering a reductive and mechanistic model of

---

49. Wolin, *Politics and Vision*, 341.

50. Enteman, *Managerialism*, 159.

51. Sennett, *The Culture of the New Capitalism*, 27.

52. Townley, *Reason's Neglect*, 47.

organizations, bureaucracy is transformed into a prescriptive model, identified with a particular form of organizational structure, and deemed to be more efficient than other forms of organization. As Weber states, from "a purely 'technical point of view', bureaucracy is 'formally' the most rational or technically superior form of organization. It is superior to any other form in precision, in stability, in stringency of its discipline and in its reliability."[53] Bureaucracy's superiority lies in its formality, that is, with its inherent reliance on an assumption of Baconian-inspired "scientific" objectivity, and with this, its guarantee of calculability. It makes possible a particularly high degree of calculability of results for heads of organizations and those acting in relation to it. Furthermore, it excludes arbitrariness[54] and promotes action in accordance with rational rules calculated along the lines of the "capacity for purposive manipulation."[55] The technical superiority of a formal rationality ensures its success.

Bureaucracy, for Weber, allows for the delivery of certainty, order, and controllability on a large scale in a comprehensive manner. The discharge of business, therefore, is according to "calculable rules." Predictability or calculability derives from a confidence in a prescribed knowledge that assumes the primacy of objectivity because of scientific analysis. To act rationally, therefore, is to act on the basis such knowledge. A bureaucratic rationality is thus the operation of "domination through knowledge." With such knowledge, a rationalized institution is thought to improve the rationality of individuals through regularizing expectations and reducing uncertainty. In addition, a properly rationalized institution embodies the visible structures and routines that make up organizations, which in modern managerial theories are thought to be a direct reflection and effect of the rules and structures that are built into the theorizing behind conceptions of what constitutes the human person.[56]

Bureaucratic rationality, drawn as it is from an analysis of the coordination of people and the deployment of such towards the meeting of specific and efficiently defined goals, carries within its premises an understanding of the organization as a kind of social body in need of management. Since modern managed organizations largely shape the activity of the worker, they set the conditions for the exercise of compliance, and

---

53. Weber, *Economy and Society*, 223.

54. Townley, *Reason's Neglect*, 50.

55. Weber, *Economy and Society*, 483.

56. Townley, *Reason's Neglect*, 101.

hence of rationality in human society. Human rationality, then, gets its higher goals and integrations from the institutional setting in which it operates and by which it is molded. Outside of the managed organization the individual is cut off from organizational membership, that is, the co-ordinating apparatus of the social body where rational action contributes to the formation of a rational person. The rational individual is, and must be then, an organized and institutionalized *individual*.[57]

The notion of "an organized and institutionalized individual" as a part of a rational, managed organization captures the ethos of manage-rialism as a form of organizational theory and practice that appropriates an instrumentalized rationality in the service of the goals of efficiency, effectiveness, predictability, and control. Such an account enlists the in-dividual subject as an active part of the overall organization in as much as the individual inhabits the formality and order of the managed institu-tion. To increase effectiveness or profitability for this "whole" becomes a task of further coordination of the parts. Shaped by the logic of manage-rialism, such coordination is ordered towards the kind of predictability and calculability that shapes an organization or any social body into a Weberian bureaucracy, complete with rationalized techniques and train-ing that instill a scientific objectivity to the plans and procedures of the organization. Rationalized institutions have become the embodiment of reason in social life.[58] Under such conditions, the social body can only be a managed body.

Behind this account is the assumption that just as the principles of managerialism are thought to operate in service to specific goals of the particular kind of organization being managed, so the individual has purpose in as much as the individual can participate and contribute to the successful operations of the organization. Under such conditions, the "rule of the body" operates as the process of rationalization that appropri-ates and deploys the parts (e.g., individual organs in the case of a physi-cal body, individual workers in the case of an organization, individual members or churches in the case of ecclesiology) through coordination

---

57. Wolin, *Politics and Vision*, 341. To this point, Enteman connects the "insti-tutionalized individual" to the way managerialism cultivates this status in order to privilege the "life of the organization" over any one worker or even group of workers. Enteman calls this the "atomization of managerialism," that is, the less-than-discrete notion that individuals have no independent "existence" outside the operations of the organization. See Enteman, *Managerialism*, 158f.

58. Townley, *Reason's Neglect*, 101.

and integration to the efficient functioning of the whole.[59] The resulting arrangement of the coordinated whole exemplifies MacIntyre's concern with how the managed organization avoids chance through the
deployment of social manipulation meant to guarantee organizational
predictability.

The "Absent Present" Body in Managed Organizations

The question of how organizations operate as social bodies has given rise
to the notion of what Chris Shilling calls, "an absent presence" of the
body.[60] The presence of the body, Shilling notes, is evident in the body
of the worker, even though it is the *function* of the worker and not the
embodiment of the worker that figures as essential to organizational
management.[61] The body has a place in the organization, even as it is
untethered from considerations of what the body signifies in reference to
the overall understanding of the modern managed organization.

The human body has been absent, however, in the sense that organizational theory and practice rarely focus in a sustained manner on
the particular embodied human as an object of importance in its own
right. As bodies, Shilling contends, the human person is regarded as an
assumed participant that lay outside of the legitimate social concerns of
analysis. Like the human heart, the body in organizational theory tends to
remain hidden from view, yet at the same time it serves ultimately to keep
alive and nourish that which surrounded it.[62] Although the physical body
is rarely an object of explicit concern, facets of human embodiment (e.g.,
language and thought, and the dispositions and emotions that motivated
action), become central to understanding the insight of Mary Douglas,
that the human body is the most readily available image of a social system. In other words, ideas about the human body correspond closely to
prevalent ideas about social organizations and society as a whole.[63]

The "absent presence" of the human body to the understanding of organization practices denies, Shilling notes, the basic and commonsensical

59. Roberts, *Religion, Theology and the Human Sciences*, 162.
60. Shilling, *The Body in Culture, Technology and Society*, 19.
61. Shilling, *The Body and Social Theory*, 15.
62. Shilling, *The Body in Culture, Technology and Society*, 17.
63. Douglas, *Natural Symbols: Explorations in Cosmology*, 69.

notion that people have bodies and act with their bodies.[64] The daily experiences of living—be they derived from learning in schools, travelling to a place of employment, working in an office, or buying and preparing food for a meal—are inextricably bound up with experiencing and understanding the body of an individual and its relation to other people's bodies. And yet, "we all have bodies," Doyal and Gough state, "and this constitutes part of what makes us human beings possessed of the ability to communicate with each other, and experience common needs, desires, satisfactions and frustrations."[65]

The body is made absent, according to Dale, through two roles specific to modern organizations. In relation to the physical presence of human bodies in organizations, the legacy of mind/body dualism has centered value, meaning, and knowledge in the mind and has largely dismissed the body as mere material—a container for the mind or soul. This is exemplified by Weber's typology of social action that associated truly human action with intellectually processed, rational action. The body was considered as a passive container that acted as a shell to the active mind (which was identified as distinguishing humans from animals).[66] The greater the emphasis on rational modes of operations, the more the human body becomes absent from the accounting of how a managed organization functions. The tendency within such accounts is to define human actors in disembodied terms as rational agents who make choices through means/ends formulae, based on "utility" criteria or "general value" orientation.

The second role is in relation to the body as a biological organism. The assumption within organizational theory is that the body of the organization is constructed following the logic of a Cartesian machine:

64. Shilling, *The Body in Culture, Technology and Society*, 20.

65. Doyal and Gough, *A Theory of Human Need*, 305. The advent of "telecommuting" further problematizes the notion of the worker as embodied, since under the conditions of telecommuting, the worker is no longer "present" in the workplace but remains "virtually" connected to the organization. As Anne Kate Smith notes, "in our slowly but surely evolving business culture, work increasingly refers to what you do rather than to where you go" (p. 62). Framed as a "solution" to work/home conflicts, and the financial strain of actual commuting, telecommuting, Smith contends, blurs the boundaries of what constitutes the "workplace" in contrast to every other place. Smith, "Make Working at Home Work." Telecommuting contributes to the absence of the body, I contend, through further instrumentalizing the material conditions of the individual body by means of reducing the human worker principally to his or her output via virtual mediums made possible with advances in internet connectivity.

66. Shilling, *The Body in Culture, Technology and Society*, 22.

already existing bits and pieces are paired and coordinated to operate smoothly. When one part fails, a replica replaces it. The goal is to keep the "machine" running efficiently. Under these conditions, the entire organism can be analyzed, dissected, and re-arranged in order to meet the principal ends of the organization.[67] The description of an organization as a mechanical organism, Dale concedes, has been incorporated into the very heart of the discipline of organizational theory.[68] The result is a vision of an orchestrated body that operates like a fine-tuned apparatus while the actual agent remains overlooked.

Dale contends that this mechanistic approach to organizational theory has contributed to a notion of the body as nothing more than the dissection and re-arrangement of body parts. This reductionism is equally evidenced, Thomas Diefenbach argues, in contemporary organizational research that employs a form of empirical epistemology that privileges the prediction and manipulation of social and natural units by means of law-like methods of control. There is a strong conviction among the proponents of managerialism, Diefenbach contends,

> that business and organisations are based on natural laws, and that these laws can be discovered, made available to managers and applied by them. Managerialism is positivistic. Indeed, in core areas of management and business studies, concepts have been developed which state theories and laws which are both applicable and even falsifiable.[69]

From within empirical assumptions, the aim of research in the field of organizational theory is to discern laws that govern the ways in which organizations operate. Such laws are for the organization to be considered prescriptive and normative. The generation of these causal relationships or laws, theorists argue, enable management to become more scientific and managers to become better able to predict and control their environments. The focus is on the observable, and the approach to the analysis of organizations assumes that their reality is objectively given, functionally necessary, and politically neutral. Thus, social interactions (e.g., between workers or between management and clients) are to be studied in the same way as physical elements: as a network of causal relations linking

---

67. Dale, *Anatomising Embodiment and Organization Theory*, 20–21.

68. Ibid., 23.

69. Diefenbach, *Management and the Dominance of Managers*, 151.

aspects of behavior to context and stimuli in the external environment thus conditioning people to behave in a certain way.[70]

Such an arrangement suggests that managers face an objective reality to which they themselves need only apply suitable methods for assessing in order to come up with the correct solution to organizational issues. This is prescriptive in itself as it implies that people and organizations should, even must, strive for "best practice" and "perfect" solutions. Managers are explicitly encouraged via these principles and best practices to organize and do business in a very specific way—and only in that way. The result is casuistic reasoning, such that: if you want to be a successful manager, you must apply this concept in that way because this will increase shareholder value and the efficiency and productivity of your business.[71]

The empirical assumptions service not only the bureaucratic rationality of managerialism, but also a conception of the organization as a mechanized body.[72] As Alasdair MacIntyre argues, managerialism treats ends as given through arranging human and non-human resources in order to achieve these pre-determined goals with maximum efficiency and effectiveness.[73] The manipulation of resources for defined ends by means of objective strategies and techniques links managerialism to an anthropology of the body that assumes the power to organize, delineate, and define the body corporate as "organs" of an organization. Thus, for the modern, managed organization, an empirical epistemology remains a vital force in shaping the function and orientation of the social body, pressuring such a body to conform to its physicalist rationality.

Material Bodies and Managed Organizations

Conceptually, reductive empiricist accounts tend towards treating the human body as simply an organism among other living and nonliving items

70. Johnson and Duberley, *Understanding Management Research*, 40. See also, Willmott, "Rethinking Management and Managerial Work."

71. Diefenbach, *Management and the Dominance of Managers*, 152.

72. Gareth Morgan names the "mechanical body" as one of the predominate "images" of organization. He notes, "when we talk about organization, we usually have in mind a state of orderly relations between clearly defined parts that have some determinate order . . . (as) a set of mechanical relations" (p. 13). See Morgan, *Images of Organization*.

73. MacIntyre, *After Virtue*, 74.

in the world.[74] As such, the human body is understood by means of the coordination and operation of physical processes and states. Moreover, through the primacy of a neural-biological description of the body, it is assumed that such an account is sufficient to defining what it means for a human body to be a *living* human person. The living human body, under this description, is an integrated system of physical operations and states that displays capacities of complex thought and behavior. Capacities that might seem to indicate a nonphysical casual description are, in the estimation of physicalist proponents, properties of the physical system that will eventually be incorporated into a physicalist account after advancements in study and research have improved. The appeal of physicalism, contends Putnam, lies precisely in its claim to be "natural metaphysics" within the bounds of science.[75]

The nature and trajectory of these reductive accounts demonstrate an analogous understanding of the human body as that displayed in a managerial account of the social body. Such an analogy, moreover, is more than simply a convenient comparison. As we have already seen, for Mary Douglas, the social body constrains the way the physical body is perceived, and vice versa.[76] The body, then, is a physical human body that is never simply "just physical," but is always already invested with certain social practices and notions. To make claims, therefore, about the particular coordination of the physical body is also to assert something about the character of the body socially understood. Likewise, to address how a social body is organized is also to gesture towards an understanding of how an organized individual is thought to operate. In other words, examining how conceptions of the human body are assumed in certain organizational understandings will reveal the depth of the analogical connection, and in doing, display the metaphysical assumptions implicit to this connection.

When examined in light of the claims of reductive physicalism, the individual/social body analogy details a set of connections that lay bare the implicit physicalist metaphysic of managerialism, and consequently the managerial logic of technique and missional-based ecclesial approaches. These connections can be highlighted by attending to three

74. Bishop, "Body Work and the Work of the Body." Bishop notes that in much contemporary metaphysics of the body, "The body is just there, almost un-thought, almost without meaning" (p. 115).

75. Putnam, "Three Kinds of Scientific Realism," 197.

76. Douglas, *Natural Symbols*, 74.

coordinating and interrelated assumptions of physicalism: first, that the human body can only be properly understood through a process of rationalization, that is, a process that reduces the operations and states of the body to that of its constitute parts. Second, that a human body requires the coordination of efficient causation. Third, the human body is primarily purposed for biological survival and growth.

The first assumption, that the body is understood through a process of reduction to its constitute parts, has its roots in the empiricism of Baconian science, which sought to classify the structure of "natural things" through observation and experiment.[77] As was addressed in a previous section, Bacon's approach to science started with a rejection of the Thomistic-Aristotelian tradition of *demonstrating* the truth of the natural world that is received through the senses and conceptualized syllogistically. For Bacon, what knowledge ought to be concerned with is *discovering* how the natural world operates through impartial experimentation through the systematic gathering of tables of experimental data. He proposed that an inductive method could be applied to the gathered facts to produce more abstract generalizations, and in this way, the edifice of scientific knowledge could be built up.[78] Bacon's experimental science, revaluated as it was through technological advancement and the deployment of mechanical approaches to natural things, entailed the rejection of alternative scientific approaches, particular approaches that understood the world of things in terms of "wholes" that form a "natural unit."[79]

Knowing is for Bacon a building or making process wherein understanding what the pieces are, and how they fit together, gives rise to a larger structure.[80] Thus, the Baconian scientific method emphasized the configuration and process of the parts of the item being investigated, which provided an account of the whole item (e.g., its overall structure and motion) by means of the causal power of the *parts*.[81] To adjust the operations of the whole becomes, through a Baconian method, a matter of understanding and manipulating the corresponding operations of the constituent pieces.

77. Turner, "The Body in Western Society," 23.

78. Rossi, "Bacon's Idea of Science," 25.

79. Perez-Ramos, "Bacon's Forms and the Maker's Knowledge Tradition," 111.

80. Rossi, "Bacon's Idea of Science," 38.

81. Joy, "Scientific Explanation from Formal Causes to Laws of Nature," 85.

The legacy of Bacon in the rationalization of scientific inquiry is evident in the growing dominance of neuroscientific accounts of living things, particularly with regard to the structure and function of the human body. For physicalists like Dennett, what neuroscience reveals is the existence of matter and physical processes that are the "building blocks" for understanding the structure and operations of the human person. As Dennett contends,

> there is only one sort of stuff, namely matter—the physical stuff of physics, chemistry, and physiology—and the mind is somehow nothing but a physical phenomenon. In short, the mind is the brain. . . . We can (in principle!) account for every mental phenomenon using the same physical principles, laws, and raw materials that suffice to explain radioactivity, continental rift, photosynthesis, reproduction, nutrition, and growth.[82]

In the estimation of the reductive physicalists like Dennett, cognitive neuroscience is in the position to address how the prefrontal cortices are responsible for human thinking, the reason for why reentrant pathways exist, and what precisely the highly determinant roles of the hippocampus and neocortex have in a human being's remembering. In other words, human capacities such as thinking, reasoning, and memory are entirely attributable to the neurobiological processes. Accordingly, for physicalism, a physical entity like a human body is accounted for by understanding the relationships of neural and other bodily systems that as *physical* systems exist in the real physical space of the body.[83]

The argument for reductive physicalism rests on its ability to explain the vast and growing body of psychophysical correlations defined and described through the neurosciences as a set of law-like physical operations. The task of physicalism consists, then, in disassembling the seemingly complicated machinery of life into its simplest components, which can then be cataloged, prodded, manipulated, and described. Accordingly, any real understanding of the body could only come from taking it apart, just as one takes apart a machine to discover its inner workings. Such a methodological style, with its emphasis on the individualistic and atomistic, whereby wholes and collectives are the equivalent to their constituent parts, displays a rationalized process. The assumption is that an accurate understanding of the parts will reveal the workings of the whole

82. Dennett, *Consciousness Explained*, 33.
83. Searle, "Putting Consciousness Back in the Brain," 118.

in its entirety, and in Dennett's estimation, this makes possible a kind of biological "reverse engineering" to improve the function of the whole by manipulating the parts.[84] The human body, under such rationalized conditions, is treated as static and open to the manipulating of its functions in order that the parts operate more effectively. Thus, the human physical body requires the deployment of rational processes.

The dominance of the neurobiological account of human life in physicalism provides the metaphysical basis for the role of the social body in management and organization theory. As was noted in the previous chapter, the assumption within organizational theory is that the managed body is constructed following the logic of a hybrid organic-machine: already existing bits and pieces are paired and coordinated to operate smoothly within a container that provides the semblance of a unified order. When one part fails to operate according to this order, a replica replaces it. The goal is to keep the "organism" running efficiently. Under these conditions, the entire organism can be analyzed, dissected, and rearranged in order to meet the principal ends of the organization.[85] The description of an organization as a mechanical organism, Dale concedes, has been incorporated into the very heart of the discipline of management theory.[86] The result is a vision of an orchestrated body that operates like a fine-tuned apparatus while the actual agent remains overlooked or simply absent.

The idea of the ordered and integrated system as being the principle arena of inquiry is common in both the physicalist examination of the body and the idea of the social body of the organization. This idea, what Dale calls the *atomizing urge,* necessarily precludes attention to the entire body as having any kind of intrinsic unity, focusing instead on dividing the body by dissection, splitting it into structured parts that have their individual functions to contribute to the whole.[87] What this present study seeks to show is that, in order to be analyzed, coordinated, and manipulated, the question of what makes a body alive has to be ignored so that the material of the body can be "fixed" in its rightful place within an objective (i.e., rational) account. Under such conditions, the *agency* and

---

84. Dennett, *Darwin's Dangeorus Idea,* 212–20.

85. Dale, *Anatomising Embodiment and Organization Theory,* 20–21.

86. Ibid., 23.

87. Ibid., 203.

unity of the living body disappears behind the mechanisms of neural-level activity.

In organizational terms, this atomizing of the "managed body" helps maintain attention on the coordination of individuals and individual units (e.g., a particular department) and their contributions, while simultaneously resisting any real notion of a unified enterprise, through the ongoing managerial manipulation of the parts to serve the established goals set forth through managerial consultation. This approach to organization contributes to a notion of the social body as an *absent presence* where those who attend to the particulars of the working parts (i.e., the workers) are subject to those that attend to the organizational vision and mission (i.e., management) such that the thrust of organizational coordination is towards the manipulation of the working parts to serve managerial ends. What looks like a whole body functioning as a kind of unity on an organizational chart resembles more accurately an anatomical assessment of a corpse that requires constant manipulation through managerial control to present the impression of a unified whole. These atomizing conditions are deemed effective for the survival and growth of the organization but the result is a social body that performs tasks and fulfils duties while lacking the conceptual tools to move beyond the atomizing state and into the status of a social unity.

The conditions of the atomizing state of the managed body leaves unaddressed the question of what constitutes a unified body. Within a managerial logic, how the parts of a social body relate is determined by their particular *function*. When a part fails, it is simply replaced or its functions are assimilated into the responsibility of an adjoining part. The task of the manager is to order the parts to create the conditions for the most efficient outcome. Any part is replaceable or able to manipulated, for what fundamentally matters is the level of production. The worker is the "building block" for the managed body, and as such, the worker exists within managerial conditions that encourage regular "adjustments" to the focus and scope of the work to improve the status of the organization in the eyes of shareholders and stakeholders.

Such a logic animates the emphasis in technique-based approaches to the church that privileges the implantation of "programs" for demographic or interest-based groups within the overall life of the community, for example, the establishment of specialized programming for young people. Increased focus on how to organize the whole body into smaller and smaller subgroups based on particular rationalized criteria allows the parts to be organized and manipulated. To the degree that the groups function to improve the established outcomes of a particular church, the groups remain part of the overall functioning of the whole. It is when a group no longer figures into the life of the community that it is replaced by another group, or simply left to atrophy.[88] As new demographics or interests emerge, new programs are established in order to continue the process of participation by means of the coordinating power of manager-like leader.

The existence of small groups or church programs is itself not a concern, for these provide for a rich variety in community life within the overall life of the community. It is the deployment of the *atomizing urge* through a process of rationalized order over such groups and programs that is questionable. Such a process requires the "dissecting" of the social body into parts, thereby atomizing the body making it possible for manager-like leaders to coordinate and manipulate the parts in service to managerial ends such as effectiveness. Under these conditions, programs become part of a "lifestyle-preference" view of religion, which, as Christian Smith notes, promotes the creation of "religious consumers" who participate in the life of the church principally through the exercise of choosing what programs or groups they prefer, and leaving aside the question of how Christian discipleship is exercised in the midst of the diversity of the entire community.[89] The rise of the "lifestyle congregation" represents a "new social community," one that reflects patterns in the broader culture towards the normalizing of self-selection when it comes to how and with whom people relate.[90] Instead of having a body whose parts are ordered and oriented to the overall life of the body, the lifestyle preference approach to the church contributes to a corpse-like ecclesial body whose life is reduced to the effectiveness of programs in contributing to the generic goals of growth and survival.

The operating assumption behind the emphasis on programs for demographic or interest groups is the same atomizing urge of physicalism and the managed organization. Individual groups, like specific neural

88. For an example of this rationalized approach to church groups, see, Ward, *Liquid Church*, 76–77.

89. Smith, "Implications of National Study of Youth and Religion Findings for Religious Leaders," 63. Fresh Expressions portrays the increase of choice as being a benefit to the overall program of *The Mission-Shaped Church*. See *Mission-Shaped Church*, 109.

90. Guder and Barrett, *Missional Church*, 66–67.

activity or individual members or departments, receive a form of priority in matters of coordination and function, while the containing body remains seemingly absent. There is a sense, under such conditions, that any appeal to the *unity* of the body, or to the body having intrinsic identity or purpose, fails to meet the criterion of the technique-based approaches to the church that emphasize function over identity. As such, the community's function is evidenced and expressed in reference principally to the values and preferences of religious consumers and not to any unifying form by which the individual programs or groups are understood to be parts of a coherent and whole body.

The second assumption of physicalism, that a human body requires the coordination of efficient causation, highlights the ambiguity of accounting for the living human body in such a way as to demonstrate its inherent value. In relation to physicalism, efficient causation names the mechanistic operation of laws and regularities that coordinate the physical body to function in a certain way. The figures of Francis Bacon and David Hume play a role in the history of the ascendency of efficient causation as the principal explanation of bodily movement and change, and, there remains a continuing and widely shared commitment by contemporary physicalists to the precepts of such causation, particularly through their attention to complete causal chains, the denial of action at a distance, and the denial of backward (downward) causation.[91] A reliance on efficient causation, in other words, gives precedence to an instrumentalized understanding of the human body as simply a biological organism that is coordinated through the mechanisms of neurobiological operations.[92]

For physicalists, the life of a human is the activity of organized matter, and the sophisticated organizational operations at the chemical, biological, and neurophysiological level.[93] To account for human feeling or thinking, for example, requires more than simply an appeal of human "reason" or "mind." As Patricia Churchland contends, a properly physicalist understanding of feeling or thinking requires a theory like that of how proteins are made. Such a theory ought to explain the main properties of feeling or thinking in sufficient detail to satisfy four conditions: an understanding of the properties and organization of the micro events, attention to how the neurobiological phenomena can be predicted, an un-

---

91. Rosenberg, "Reductionism (and Antireductionism) in Biology," 131.

92. Bishop, "Rejecting Medical Humanism," 19.

93. Churchland, *Matter and Consciousness*, 147.

derstanding of how the system can be manipulated, and clarity regarding the location of the phenomena in the brain itself.[94] Equipped with such a theory, proponents argue, physicalism will fully account for the properties of bodily phenomena by means of understanding the neurobiological mechanisms.[95]

Physicalists maintain that humans are merely a physical substance (a brain and central nervous system plus a body) that has physical properties and in which occur physical events.[96] This arrangement, Paul Churchland notes, is simply the result of the processes involved in human evolution. The important point about the standard evolutionary story, Churchland states,

> is that the human species and all of its features are the wholly physical outcome of a purely physical process. . . . If this is the correct account of our origins, then there seems neither need, nor room, to fit any nonphysical substances or properties into our theoretical account of ourselves. We are creatures of matter. And we should learn to live with that fact.[97]

In other words, what comes from the physical by means of physical processes will also be physical. The human body, in the estimation of physicalists, is a physical thing with physical processes, and is best understood as an ordered aggregate, a set of parts put into external relations by some ordering principle (e.g., the laws of efficient causation within "nature") to form a whole.[98] To account for a living human body is a matter of attending to how the constitute parts to the body are ordered, and how they relate as an integrated neurobiological system.

The physicalist notion of the human body as a neurobiological ordered system of aggregate parts means that the physicalist account pays little attention to the human body as a particular kind of *unified* thing. Physicalists approach the human body in much the same way that the bronze of a statue might be considered, as mere stuff that has experienced some force of organization and remains potentially manipulated. As such, the body of physicalism is itself no different from a *corpse*, animated by metaphysics of efficient causation, a mechanism when matter

94. Churchland, "A Neurophilosophical Slant on Consciousness Research," 288.

95. Ibid., 289. Also, Searle, "Consciousness," 576.

96. Moreland, "The Mind-Body Problem," 567.

97. Churchland, *Matter and Consciousness*, 21.

98. Moreland, "Should a Naturalist Be a Supervenient Physicalist?" 46.

that is definitively identical to dead matter is ordered and able to move by virtue of the force of its prior efficient (and "natural") causes.[99] The human body is therefore a malleable object subject to the instrumental causation of neurobiological systems, which is where what counts as "life" can be observed and examined. In brief, the body of physicalism is the site of rational organization.

The notion of "an organized body" as a part of a rational, managed organization captures the ethos of managerialism as a form of organizational theory and practice that appropriates an instrumentalized rationality in the service of the goals of efficiency, effectiveness, predictability, and control. Like the rational investigation of physicalism, managerialism views the individual subject as a generic body that has no particular history and comes from no particular culture. The managed body "matters" only in as much as the individual inhabits the formality and order of the managed institution. To increase effectiveness or profitability, the individual worker needs coordination. Shaped by the logic of managerialism, such coordination is ordered toward the kind of predictability and calculability that shapes an organization or any social body into a Weberian bureaucracy, complete with rationalized techniques and training that instill a scientific objectivity to the plans and procedures of the organization. Rationalized institutions have become the embodiment of reason in social life.[100] Under such conditions, the social body can only be a managed body.

The claims of managerialism to order and organize the social body include two major assumptions: existence of a domain of morally neutral fact, about which the "manager" is to be "expert," and the ability to identify and utilize law-like generalizations about human and institutional life sufficient to mold, influence, and control the social environment.[101] When enacted, a managerial logic inspires the appropriation and deployment of instruments of coordination and integration that exercises power by means of "scientific" (and hence, objective) and law-like generalizations designed to account for the entire operation of the social body. The person tasked with such appropriation and deployment is the managerial leader.

99. Bishop, "Body Work and the Work of the Body," 114.

100. Townley, *Reason's Neglect*, 101.

101. MacIntyre, *After Virtue*, 77.

In the life of the church, the managerial leader who orders and orients the social body towards the generic goals of managerialism is evidenced in the emphasis certain church theorists and practitioners give to charismatic or entrepreneurial leadership. As Richard Roberts notes, managerialism is fundamentally about power, obedience, and conformity in a low-trust environment that is often masked by appeals to reflexivity and empowerment.[102] In times of crisis, the church entrepreneur takes responsibility for customizing the learning track for the church's life context and goals.[103] Such leaders promise "salvation," and require a rejection of ties to the external order so that the message itself becomes the only route of escape from a perceived crisis.[104] This is particularly apposite at times of social anxiety, when the fundamental aims and methods of an organization are in question. Into this scenario, the leader who manifests the power to direct the entire mission of a church can enter with dynamic self-defining authority that dictates reality for and on behalf of others.[105]

Emulating the rational process of the managed body, the entrepreneurial church leader asks: what does the church need to be more effective? Then, using the position of "expert," the leader employs methods and techniques designed to meet the criterion of being coherent, systematic, and justifiable. With the appropriate tools in place, the leader can begin a process, "designed to assist congregations in entering this critical place of dialogue and discernment."[106] Success in "bringing in a new order of things or responding to circumstances that demand different ways of doing and being" is, in the end, the hallmark task of the entrepreneurial leader who operates by means of personal "skill, discernment and wisdom."[107] Under such conditions, the social body of the church is ordered and oriented to a "new order of things," but an order that is nonetheless predictable for the outcomes remain measurable as examples of efficient and effective management.[108]

The third assumption of physicalism pertains to how the human body is primarily purposed for biological survival and growth. For the

102. Roberts, *Religion, Theology and the Human Sciences*, 71.

103. Bandy, *Mission Mover*, 47.

104. Percy, *Words, Wonders and Power*, 53.

105. Roberts, *Religion, Theology and the Human Sciences*, 168.

106. Roxburgh and Romanuk, *The Missional Leader*, 75.

107. Davies and Dodds, *Leadership in the Church for a People of Hope*, 79.

108. Wimberly, Jr., "The Challenges of Incarnational Life."

strict physicalist, the human body consists of matter, atoms (or maybe genes) that have a *function* by means of neurobiological systems the activity of which can be translated into physicochemical explanations, and a *program* for biological adaptedness that is operative in service to the continuation of the human species.[109] Beyond the neurobiological function and adaptive program, there is, proponents contend, no additional account required regarding human goal-orientation or the mechanisms whereby overall human purposefulness might be understood.[110] As long as humans can adapt as one organic species among many, the story of the human body will be one of growth and survival.

In the estimation of Ernst Mayr, since the ascendency of the synthesis of evolutionary theory and neurobiological research, most endeavors to explain a general goal for humans and other organisms has focused on physiological functioning in light of Darwinian and Neo-Darwinian developments around the notion of natural selection.[111] Within this conceptual scheme, all biological phenomena, including minds and consciousness, can be understood to have evolved from insensate matter via natural selection in a series of progressive steps. These conditions, notes Stephen Gould, mean that no reason for how organisms function or survive comes from outside the organism,

> no divine watchmaker superintends the works of his creation. Individuals are struggling for reproductive success, the natural analogue of profit. No other mechanism is at work, nothing "higher" or more exalted. Yet the result is adaptation and balance.[112]

The priority of biological adaptation and balance, Dennett contends, is part of Darwin's legacy, and shows how evolution as an operating principle within organic growth and survival is not restricted to maintaining conditions that are always suitable for the survival of that organism. Where the neurobiological function and adaptive program of natural selection leads is to the conclusion that organic life is determined by an "impersonal, unreflective, robotic, mindless little scrap of molecular machinery" that functions as the "ultimate basis of all the agency, and

109. Mayr, *What Makes Biology Unique?* 45.
110. Gould, *Full House*, 136.
111. Mayr, *What Makes Biology Unique?* 42.
112. Gould, *Eight Little Piggies*, 164.

hence meaning, and hence consciousness, in the universe."[113] This non-teleological approach of Darwin, Dennett writes, operates as a "universal acid" that "eats through just about every concept, and leaves in its wake a revolutionized world-view, with most of the old landmarks still recognizable, but transformed in fundamental way."[114]

Within this "revolutionized world-view," an animal might be said to *act* for a purpose (e.g., it hunts to find food) due to its biological programming, but it does not *exist* for a purpose, unless the explanation of existence is *casual* in relation to the animal's genetic success and evolution. An example of the kind of purposeful action innate to an animal is the internal and external functioning of body parts. The internal organs of an animal are, for the most part, not under the voluntary control of the animal. They are needed for the natural motor, sensory, and reproductive activities of the animal. Their normal functioning is a condition for the animal's possessing and being able to exercise its faculties optimally.[115] As such, all physical effects of the animal are fully caused and ordered by purely physical conditions. It is possible, then, that adjustments to the physical conditions by either natural selection or technological enhancement could improve the functioning of the animal, and consequently, its growth and survival.

This possibility of enhancement to the physical conditions of, for example, the human body, follows from the physicalist logic that gives precedence to the body as an integrated neurobiological organism that has no "higher" purpose than physiological functioning and reproduction. This non-teleological logic is adopted into the general approach to "improve" human life by means of technology-driven enhancements, an approach that is generally referred to as *transhumanism*.

In the "revolutionized world-view" of physicalists like Dennett and Gould, the notion that a human life has function by means of its genetic program, and therefore with no purpose other than biological survival, provides the metaphysical basis for the use of technology to enhance bodies to function more efficiently. Such enhancements come by means of advancements in biotechnology (genetic engineering, and methods of regenerative medicine, i.e., stem cell cloning and regenerative cells growing organs), nanotechnology (nanomedicine, nanorobotics, and

113. Dennett, *Darwin's Dangeorus Idea*, 203.

114. Ibid., 63. For a critique of Dennett's reading of Darwin on teleology, see, chapter 4 of Cunningham's, *Darwin's Pious Idea*.

115. Hacker, *Human Nature*, 171.

molecular manufacturing) and human-computer interaction, including artificial intelligence, and processes for whole brain emulation.[116] According to transhumanist proponents, the goal of enhancement is not to be well, that is, to achieve the optimal level of health possible within the limits of a naturally given human embodiment, but to become better than well, by using technologies to redefine or remove the naturally given limits of human embodiment that have historically shaped definitions of health and wellbeing. This is, in bioethical terms, human enhancement, defined in terms of transcending biological limitations. Transhumanist objectives of enhancement explicitly include the pursuit of longevity and the elimination of aging, disease, pain, and suffering.[117] Under the vision of transhumanism, the human body exists as a site for endless manipulation in pursuit of being "better than well."

The ability to augment the physical conditions of the human body has given rise to both the promise of "molecular manufacturing" that proponents suggest will eventually enable precise, inexpensive control of the structure of matter, and the rise of the promotion of personal wellness and success by means of elective forms of medicine like cosmetic surgery.[118] In an age of "biomedical culture" that engages in genetic and cosmetic enhancements, the human body, from the levels of surface flesh all the way to molecule, neuron, and gene, are understood as the key site for practices of self-enhancement and survival. Such an emphasis, notes Victoria Pitts-Taylor, is unsurprising given the non-teleological understanding of human persons who, as *generic* bodies, are encouraged through

116. Vita-More, "Life Expansion Media," 74.

117. Thweatt-Bates, *Cyborg Selves*, 43. Though the focus here is on human enhancement, *transhumanist* proponents extend the identity of an agent to entities with similar levels of sapience, sentience, and personhood, whether they are humans, animals, cyborgs, machine intelligences, or aliens. See More, "The Philosophy of Transhumanism."

118. Pitts-Taylor, "Medicine, Governmentality and Biopower in Cosmetic Surgery," 163.

"technologies of the self" to establish their own identities and purposes.[119] In sum, bodies are malleable and, therefore, "constructable."[120]

The promise of enhancement through molecular or cosmetic augmentation rests on the assumptions of a physicalist logic that reduces human identity and purposefulness to biological function and programming that result principally in the growth and survival of the body. If the human agent is just one more example of a generic organic body then enhancements that are understood to "improve" the function and longevity of organic life can be seen as benefits to the already established biological end of adaptation that is in service to the continuation of the species. An "enhanced human" or even *post*human, therefore, is seen by transhuman proponents as the necessary next phase in human evolution and development.[121]

The physicalist logic at work in transhumanism, a rationality that treats the human body as lacking in an essential and innate purpose beyond biological survival, is operative in managerialism, in particular, in the notion that all organizations as particular managed bodies share the same generic goals of growth and survival. Like the human body, the social body has coordinating features and functions by means of an integrated system of working parts. And like the human body of physicalism, the social body of managerialism has no purpose other than the goals associated with growth and survival expressed through maximizing techniques that promote efficiency, effectiveness, predictability, and control. These techniques, like body enhancements, are designed to make an organization operate "better than well." The shape and function of the organization, as with transhumanism with respect to the human body, is open and malleable, undermined by any sense of a notion of inherent purpose.

One of the defining features of a managed organization is that it is purposeful inasmuch as it is oriented to the pursuit of relatively specific goals, which are presumed to be rational, clearly defined, and explicit. Organizations must be centrally coordinated for the pursuit of these,

119. Ibid., 168. The notion of "technologies of the self" belongs to Foucault. For him, technologies of the self, "permit individuals to effect by their own means or with the help of others a certain number of operations on their own bodies and souls, thoughts, conduct, and way of being, so as to transform themselves in order to attain a certain state-of happiness, purity, wisdom, perfection, or immortality." Foucault, *Technologies of the Self*, 18.

120. Elshtain, "The Body and the Quest for Control," 155.

121. Bostrom, "Why I Want to Be a Posthuman When I Grow Up."

and there must be unambiguous criteria for selecting among activities to achieve predetermined goals with maximum efficiency.[122] Under these conditions, the managed body is presented as a single, unified, rational decision-maker, purposive and intentional, with clear goals and identifiable preferences for outcomes. Moreover, unlike earlier societies where it is thought that autocracy and primitivism kept people in general, and workers in particular, in various forms of social and economic bondage, the logic of managerialism is thought to be democratic and transparent, premised on the notion that an efficient ordering of people and things is what makes the achievement of collective goals possible. Under the "new order" of managerialism, accountability is maintained, human energy reserved, and economic progress is made available to all. [123]

What this "new order" of managerialism has made possible is the colonization of virtually all organizational contexts, being flexible enough in its ordering that even public sector organizations have to demonstrate market and profit orientation, professional management, and the ethical change in governance from the traditional principle of public welfare to the commercial norm of value-for-money.[124] Both private and public sector organizations must adapt in order to match the ever-changing business environment; they must, in the estimation of Tom Karp, accept that they need to adjust by means of shifts in process, strategy, practices, and systems in order to be successful.[125] And, crucially, they can only adapt in the way managerialism and its proponents think is right because managerialism represents the baseline on which techniques for further growth can be applied.

The managerialistic paradigm presumes the legitimacy of established managerial priorities and is dedicated to identifying more effective and efficient means for their realization. Like the body of physicalism, the managed body is a *generic* body that awaits the introduction of identity and purpose by means of managerial techniques and strategic orientations. In pursuit of the maximization of value or growth, managers deploy technique after technique to improve the organization status. With the fundamental goals of growth and survival predetermined, the managed body is enhanced through such things as strategic planning and

122. Townley, *Reason's Neglect*, 32.
123. Parker, *Against Management*, 4.
124. Diefenbach, *Management and the Dominance of Managers*, 20.
125. Karp, "Unpacking the Mysteries of Change," 88–89.

the adoption of mission/vision statements that focuses the attainment of these goals through adopting specific language and outcomes that are designed to provide an organizational vision that through managerial control can be measured by means of performance criterion and other measurement systems.[126] Thus, the managed organization, though it is presented by means of a specific vision for each organization, seeks to protect its generic function and organizational rationale (or program) from conditions that might threaten the social body's survival. In other words, as an instrumentalized institution, the managed body can only exist in service to self-preservation and reproduction.

The managerial logic of enhancement through the deployment of strategies and techniques of purpose and identity is an active part for technique-based approaches to the church that see in such activities a response to decline. Against the fear of irrationality and randomness, strategic planning, for instance, works toward possibilities that implicitly assume that right planning will produce favorable results. Through the use of "development teams" whose work is to help form the "spiritual foundation" of the church, the strategic process is designed to establish a church's core values, mission, vision, and a strategy that can be implemented to assist a particular church in establishing its unique identity and purpose.[127]

The objectives that emerge from the strategic process, note Gilbert and Mann, state what the congregation and its leaders must commit themselves to do or to be in order to address the unique future being shaped. Consequently, the related goals state how the congregation will accomplish those objectives.[128] For the goals to prove helpful, they must be specific, measureable, attainable, relevant, and time-bound. In other words, the objectives and goals must flow out of the uniqueness of the parish and establish in clear and unambiguous terms the direction that the parish will take in the future. Far too many churches, notes Aubrey Malphurs, ignore the promises of a probably organized strategic process with efficient and measurable objectives and goals, and have instead, "offered up ministry mediocrity under the guise of 'It's a spiritual undertaking for God!'"[129] In other words, a congregation's survival rests in

---

126. Diefenbach, *Management and the Dominance of Managers*, 23.

127. Malphurs, *Advanced Strategic Planning*, 285.

128 Rendle and Mann, *Holy Conversations*, 86.

129. Malphurs, *Advanced Strategic Planning*, 286.

the deployment of appropriate rationalized techniques that are designed to enhance each individual community. The social body of the church, since it is a generic body, requires enhancement by means of the strategic process if the church is going to be "better than well." In doing so, the church reflects the malleability of the managed body that is oriented to the maximization of efficiency and related goals.

The managerial notion of a social body having goals of survival and growth is further evidenced in the process of applying specialization to particular church communities. The notion of the need for enhancement establishes the conditions in which the definition of the church is determined by characteristics of function that distinguish one church from another. In this atomized state, the ascendency of "niche ministries" becomes the coordinating factor for the identity of the church. One church, for example, might have a strong commitment to justice, another to outreach within the local community, and another to ministry with seniors or teenagers or adoptive families.[130] These particularities are not simply the response of the church to its environs, but as functions, become the focal point of ecclesial practice.

In the estimation of missional approaches to the church, there is a need to understand the church through a diversity of structures and modes. As the "Mission-Shaped Church" and "Fresh Expressions" movements in the UK stress, the essential aspect of church is its "missionary nature" expressed through how particular faith communities, unified by particular interests and preferences, become "networks" that attract people who share similar interests and preferences.[131] In this "post-congregational era of Christianity,"[132] what is required is attention to the "context and incarnational reality of each church."[133]

The way the church expresses itself through a diversity of structures and modes is dependent on the values within the context where the church operates. As Duraisingh suggests, the key to a missional-approach is the emphasis the particular church communities give to the perceived needs outside the current church structures. Such attention is designed to align the church more closely with the interests and preferences of the wider community over the maintenance of forms of "being church"

130. Baab, "Myths."
131. *Mission-Shaped Church*, 63.
132. McNeal, *Missional Communities*, 2.
133. Spellers, "The Church Awake," 38.

that have ceased to inspire.[134] No longer does one size fit all. The market wherein a church exists, the *Mission-Shaped Church* report emphasizes, requires diverse forms of church, including cell church, in which committed relationships can develop outside the established walls of the church.[135] The guiding principle for understanding the specific mission of the church community begins by not deciding "where we want to go or exploring what is working for other churches but understanding how we are unique."[136] In other words, to become a unique missional community is the task of every individual church.

In sum, the efficient body of managerialism evidenced in the technique and missional approaches to the church performs tasks and fulfils duties following the pre-determined goals of survival and growth. The managed body, resting as it does on the coordinated body of physicalism, risks making the body "absent" through attending primarily to what the body does by privileging activity over identity. In other words, in the way physicalism (and by extension, managerialism) reduces the body to the functions of its constituent parts, it is uncertain whether these theories can provide a holistic account of a human being as a living, sensitive, reasoning body that transcends its individual materiality through meaningful activity.[137]

Beyond the Managed Body

The "managed body" of the modern organization and contemporary church is the result of conceptual moves that were initiated in the sixteenth century through the work of Bacon and Descartes, and through a development of mechanistic and reductive methods and practices in relation to the human body, created the conditions for the emphasis of the

134. Duraisingh, "From Church-Shaped Mission to Mission-Shaped Church," 12–13.

135. *Mission-Shaped Church*, 54.

136. Mancini, *Church Unique*, 6.

137. Klima, "Thomistic 'Monism' vs. Cartesian 'Dualism,'" 99. According to Herbert McCabe, a "meaningful activity" in a Thomistic sense is a single activity that is relevant to the entire body. McCabe considers the act of seeing as an example. Seeing, he argues, is an operation done with the eye but it is an operation of the entire body. "So the eye has an operation of its own which is itself also an operation of the whole body. . . . The eye does not undergo electrochemical changes and also do something else which is seeing; its sight just is its physiological modification as meaningful for the whole animal." McCabe, *On Aquinas*, 13.

past century on a more rationalized notion of the social body. The emergence of bureaucratic and instrumentalized approaches to workers and work places, and the heritage of scientific empiricism, have contributed to the concept of the "absent present" body that requires management if it is to be an efficient and effective body. The coordination of this body, both the individual human and the social organization, is vital for maintaining the goals of efficiency, effectiveness, predictability, and control. This social arrangement follows the logic of managerialism and displays the assumptions of physicalist accounts of the human body that reduce the complexity and purposefulness of the living human body to carefully coordinated physical processes. Thus, the social body of an organization is understood in light of pre-determined ends that stipulate continued coordination.

As will be developed in next two chapters, a contrasting position argues that managerialism and the assumptions of physicalism contribute to a confused status for the body, both individual and social. This confusion begins with a description of the human body in mechanical and functionalist language. A biological entity, like that of a human person, is not an arbitrary grouping of parts organized towards a whole, an artifact or synthetic entity that Thomas Aquinas refers to as an "accidental form" (*ens per accidens*). Rather, a human body in Aquinas's anthropology is a living member of a species understood to be natural unit, or more precisely, an example of a living organism that has the particular substantial form (*ens per se*).[138]

The investigation of this book now turns to a retrieval of a Thomistic anthropology and sacramental theology as an alternative to the mechanistic and reductive tradition of individual and social bodies. Having jettisoned the Thomistic-Aristotelian tradition, Bacon, Descartes and the subsequent tradition based their methods and metaphysics on technological metaphors and concepts for understanding the human and social bodies. The continuity in this tradition between physics, biology, and technology furthered the conceptual shift through reducing the definition of human life to the operation of the body's constituent parts.

138. Aquinas's use of accidental and substantial forms will be addressed in the next chapter. For the time being, it is sufficient to define a substantial form as being how a material thing is configured in order for it is have actuality (to exist), whereas, an accidental form configures something which is an actually already existing thing (e.g., building a house out of existing bricks, where the bricks are understood to have separate existence from being incorporated into a house). See Stump, *Aquinas*, 38. Also, McCabe, *The Good Life*, 100.

This instrumental-rationalized approach has proven caustic to general accounts of human and social life, and in particular, to accounts of the church as the body of Christ. A retrieval of a Thomistic account, I suggest, is necessary to provide a metaphysical framework to account for how the church exists as the social body in which human persons can, through sacramental participation, be made members of Christ and each other.

4

What Difference Does a Body Make?
A *Holistic* Alternative according to a
Thomistic Theological Anthropology

L IFE, SAYS THOMAS AQUINAS in his commentary on Aristotle's *De Anima*, is essentially that by which anything has power to move itself—taking "movement" in its wide sense.[1] Having an *anima* or "soul" means being, at some level, able to move oneself. This kind of "soul talk" begins with the premise that for a thing to have a soul means for that thing to be alive. Rocks, in this case, do not have souls; however, humans and plants do.

This chapter provides an account of the human person as an *ensouled* body following the anthropology of Thomas Aquinas and scholars in the Aristotelian-Thomistic tradition. The purpose is to demonstrate how a Thomistic account of the human person operates as an alternative metaphysic of the body that contrasts with the assumptions of a reductive physicalism, and yet provides the necessary grounds for a vision of the church as Christ's body: a vision that is more than a metaphor but one that conceives how human lives are by grace incorporated into the divine life of God. Such a vision requires exploring questions of the quiddity of the human body, the purpose of human life, and how the church is understood as the site of membership for humans into the glorified humanity of Jesus. This course of inquiry seeks a constructive alternative to the assumptions of managerialism and the metaphysics of physicalism that reduce the body to an instrumentalized organism that exists solely

1. Thomas Aquinas, *Commentary on Aristotle's De Anima*, Book II, chapter II.

119

to survive and grow. Such assumptions, as was argued in the previous chapter, occupy the imaginary within contemporary forms of ecclesiology that privilege technique and missional-approaches to the church.

Human Nature in the *Summa Theologiae* (1a.75–83)

In 1a.75–79 of the *Summa Theologiae*, Aquinas argues that human beings are things with souls—things with bodily functions and sensations, things with the ability to move, and things with the ability to understand and choose. Following the general anthropology that he has developed elsewhere,[2] this section in the *Summa* represents the most comprehensive account Aquinas provides on the question: what is a human being? For Aquinas, to address this question is to be engaged in *theological* anthropology for, as he notes in the prologue to 1a.75, humans are created "corporeal beings" with a "spiritual substance" (i.e., the soul) by God. They are bodies of a certain kind, with a certain kind of life (i.e., soul). The kind of soul that makes possible humanness, and the capacities and perfections associated with being a particular substance that embodies that soul, are allied with Aquinas's notion that of all created things, human beings are capable of sharing in the joy of God, which Aquinas thinks of as the true and final purpose of human life.[3]

In 1a.78.1 Aquinas asks about the *potentiae* (i.e., abilities or powers or capabilities) that defines how a human person exists (i.e., what it takes for a soul to be said to be a *human* soul). Following Aristotle, he names five such *potentiae*: vegetative, sensitive, appetitive, locomotive, and intellective. Something has vegetative powers, he thinks, if it is able to feed or nourish itself, if it is able to grow, and if it is able to reproduce.[4] Sensitive powers, thinks Aquinas, lead things to be able to latch onto the world at a sensory level (by touch, sight, taste, hearing, or smell).[5] Something with appetite is an individual that is naturally drawn to goods of various kinds, while something capable of locomotion is just able to move around under

---

2. In particular his treatises: *De Anima, Et Ente et Essentia,* and *De Principiis Naturae;* his commentary on Aristotle's *De Anima;* and his major theological works, *Summa Contra Gentiles* (particularly in book 2), and *Scriptum super Sententiis* (book 2).

3. On human purpose and sharing in God's joy, see *ST* 1a2ae.1–5.

4. *ST* 1a.78.2.

5. *ST* 1a.78.3.

its own steam (as it were).[6] As for being intellective, Aquinas takes something with intellect to be able to understand the world in which it lives.[7]

One might think, for instance, of a cow. It has "vegetative" abilities, not to mention sensitive, appetitive, and locomotive ones. However, cows cannot give you a lecture on what cows are. They are not things with understanding expressible linguistically, that is, with abilities associated with understanding and giving symbolic structure to *what* things are and *how* things are (i.e., the essence of something) as abstracted from any particular material conditions (e.g., the ability to recognize and speak about *cowness*, not simply respond by some sensual means to a particular cow in a specific barn—by not walking into it, for example).[8]

It is worth noting that for Aquinas there is a kind of continuum between the lower kinds of life, the plants, which have certain vegetative abilities such as metabolism and growth, on through the animals with sensual capacities, which behave in this way or that because of their sensual interpretation, on up to the rational animals, which with intellective capacities interpret the world through symbols that they have themselves created. The intellectual powers associated with rationality are, for Aquinas, what allows humans to transcend the lower capacities, but in a way coextensive with them.[9]

6. *ST* 1a.78.4.

7. *ST* 1a.79.1. The Latin word *intellectus* is connected with the verb *intellegere*: this is commonly translated "understand", but in Aquinas' Latin it is a verb of very general use corresponding roughly to our word "think." As Anthony Kenny explains,

> we employ the word "think" in two different ways: we talk of thinking *of* something, and we talk of thinking *that* something. Thus, in the first way, we may say that someone abroad thought of home, or thought of his family; in the second way we may say that someone thought that there was a prowler downstairs, or that inflation was on the increase. Aquinas makes a corresponding distinction between simple thoughts (thoughts of) and complex thoughts (thoughts that); both of these were acts of intellect. All thoughts, according to Aquinas, are expressible in language.

Kenny, "Body, Soul, and Intellect in Aquinas," 34.

8. *ST* 1a.79.3. Also, Eberl, "Aquinas on the Nature of Human Beings," 341.

9. *ST* 1a.79.4. Also, McCabe, *On Aquinas*, 31–32. The body, McCabe maintains:

> is a complex organism in which each is relevant to every other part. The eye is not just itself, it is also part of a higher order, the whole functional complex of the body. . . . Each part of the body is in a sense raised beyond itself and in sensation other things are given the opportunity of sharing in this sensitive world.

Herbert McCabe, "Appendix 1: Knowledge," in Aquinas, *Knowing and Naming God: (1a. 12–13)*, 19.

When it comes to the souls of human beings, Aquinas is concerned with the question, "What makes human beings different from other living things?" In 1a.75.1, he reiterates the claim (following Aristotle) that the soul is the actuality of the body, the "first principle of life" in the things that are alive around us. People, he thinks, are alive (as human beings) insofar as they have a soul with the appropriate capacities. They are bodies of a certain kind, bodies with a certain kind of life (or soul). As such, Aquinas maintains that human souls are not distinct from human beings (considered as parts of the material world). In 1a.75.1–4, for instance, many of the arguments Aquinas responds to as incomplete, give an account of the soul as something that exists quite independently of the body. For these interlocutors, the soul is a thing or substance to be distinguished from what a body is in something like the way in which the driver of a car is to be distinguished from the car. One driver plus one car equals two individual things, for example. And, so it has been argued, a soul plus body equals two distinct things. Yet, Aquinas does not think of human souls (or any souls at all for that matter) in this way. For instance, to move around a room, and to think about what wallpaper should go up, are different capacities *of* the soul, but both moving and thinking are part of a single definition of what it means to be human (i.e., to have a particular kind of living or *ensouled* body).[10] In Aquinas's anthropology, the living human body has the kind of integrity that is missing from the physicalist notion of the body as being merely *generic* that it requires forms of enhancement and the imposition of a rationalized order.

The human soul, Aquinas maintains, is the form of the human body.[11] He means that human beings are what they are (i.e., have a particular essence) because of their substantial form, one that he takes to be what makes people to be alive as the things that they are, and not as a "something extra" to human existence.[12] He does not mean that human bodies are somehow connected to independently existing substances called "souls." He means that human beings (as physical items in the world able to be examined and classified with respect to other living

10. Klima, "Man = Body + Soul: Aquinas's Arithmetic of Human Nature," 258.

11. *ST* 1a.76.1

12. In the sense of a "Platonic" or substance dualist account of the soul. Richard Swinburne, for instance, maintains a "simple dualism" that defines the person as a "pure mental substance," which accounts for a "thisness" that is in addition and distinction to the "thisness" of the matter of which bodies are made. See Van Inwagen, Zimmerman, and Swinburne, "From Mental/Physical Identity to Substance Dualism."

things) are things with a substantial form, though one that does not leave them totally material. "Matter . . . of itself exists incompletely," thinks Aquinas, and

> Form gives existence to matter . . . just as everything which is in potency can be called matter, so everything by which a thing has (substantial) being . . . can be called (a substantial) form; . . . sperm which is potentially a human is made actually a human by the soul.[13]

In other words, a substantial form actualizes matter, and this unity (i.e., form and matter) makes something exist as a particular thing in the world. Aquinas takes God to be form without matter, and in one respect, angels too.[14] Yet, he does not say that people are wholly immaterial, as if the term "human person" could be properly understood without encountering and interacting with a physical human. As such, Aquinas thinks that people are evidently particular living bodily things (i.e., having the essence of humanness as a *compositio* of form and matter) that cannot be properly defined by reference only to form (immaterial soul) or matter (material body).

Aquinas distinguishes between a living and a non-living thing by saying that a living thing moves of itself. Under this description, he thinks that to speak of people as having souls is primarily to say that they move of their own accord. He also states, however, that the soul of a human being differs, for example, from the soul of a dog. Life manifests its presence through different activities at different levels,

> But the soul is the ultimate principle by which we conduct every one of life's activities; the soul is the ultimate motive factor behind nutrition, sensation and movement from place to place, and the same holds true of the act of understanding.[15]

When it comes to soul, Aquinas recognizes a kind of hierarchy in terms of which some things can be thought of as being more in control of

---

13. Aquinas, "On the Principles of Nature," ch. 1. Brian Leftow states that the logic of substantial forms is revealed in what they do: x's form is that, intrinsic to x, which "makes" x's matter constitute x—that is, makes that matter actually what it could have been or had been merely potentially. See Leftow, "Souls Dipped in Dust," 125–27.

14. *ST* 1a.3.1–4. In 1a.3.1, Aquinas notes that, as the "unchanging first cause of change," God cannot be "material" (i.e., having the potential to change). Any time Scripture refers to God having bodily parts (e.g., the hand of God), this use is metaphorical, for, as Aquinas maintains, God is everywhere and without "parts."

15. *ST* 1a.76.1.

themselves than others are. Human beings, in his estimation, are things with souls that enable them to live in ways that other things in the world do not, as things having not just the ability to feed, move around, and sense, but as things able to understand, that is, to think.[16]

Aquinas draws a distinction between sensation and understanding. He takes sensation, particularly when applied to animals, to occur as a felt physical change is brought about—as when pain is felt after a cut. Sensation, for Aquinas, is something material—a change in a body.[17] When it comes to understanding, however, it is not a bodily process or a change in a body. He maintains that humans can be thought of as bodily things who understand. As such, Aquinas denies that understanding itself is something material or that its occurrence involves people undergoing a physical change.[18]

In effect, Aquinas thinks that understanding what something is involves having the form of something without actually being the thing whose nature one understands. Aquinas's position is that understanding what a cow is amounts to having what it takes to be a cow *in mind*,[19] having the nature of a cow "intentionally" or immaterially. Aquinas thinks, therefore, that human beings have souls as individuals able to "know the

16. Understanding—thinking—is, for Aquinas, a perfection of the human soul, which is only achieved through being joined with a body that can allow for sensory experience. See Aquinas, *Questions on the Soul*.

17. *ST* 1a.78.3.

18. *ST* 1a.76.5.*ad*.2.

19. The use of the term "mind" is limited in this section due in part to the modern conception of the mind as pertaining to certain operations (e.g., thinking, reasoning, and the activities associated with consciousness), which physicalists claim are identical with brain-states or emergent qualities of a neural state, while dualists tend to claim the mind as causally related to, but not identical with, the body. Aquinas's, as this chapter articulates, holds something of a middle position: the intellectual principle of human persons is what Aquinas means by a person having a particular kind of soul that with the body is how human existence is defined. While the soul is thought to be immaterial, the operations of the soul animate the full bodily life of the human person, without ever being reduced to simply an action of the soul or the body. For a good summary of "mind" talk, see, Lowe, *Introduction to the Philosophy of Mind*, 8–36. Anthony Kenny, in *Aquinas on Mind*, attempts to clarify how Aquinas's position on the soul can be understood in light of modern conceptions of mind; yet, as John O'Callaghan has shown, Kenny's "mind" is a distinctive quality of human life that, unlike Aquinas's account of the human soul, is somehow different from the animating principle of the soul that distinguishes all living things from nonliving things. See O'Callaghan, "Aquinas's Rejection of Mind, Contra Kenny."

natures of all bodily things."[20] This means that the intellective soul has the potential to reach an understanding of the essence of anything corporeal, of the defining features of bodily things. What it means to understand a cow, for example, is for the form of the cow to be intelligible in light of the kind of thing a cow is essentially (an animal with form and matter that corresponds to the essence of *cowness*) and the kind of world that exists. This capacity, Aquinas contends, is not dependent upon any material operation (i.e., any specific operation of the body) for its functioning. In contradistinction to the claim of contemporary physicalists that "every mental event (state, property) is related to some brain event,"[21] intellective capacities, for Aquinas, surpass the limits of matter in their ability to understand the forms of things; such forms are the natures of things understood as abstracted from any particular material conditions. Since intellective capacities surpass the limits of matter, no purely material process can be responsible for the generation of substantial forms with such capacities.[22]

Having intellective capacities, the kind of soul that is a human soul allows human beings to not only interact with other material things (via bodily senses), but to understand how these things fit within the structure and organization of the world at large. Aquinas refers to this capacity as the "agent intellect" (*intellectus agens*). The agent intellect, argues Aquinas in 1a, 79, is the active power by which people are able to proceed from sense experience (via *phantasmata* or sense data) to an interpretation of the world as meaningful, an interpretation that allows for the recognition of what things are and to form accurate judgments accordingly. In other words, the agent intellect "abstracts universal forms from particular conditions."[23] Since he thinks of people as essentially material

20. *ST* 1a.75.2.

21. Murphy, "Nonreductive Physicalism," 132. In reference to the physicalist claim of the irreducibility of all states to physical causes, Norris Clarke, reiterates the Thomistic position that "the lower" activities (i.e., physical) cannot be the source of "the higher" activities (i.e., intellectual). This position, Clarke notes, allows for a truly nonreductive account of human life and activity by means of an intellective soul being the source of intellective activity, beginning from the body and stretching out beyond the bodily capacities. This is the image of an agent operating on two levels, one higher, one lower, one on the level of bodily operation, the other of intellective—*a dualism of levels of activity within one substance or nature*. See Clarke, *Creative Retrieval of Saint Thomas Aquinas*, 183–84.

22. *ST* 1a.79.4. Also, Eberl, "Aquinas on the Nature of Human Beings," 341–42.

23. *ST* 1a.79.3.*ad*.3.

objects, Aquinas maintains that all human knowledge arises as a result of encountering the world at a sensory level.[24] Yet, he also thinks that sensory experience is of material things that, considered only as objects extended in space, are not intelligible precisely because intelligibility is a non-material category.

According to Aquinas, what something is (i.e., its form) is the intelligible content that is the basis for human understanding. The agent intellect, thinks Aquinas, is what allows people, based on sensory experience, to form concepts or language. His idea (expressed in semantic terms) is that the agent intellect is a power people possess by which concepts and language are possible. In an important sense, people, in light of living in a material world as creatures with an intellective soul, are capable of creating concepts and language. Meanings, Aquinas contends, are not *in* the objects encountered at the sensory level; rather the capacity of the agent intellect allows sensory objects to become the source of conceptual knowledge expressed through language (broadly understood). Humans can understand things in the environment on the basis of their sensory acquaintance with them because, as Aquinas says, the combination of an intellective soul of human beings and a world of existing things that are the essence of one thing or another (and consequently, are a particular form of something), creates the conditions for intelligibility.[25] Such capacity is not to be confused with a bodily organ (e.g., a heart).[26] The soul, for Aquinas, does not replace the processes of the brain (as some physicalists claim Aquinas's position to be),[27] but rather organizes these processes in particular acts of knowing. Unlike other living and non-living things, human beings, Aquinas contends, are able to think, that is, able to proceed from sensation to reflection and argument by means of a capacity that surpasses the limits of matter. People, concludes Aquinas, straddle the realm between the material and the immaterial. Like materials things (living or nonliving), humans are essentially material objects. Nevertheless, like immaterial thing (e.g., angels[28]), they are things that

24. *ST* 1a.87.1.

25. *ST* 1a.79.4c.

26. *ST* 1a.79.6.

27. See Murphy, *Religion and Science*, 15; Post, "A Moral Case for Nonreductive Physicalism," 198.

28. *ST* 1a.12.4. Angels are immaterial, but they are created as such. In brief, Aquinas understands angels to be incorporeal (1a.50.1); "spiritual" rather than "bodily" substances (1a.90.3); "more perfectly intelligent" than humans (1a.93.3); "separated

operate at a non-material level due to having an intellective soul that simply is a substantial form able to function immaterially.[29]

Aquinas holds that a purely physical account of what people are is incoherent, given that people, through the capacity of understanding, can receive the *forms* of intelligible things.[30] For him, matter is always the big obstacle when it comes to understanding. With this in mind, it might sound as if Aquinas is denying the body any role as an intermediary in intellectual cognition. Yet clearly, there is a sense in which the intellect does operate through the body, inasmuch as the intellect receives information about the world through the senses.[31] In this regard, the senses do mediate intellectual thought, yet not in the way in which physicalists reduce thought to physical processes.[32] Aquinas is clear that the intellect does not have an organ in the way that the sensory powers do. The soul's sensory powers are forms and not bodies, but still the sensory part of the soul operates "through a bodily organ" in that these powers actualize the sensory organs. Sight, for instance, is a composite of a form (the visual power) and a bodily organ (the eye). Seeing, therefore, is not simply an operation of the physical organ (the eye), but a capacity or operation of a particular soul.[33]

To say, for example, that seeing is an operation of the soul is to express first, that seeing is the operation of an organ, the eye, precisely as a

---

substances" (i.e., subsistent forms that can exist without being realized in matter); and able to understand without the need for sense images (1a.94.2). In comparison, God is not only immaterial, "only God is his existence; in all else essence and existence are distinct" (1a.61.2).

29. The immateriality of human beings as intellective souls is one aspect of what it means to say that humans are created in the image of God. See *ST* 1a.3.1.*ad*.2. As a *composito* of matter and form who have an intellective soul, humans engage in such things as managing and scientific research as part of the exercise of reason. The contention of this book is not with these activities as such, but with how managing and scientific inquiry can create the conditions so that their output is privileged over other accounts of human and social living.

30. In the jargon of contemporary epistemology, one might say that Aquinas is something of a "strong externalist." See O'Callaghan, *Thomistic Realism and the Linguistic Turn*, 237–74.

31. *ST* 1a.84.4–6.

32. Alvin Plantinga argues that just because we cannot fully understand how a change in a physical thing can be a mental change and thus could constitute a sensation or thought, it is not matched by an equal inability to imagine how an immaterial thing could be thinking. See Plantinga, "Materialism and Christian Belief," 116.

33. *ST* 1a.76.1.*ad*.2–3. Also, see Pasnau, *Thomas Aquinas on Human Nature*, 53–54.

physical organ of the body. Second, it is to express that seeing is a mean-ingful activity for the whole body, for the life of the animal. What hap-pens in the eyeball is meaningful for the whole animal when in response to stimuli in the visual field, the animal responds by running away, for example, or by walking through a doorway (rather than walking into a wall). All the organs of sense are functioning parts of the body that when affected, make the world meaningful for the animal. To act meaningfully is for the animal to respond in appropriate ways to its environment. It is because the organs are themselves significant parts of the whole body that what affects them is taken up into the structure of the whole body and is thus meaningful. In other words, the photoelectric effects on the retina of the eye are bodily sensations because the eye is a functional part of a complex structure, the operation of which is not reducible to any one part of the structure.[34]

For a dog to see is for it to behave in a certain way in response to its environment (and hence to be said to have a particular soul, which includes sensing capacities). For a person to see, Aquinas argues, is to have a similar capacity as the dog in reference to responding to its envi-ronment, but in distinction to the dog (and all other living animals), the human person has the capacity[35] to conceptualize (i.e., to abstract from sense data—*phantasmata*—an understanding—*intellectus*—of the form of what the person sees) its environment through language and scientific study and in using parts of the environment within the visual field to, for instance, arrange artifacts (e.g., bones or sticks) in an artistic way (that is, for the sake of symbolizing or for pure enjoyment). Both a dog and a person can be said to see, and for both, seeing is meaningful to the entire body; however, for Aquinas, the difference between seeing as an operation of a *canine* soul and that of a *human* soul, is that the intellective capacities of humans makes the activity meaningful not only to the whole person, but potentially to a range of symbolic activities such as those as-sociated with the formation of culture, art, and language.[36]

34. McCabe, *Faith Within Reason*, 131–33.

35. In 1a.79.2, Aquinas reiterates that a capacity of the soul moves from potential-ity to actuality. There is the need for learning and even practice for the capacity to be properly actualized. He writes, "human understanding . . . is in a state of potentiality in relation to what it can understand, and is initially like a blank page on which nothing is written, as Aristotle writes" (*ST* 1a.79.2c).

36. *ST* 1a.79.4 & 9. Alasdair MacIntrye writes of the human body as being "expres-sive"; by this he means that humans deploy social and linguistic characteristics that operate in virtue of the human capacity to communicate, interpret, and categorize the

In short, Aquinas's treatment of the human person in 1a,75–79 steers a middle course between the extremes of concluding, (a) that people are simply and wholly material, and (b) that people are non-corporeal substances related to bodies as substances in their own right. That by which they are the living things that they are (their soul) animates them at all levels of their being—from their ability to feed, walk, and sense, to their ability to acquire knowledge or understanding. He is aware that some of his predecessors and contemporaries argue that people have several souls (one which informs them at a "vegetative" level, one that informs them at a sensory level, and one that informs them at an intellectual level). Yet, Aquinas remains resolute that people are individual things (even though they can be thought of as things with parts) that must therefore live as the individuals that they are by virtue of a single principle of life (substantial form). As such, in 1a.76.3 and 4, Aquinas argues that human beings have a single substantial form or soul. Since he takes this soul to be something non-material but also subsisting, he thinks of the human soul as able to survive the death of the body it informs.[37]

That human souls survive death is not, for Aquinas, to suggest that the human soul is fundamentally what a person is, in life or death. As created by God, a human soul cannot perish since it is a subsisting substantial form. Yet, he also thinks that a human soul surviving the death of a human being is not that full human person. The human soul is what remains of a human person it once informed, in that it is an aspect of what is properly a matter/form composite.[38] In 1a.75 he asks whether the soul of a human being is that particular human being. He answers that it is not, in that Fred's soul is not Fred but something that informs the human being identified as Fred. Before death, a human being "is" his/her soul, meaning that he/she is composed of an informed material body, the existence and nature of which is provided by his/her soul. A human being exists—is—as composed of their soul as a part, but they are not identical to either it or the matter it informs.[39] For Aquinas, Fred is something material, so his immaterial soul (which Aquinas takes to be something that subsists immaterially) is not Fred. Or, as Aquinas writes: "Man is no

material world into meaningful concepts that are shared with other humans through culture, art, etc. See MacIntyre, "What Is a Human Body?"

37. *ST* 1a.76.6.

38. *ST* 1a.76.1.

39. Eberl, "Aquinas on the Nature of Human Beings," 340.

mere soul, but a compound (*compositum*) of soul and body"[40] and in the next article, Aquinas states, "it belongs to the very essence of soul to be united to a body. . . . The human soul, remaining in its own existence after separation from the body, has a natural aptitude and a natural tendency to union with body."[41] In Aquinas's view, then, disembodied existence is not natural to the soul.

Death, for Aquinas, is the loss of form from the body, and form is that in terms of which we analyze perishing. He therefore concludes that it makes no sense to speak of form as such perishing. Moreover, if the form in question subsists, he reasons, it continues to exist as something subsistent. Not being a body capable of perishing (like matter), and yet being subsistent, the human soul cannot perish. This position is in line with Aquinas's overall nonreductive anthropology. People, for Aquinas, are rational, understanding animals, and they are what they are by virtue of what is not material, a position that stands in stark contrast to the general physicalist understanding of humans as simply a coordinated neurobiological organism. This aspect of people must, Aquinas concludes, be capable of surviving the destruction of what is material. In death, what remains is not something able to know by means of sense experience, nor undergo the feelings or sensations that go with being bodily. On Aquinas's account, therefore, the human soul can only be said to survive as something purely intellectual, as the locus of thought and will, even though there remains for the soul a "natural tendency to union with body."[42]

When the soul of a person is separated from the body, Aquinas thinks, the cognitive powers that person had are curtailed and restricted and, for certain intellectual functions (i.e., operations of an intellective soul), Aquinas feels constrained to give complicated considerations

40. *ST* 1a.75.4. There is debate among readers of Aquinas on this point, particularly in relation to the persistence of human nature after death. Robert Pasnau, for instance, contends that Aquinas denies a human being's substantial existence between death and resurrection; rather, a human being exists *partially* by virtue of the soul's continued existence. Eleonore Stump, on the other hand, contends that Aquinas attributes to disembodied souls properties that he takes to be *most characteristic* of human persons, including intellectual understanding and love. See Pasnau, *Thomas Aquinas on Human Nature*, 387–88; Stump, *Aquinas*, 52–53.

41. *ST* 1a.76.1.*ad*.6. Or, as Aquinas puts it in his commentary on 1 Corinthians, "my soul is not I."

42. *ST* 1a.75.6.*ad*.3 and 1a.77.8. Also, Davies, *The Thought of Thomas Aquinas*, 216.

to show how the disembodied soul could engage in them at all. As for knowledge of material things in the world that would ordinarily be abstracted from sense perception, Aquinas attributes the disembodied soul's ability to cognize such things to divine intervention.[43] The separated soul, Aquinas writes,

> does not understand by way of innate species, nor by species abstracted then, nor only by species retained, ... but the soul in that state understands by means of participated species arising from the influence of the Divine light, shared by the soul as by other separate substances; though in a lesser degree. Hence as soon as it ceases to act by turning to things corporeal, the soul turns at once to the superior things; nor is this way of knowledge unnatural, for God is the author of the influx of both of the light of grace and of the light of nature.[44]

The appeal to divine influence and order when it comes to the disembodied soul continues the thrust of what Aquinas thinks to be true of people: that the human soul, as he says in 1a.77.2, is "at the boundary between spiritual and corporeal creatures." What he calls happiness or beatitude (*beatitudo*) is a matter of the human soul's final union with God, which Aquinas recognizes as a divine gift.[45] Yet, Aquinas acknowledges,

43. Stump, *Aquinas*, 211–13.

44. *ST* 1a.89.1.*ad*.3

45. *ST* 1a2ae.3.8. The distinction between human happiness (*hominis beatitude*) by means of nature *per se* (*per principia suae naturae*), and graced human nature obtained by the power of God alone (*ad quam homo sola divina virtute pervenire potest*) is, Steven Long notes, an area of great complexity and controversy among readers of Aquinas. In the modern period, focus on questions of nature and grace has been due in part to the *la nouvelle théologie* school of Catholic thought, which held (often in reference to the work of Henri De Lubac, Yves Congar, and Hans Urs von Balthasar) that "supernatural beatitude is the natural end of man." How "natural" such beatitude is defines the contours of the enduring debate The position of a supernatural beatitude as the natural end of humans, argued the *la nouvelle* school, countered a tradition of thought (associated with the "scholastic" writers: Cardinal Cajetan, Luis de Molina, Domingo Báñez, and Francisco Suárez) that ignored the supernatural order by means of concentrating on the development of the merely natural order. For, if there is a sharp distinction between nature and grace, then development can be made with regards the natural order of things (e.g., politics, social science, and economics) without recourse to theological accounts that seek to understand all reality in the light of faith. Yet, as proponents of the position critique by De Lubac argue (from Aquinas, in particular), natural understanding of God—if taken seriously and straight forwardly—is necessarily limited with respect to God because such knowledge (*scientia*) is conditioned by the material nature of human existence. As such, there is no natural *finis ultimus* of

"so long as the soul enjoys God without its partner [i.e., the body], its desire, though at rest with what it has, still longs for the body to enter in and share."[46] The answer to the human soul's "desire" for the body is bodily resurrection; a theological move consistent with Aquinas's Christology wherein the human Jesus, in every element pertaining to the nature of a human body, is raised from the dead. In order for it to be a true resurrection, Aquinas maintains,

> it was necessary for the same body of Christ to be once more united with the same soul. And since the truth of the body's nature is from its form it follows that Christ's body after His Resurrection was a true body, and of the same nature as it was before.[47]

Aquinas does not claim to know what processes must occur in the resurrection of an individual human being, yet for him, personal identity requires bodily continuity.[48] The essential point for him is that the human

---

human nature that is separate from the desire for God. As Arron Riches contends, for Aquinas, the one *finis ultimus* of human nature is always "supernatural," an end human nature cannot achieve by any self-sufficing power of nature. See Riches, "Christology and Duplex Hominis Beatitudo," 49. For an overview of the debate, see, Feingold, *The Natural Desire to See God according to St. Thomas Aquinas and His Interpreters*; Long, *Natura Pura*, 10–50. Long is critical of *la nouvelle théologie*, yet he acknowledges the importance De Lubac and others have given to resisting the *ghettoizing* of theology to the "private" realm of a spiritual grace that is unnecessary for human goodness. For a sympathetic account to De Lubac's view of the supernatural as a fulfillment of a natural human desire, see, Milbank, *The Suspended Middle*. In a clarifying summary, A. N. Williams argues that Aquinas's doctrine of *duplex beatitudo* works in terms of a twofold trajectory: (1) theological virtues completing the natural virtues to lead humanity to its final end, and (2) divine assistance completing the natural capacities of the human creature through illumination in order to draw the human will into union with God. See Williams, *The Ground of Union*, 37.

46. *ST* 1a2ae.5.*ad*.4. To combine physicalism with the Christian doctrine of resurrection, as, for example, Nancey Murphy does, creates, Matthew Levering argues, an untenable situation whereby the human lacks the immaterial faculties to share in the immaterial life of God. Without a subsisting substance, the vision of God is unavailable. See Levering, *Jesus and the Demise of Death*, 106.

47. *ST* 3a.54.1c.

48. Lynne Rudder Baker takes issue with any sense of personal identity being limited by bodily continuity, if the body in question is somehow the same body from before death. For Baker, the resurrected body is incorruptible, thus it cannot be numerically identical to a biological carbon-based body. There is no identity preserving transformation from one to the other. Eleonore Stump agrees. Since the soul is what is made unformed prime matter into a human being configured in such a way that the matter is this living animal capable of intellective cognition, presumably in the

soul, though subsisting immaterially, is ordered towards union with the body, and through the gift of *caritas*, union with God. Such an ordering, Aquinas maintains, is a result of the body being a good (or desirable) of the soul,[49] and God being the ultimate end for human perfection insofar as God is "uncreated good . . . who alone by God's infinite goodness" can perfectly satisfy the desire and perfections of humans.[50] We will see this spelled out in terms of a sacramental union with Christ in the next chapter.

In summary, in his definition of the human person, Aquinas provides a holistic account of a living, rational animal that exhibits an essential unity as a particular kind of informed matter in which the necessary capacities for sensitive and intellectual activity is contained within what "human nature" makes possible. Aquinas's anthropology spells out an account of the living human body that lacks the physicalist and reductive notion of the body as being a *generic* thing that requires forms of enhancement and the imposition of *a rationalized order*. As a particular living thing with a particular kind of nature, human persons recurrently exhibit in their activity a teleological organization of their structures and powers: projects aimed at the achievement of sensitive and intellective understanding that are *secundum modum suae perfectionis* (according to the mode of its perfection, i.e., the achievement of what is good in relation to being a human).[51] For Aquinas (and the classic Christian tradition), the bodily, intellective, and teleological existence that defines human persons is a result of God's creative ends, which includes humanity's ultimate purpose as union with God as members of Christ's body.

---

resurrection of the body the soul can again make the unformed matter it informs *this* human being. Thus, identity preservation is not a case of the same matter being configured for a second time as a resurrection body, but the soul performing its principal organizing principles for a (graced) body. See Baker, "Persons and the Metaphysics of Resurrection"; Stump, *Aquinas*, 208–13. For an account of the persistence of an identical material body in reference to resurrection, see, Corcoran, *Rethinking Human Nature*, 119–34.

49. Following Aquinas's principle: *Forma date esse materiae*—Form gives existence to matter. See Thomas Aquinas, "On the Principles of Nature," ch. 2. In a suggestive formulation from Graham McAleer, form and matter always ecstatically reach out the one to the other. See McAleer, *Ecstatic Morality and Sexual Politics*, 115–35.

50. *ST* 1a2ae.3.1.

51. *ST*, 1a.4.2.

The Goal of Human Bodily Life

In the previous section, reference has been made to the perfection and purposefulness of human beings as a particular kind of ensouled body. This has earthly and heavenly implications, as it pertains to how human life is ordered as a material substance with a subsisting immaterial soul. This notion of human bodily life having purpose (in particular, ultimate purpose) goes beyond physicalist accounts, which tend to limit discussion on teleology to specific human capacities.[52] As such, these accounts lack the resources to properly address what constitutes human goodness and happiness.

In 1a.79–83, Aquinas articulates and defends a particular notion of human understanding and action. In his estimation, intellectual beings are able to know and employ understanding in order to act. The basis for Aquinas's explanation of human action is his metaphysical commitment to the notion that every form (living and nonliving) has some tendency or inclination (*inclinatio*) associated with it.[53] "On the basis of its form," Aquinas maintains, even, "fire, for instance, is inclined toward a higher place and toward generating its like."[54] When one considers the form related to being human, Aquinas notes later, natural inclination operates to include the senses and the intellect, since both are proper to an account of what defines a human person.[55]

Inclination, for Aquinas, is the genus of appetite, and appetite is associated with goodness. In contrast to the physicalist account of the human that limits inclination to organic survival because of blind evolutionary processes, for Aquinas all things are created by a good God who

52. Physicalists, in particular, religiously minded non-reductive physicalists, speak of *capacities* of the physical human person for human friendship and divine relationship (or, religious experience); however, there is nothing teleological to these capacities that would make the human person *ordered* in any sense towards such human and divine interaction. See Brown, "Human Nature, Physicalism, Spirituality, and Healing"; Murphy, "Physicalism without Reductionism." In addition, the decidedly teleological move Aquinas makes in considering the rational creatures advance toward God is missing from the recent "philosophical study" by Robert Pasnau. Robert Miner argues that leaving aside the theological concerns of Aquinas hinders any attempt to grasp the full implications of Aquinas's anthropology as it relates to his theological project. See Miner, "Recent Work on Thomas in North America," 151–52.

53. Kretzmann, "Philosophy of Mind," 144. Also, Lombardo, *The Logic of Desire*, 25.

54. *ST* 1a.80.1.

55. *ST* 1a.80.1c.

wills what is good for the creation. Therefore, all things are created with an inclination of their own to the good. As such, things that lack understanding or intellective faculties, and even inanimate things, as existing things, have simple inclinations, sometimes called "natural appetites" (for example, the gravitational attraction of a rock to the ground). Living beings with merely nutritive souls have no cognition at all, but they do have natural appetites beyond those associated with inanimate things (such as phototropism in green plants). At the level of nonhuman life there is sensory cognition, and with cognition comes accidental goals, dependent on what happens to be presented to the animal's senses as desirable, or good for it: "an animal can seek (*appetere*) things it apprehends, not only the things it is inclined toward on the basis of its natural form."[56] It has not only natural but also sensory appetite, which Aquinas often calls "sensuality" (*sensualitas*), "the appetite that follows sensory cognition naturally."[57]

People have appetite (*appetitus*), Aquinas argues, since humans are the kinds of living things that are able to assimilate the forms of things outside themselves (via understanding) and are drawn to what they find good (i.e., desirable). For humans, appetite is twofold: sensitive and intellectual—appetite that arises as via human senses and appetite that arises via human understanding.[58] Aquinas regards sensuality as attraction that arises at the sensory level (as a matter of sense appetite). Human senses, Aquinas maintains, can lead people to revolt against what they sense as well as to enjoy it. Sense appetite, therefore, can amount to a leaning to some objects of sense and a backing away from others. It can also lead to a complicated interaction of leaning to and avoiding (as, for example, when a hungry person eats a less-than-satisfying meal—satiating the hunger, a sensual desire—but not in a way that might ordinarily be considered humanly desirable). Such desire, contends Aquinas, can sometimes be controlled by reason.

56. *ST* 1a.80.1c.

57. *ST* 1a.81.1c.

58. *ST* 1a.81.2. Herbert McCabe sees the distinction between sensory and intellectual appetite as being analogous to what it means to say that the appetite of nonhuman animals is a matter of DNA and evolution (and thereby, *given*), while humans with both sensory and intellectual appetites have, in addition, culture and tradition (i.e., meaningful activity beyond the sensory level in that, in a fundamental sense, people *make* culture and tradition) to shape human desire. See McCabe, *Faith within Reason*, 137.

The notion of reason as playing a role when it comes to what people are drawn to at the sensory and intellectual level is what leads Aquinas to his discussion of will (*voluntas*) in 1a.82. He takes willing to be a rational power, a matter of being drawn to a good as understood. Understood as *rational* appetite (i.e., activity done for an aim, a reason), the will is the primary mover of all the powers of the soul (including itself) except the nutritive powers, and it is also the cause of motion in the body, and, in some cases, the will has primacy over the intellect.[59] As appetitive, the will is incompatible with coercion since Aquinas takes coercion to involve forces acting on a person to prevent them from moving towards what they want (which is what he takes us to be doing when acting by will, when acting voluntarily). When a person acts voluntarily, thinks Aquinas, they are, so to speak, doing something of their own accord— something Aquinas takes to be different from acting when being forced to act.[60] Yet, Aquinas also recognizes that people can be subject to necessity of a kind when acting voluntarily. In this sense, thinks Aquinas, voluntary action can be constrained by factors beyond the control of the person. And, he adds, a person cannot but will what one's absolute good is if one is aware of what that amounts to. There are certain individual goods, Aquinas reasons,

> which have not a necessary connection with happiness, because without them a man can be happy: and to such the will does not adhere of necessity. But there are some things which have a necessary connection with happiness, by means of which things man adheres to God, in Whom alone true happiness consists. Nevertheless, until through the certitude of the Divine Vision the necessity of such connection be shown, the will does not adhere to God of necessity, nor to those things which are of God. But the will of the man who sees God in His essence of necessity adheres to God, just as now we desire of necessity to be happy.[61]

59. *ST* 1a.82.3.

60. *ST* 1a.82.1. A human will is associated, for Aquinas, with the exercise of freedom of choice (*liberum arbitrium*), though its operations are not reducible to such choice. The will, Aquinas maintains, is operative in choice but the choice is free because the will is attracted by what is understood to be in some way or other good. So unless it be confronted by sheer goodness itself, which is God, the will may have a variety of reasons for being attracted; and thus the choice or decision is free. For Aquinas, "we are free not because we act at random or unpredictably, but because we act for reasons, and there are many possible available reasons." McCabe, *On Aquinas*, 68.

61. *ST* 1a.82.2c.

In other words, just as people do not have to assent intellectually to propositions that are not necessarily true; likewise, they do not have to will what is not perceived to be necessary to their ultimate or complete happiness. It is reasonable, Aquinas maintains, to think that a human being can be happy without good things that are not necessary for such happiness. Yet, there are some necessary conditions when it comes to appetite and human happiness. The vision of God, Aquinas assumes, leaves one unable not to want God or be drawn to God. As the ultimate good for human appetite, the vision of God is necessarily a goal for human (ultimate) joy. Failing such certain knowledge of that in which final happiness lies, people do not, Aquinas reasons, have to will as they do. In this sense, willing (acting voluntarily) is subject to our understanding of what is good for us. As will be discussed in the next chapter, this inclination of all that is properly said to be human to the divine good as ultimate good has implications for how the church is said to have an explicit supernatural orientation.

Aquinas recognizes a kind of interweaving of intellect (understanding) and will (wanting and moving toward some goal) in human action. For the most part, Aquinas thinks that people are drawn to what they take to be good as they think about such things. He also considers, however, that how someone thinks about things can be affected by his willing or desiring. Consider, for example, a person reading about an organization that is asking for money to help with orphans of war.[62] The intellect of the person recognizes that if they look at the advertisement for very long, they are likely to succumb to its emotional force. Intellect sees the goodness of contributing to the organization, but it also recognizes that if the person gives money to this organization, they will not have it for the new computer they have been wanting. The person's desire for the new computer is strong and influences intellect to rank saving money for the computer as the best for them considering their current circumstances. In consequence of the findings on the part of the intellect, the will directs the intellect to stop thinking about the advertisement and the organization, and (after a further interaction of intellect and will) the person turns the page of the magazine. This, Aquinas reasons, is not two instants, one, the operation of the intellect perceiving something attractive, and the next, an operation of the will overriding the intellect through an action. It is a single complex operation involving both will and intellect (i.e., both

62. The example is adapted from one provided by Eleonore Stump. See Stump, *Aquinas*, 279.

desire and thinking).[63] For Aquinas, what a person knows can sometimes shape or be shaped by what they desire.[64]

The interaction of will and intellect is fundamental to matters pertaining to human goal-directedness, a topic Aquinas addresses in 1a2ae. In brief, the *Secunda Pars* focuses on human beings and how they can be thought to be brought by God to union with God. Aquinas takes union with God to be something we should aim for as a goal. The opening articles begin with a reflection on what it means to say that goal-orientation is integral to understanding human nature and human purpose.

Aquinas suggests in 1a2ae.1.1 that sometimes people seem to act without thought or deliberation—as, for example, when a person scratches their arm when talking to someone while focused on what is being said, rather than the arm. An insect bite might result in a deliberate scratching of the arm to relieve an irritating itch, yet, Aquinas notes, people often pass and go through other bodily behavior without deliberation. As such, Aquinas suggests a distinction between "acts of a human being" (*actiones hominis*) and "human acts" (*actiones humanae*). Of actions done by people, argues Aquinas,

> those alone are properly called "human," which are proper to man as man. Now man differs from irrational animals in this, that he is master of his actions. Wherefore those actions alone are properly called human, of which man is master. . . . And if any other actions are found in man, they can be called actions "of a man" (*actiones hominis*) but not properly "human" actions, since they are not proper to man as man. Now it is clear that whatever actions proceed from a power, are caused by that power in accordance with the nature of its object. But the object

63. *ST* 1a.82.4.

64. The role of emotions (*passiones animae*, "passions of the soul") figures into Aquinas's anthropology, and is presented in the *Prima Secundae*. In brief, emotions, or passions, are the bodily and psychological expressions associated with sensual appetites. As passions of "the soul," an emotion like fear is not localized to one aspect of bodily or mental life (as, for example, a broken ankle is a problem of the ankle); rather, fear, like all emotions, is referenced to the whole of human vital activity. Emotions, for Aquinas, are part of the appetive and cognitive operations of a person, in that they play a part in how a person lives a human life. But emotions, Aquinas maintains, are part of human receptivity to the world in that they are defined by their *object* (e.g., the specific thing a person is afraid of) rather than through some *cause* (e.g., the thought and action that leads a person to the object of their fear). For a recent and well developed study of Aquinas on emotions, see, Lombardo, *The Logic of Desire*, particularly chapter 3.

of the will is the end and the good. Therefore all human actions
(*actiones humanae*) must be for an end.[65]

This acting for an end is, Aquinas argues, peculiar to human beings
considered as things in the world with rational faculties. He agrees that
the world contains non-thinking things that act so as to achieve various
ends, for example, that tigers are truly acting for an end as they seek out
prey on which to feed. Nevertheless, there is a difference between tigers
acting and people doing so. For people, unlike tigers and other living
things, can think or reflect about what they are doing (or are about to do)
and can therefore be thought of as deliberately acting for ends.[66] In addition, thinks Aquinas, there has to be a final end aimed at as people act.[67]
He means that when a person aims for an end they have to be aiming
at something specific, even though, Aquinas maintains, it may involve a
series of intermediate actions for an end.

As previously noted, Aquinas held willing to be the rational power,
by which the good, as understood, is sought or desired. Under this description, nobody can fail to desire what he or she takes to be good.[68]
People might, Aquinas admits, be wrong when it comes to what is good
for human life, but he thinks that people naturally gravitate to what they
understand to be good. In this sense, he argues, humans always aim at
goodness and have an innate tendency to desire what is good.

The good for a given thing, Aquinas maintains, will depend on what
it is. What is good for a cat is not necessarily what is good for a lizard.
With this point in mind, Aquinas stresses that to see what fulfills people
(i.e., see what is good for them), it has be considered what makes them
different from other things in the world. Aquinas thinks that noting the
answer to this question will reveal what is fulfilling for them.[69] As such,
for Aquinas, "happiness is the perfect good, which lulls the appetite altogether, else it would not be the last end, if something yet remained to be
desired."[70] As noted above, the one thing that makes people different from

65. *ST* 1a2ae.1.1c.

66. *ST* 1a2ae.1.2.

67. *ST* 1a2ae.1.4.

68. *ST* 1a2ae.1.6–7. "If the intellect does present something to the will as good,"
notes Eleonore Stump, "then, because the will is an appetite for the good, the will wills
it—unless the will directs intellect to reconsider, to direct its attention to something
else, or to stop considering the matter at hand." Stump, *Aquinas*, 281.

69. *ST* 1a2ae.2.8.

70. *ST* 1a2ae.2.8c.

everything else in the world is the fact that they are able to understand. The characteristic activity of people, Aquinas says, is understanding. Consequently, the ultimate good for humans must lie in understanding, which, for him, means that people cannot be finally satisfied until they have somehow understood the source and goal of all things, i.e., God. The ultimate good for humans, what Aquinas calls beatitude, is an operation of the mind by which the mind is united to God in knowing God.[71] "For perfect happiness (*beatitudo perfecta*)," Aquinas explains, "the intellect needs to reach the very Essence of the First Cause. And thus it will have its perfection through union with God as with that object, in which alone man's happiness consists."[72] Such understanding, Aquinas notes later, is a real potentiality in humans, even as it remains beyond human means alone to grasp the fullness of this happiness.[73]

The word *beatitudo* is often translated as "happiness," as can the Latin word *felicitas*. Aquinas holds that human goodness ultimately lies in being happy. When he uses the term *felicitas*, however, Aquinas is thinking of what might be termed "earthly happiness" (*beatitudo imperfecta*), it is "that which is had in this life" (*quae habetur in hac vita*) and it is not this that he has in mind when saying that human fulfillment lies in humanity's last end, "the thing in which the last end is found (*id in quo finis ultimi ratio invenitur*)," which he calls *beatitudo*.[74] This is not to discount "earthly happiness," nor does it suggest that the only happiness that counts is the vision of God.[75] As embodied souls, happiness can be had, Aquinas maintains, through the speculative and practical uses of human intellect in a life of intellectual and moral virtue.[76] All knowledge

71. Kerr, *Aquinas*, 158.

72. *ST* 1a2ae.3.8c.

73. *ST* 1a2ae.5.1. Wang refers to this notion as a natural desire that cannot be fulfilled naturally. See Wang, *Aquinas and Sartre*, 270. On this point, Kerr adds that the gift of God's self-disclosure through the gift of faith, means that "not only are we not frustrated in our desire to know what lies infinitely beyond us but we are drawn to a destiny we could never of ourselves have even imagined". Kerr, *Aquinas*, 159.

74. *ST* 1a2ae.1.7.

75. On this point, Stephen Wang notes that, for Aquinas, the good is not always beyond us—sometimes it is present and possessed. See Wang, *Aquinas and Sartre*, 256.

76. The concept of virtues in Aquinas's theological project deserves more attention than space allows in this book. In brief, the virtues are a kind of disposition (*habitus*) the acquiring of which forms the fundamental principle of human acts. In other words, virtues are one of the constitutive principles of a properly human kind of causality. In effect, the *Secunda Pars* of the *Summa* is an exercise in moral theology where Aquinas

in this life, whether in speculative or practical matters, has its origin in sense experience. As such, *felicitas* involves the entire human person.

When considering happiness in general, Aquinas believes that human desire, in this life, never ends. The desire for a good always reflects a desire to become what people are not, because in every good they seek they are seeking their own good, that is, their perfection particular to being human.[77] Aquinas is arguing that in earthly life, people seek to go beyond the present to a future perfection that they do not yet possess. It is an essential part of human nature as creatures in time to be incomplete, yet as existing things that seek to exist beyond individual materiality through understanding and desire. To be human is to lack the fullness of being complete.[78] "But speaking of perfect happiness (*beatitudo perfecta*)," Aquinas argues,

> some have maintained that no disposition of body is necessary for happiness; indeed, that it is necessary for the soul to be entirely separated from the body. . . . But this is unreasonable. *For since it is natural to the soul to be united to the body; it is not possible for the perfection of the soul to exclude its natural perfection.* Consequently, we must say that perfect disposition of the body is necessary, both antecedently and consequently, for that happiness which is in all ways perfect. Antecedently, because, as Augustine says (*Gen. ad lit. xii, 35*), "if body be such, that the governance thereof is difficult and burdensome, like unto flesh which is corruptible and weighs upon the soul, the mind is turned away from that vision of the highest heaven." Whence he concludes that, "when this body will no longer be 'natural,' but 'spiritual,' then will it be equaled to the angels, and that will be its glory, which erstwhile was its burden." *Consequently, because from the happiness of the soul there will be an overflow on*

---

seeks to develop an ethics based, not on obedience to this or that divine command, but in terms of the formation of the kind of person who appropriates and develops the gifts required for a moral life in view of the promised enjoyment of divine beatitude. For a concise introduction to virtues (and vices), See Porter, "Virtues and Vices." A more comprehensive analysis of Aquinas's moral theory and theology is found in Pope, *The Ethics of Aquinas*; Pinches, *Theology and Action*. Mark Jorden suggests that the Summa as a whole provides a "pattern for an ideal pedagogy" in moral learning. In his estimation, the *Secunda Pars* with its descriptive and prescriptive analysis of the virtues and vices constitutes the ideal of a clarified and unified theological ordering for human flourishing. See Jordan, *Rewritten Theology*, 116–35.

77. *ST* 1a2ae.18.1.

78. Wang, *Aquinas and Sartre*, 259.

to the body, so that this too will obtain its perfection.[79] (Emphasis added)

In other words, Aquinas finds it hard to believe that ultimate human happiness (*beatitudo*) is fundamentally a matter of corporal existence; however, in line with his commitment to the resurrection of the body, the human body (as the "spiritual" or resurrected body) must eventually be reunited with the soul in the beatific vision for people to be able rightfully to call this perfect *human* happiness.[80] Beatitude, says Aquinas, amounts to "seeing God just as he is."[81] The body, inasmuch as it is necessary for the excellent working of the intellective soul as a subsisting substance is, therefore, a part of what Aquinas means when discussing perfect happiness of the human person.[82] In this, his anthropology is decidedly theological.[83]

An Anthropology of the Whole Body

To summarize: Aquinas's anthropology provides a framework to approach human persons as substances that exist, have sets of specific capacities, acts, and cannot be reduced to their parts, taken individually or aggregately. While the existence and nature of a human being is dependent upon his or her having a substantial form actualizing a sufficiently complex organic material body, such parts are not acting substances in

79. *ST* 1a2ae.4.6,c.

80. Trabbic, "The Human Body and Human Happiness in Aquinas's Summa Theologiae," 562. On this note, Peter Dillard stresses that for Aquinas, it is the soul's act of understanding—an act not reliant on a "bodily organ"—that figures preeminently in an account of the resurrected body. The soul's being reunited with its resurrected body will not bring it about that the soul understands but only that the glorified body no longer impedes the soul's act of understanding, as it did when the same body was material, and therefore, corruptible. This position, Dillard contends, maintains the logic of Aquinas's anthropology and operates in contradistinction to physicalist accounts (e.g., Dillard takes issue with Caroline Bynum's objection to Aquinas's position on the resurrected body and beatitude) that seek to restrict any non-physical operations of the human person, particularly after death. See Dillard, "Keeping the Vision."

81. *ST* 1a2ae.3.8.

82. Torrell, *Saint Thomas Aquinas, Vol. 2*, 12.

83. Anthony Celano argues convincingly that in formalizing the distinction between *beatitudo imperfecta* and *beatitudo perfecta,* Aquinas draws out theological implications of Aristotle's ethics without betraying Aristotle's thought. See Celano, "The Concept of Worldly Beatitude in the Writings of Thomas Aquinas."

their own right. A human being exists and acts by means of his or her soul and body, which together compose the individual person.

As a "rational animal," the human person, for Aquinas, is a living, sensitive, reasoning body that transcends its individual materiality through meaningful activity. Consequently, Aquinas's anthropology resists both the reductionism of mechanistic physicalism, which relies on the rationalization of the human body to its constituent parts, and the lack of human purposefulness in physicalism, which sets human inclinations adrift from the attributes and capacities that are particular to human bodily life, thereby requiring purpose to be imposed through various physical enhancements.

Such a rationalization of the body proves inadequate, in terms of Aquinas's anthropology, in reference to how the rationalized human body resembles mere stuff that is said to be alive through the operations of neurobiological forces of organization. As such, the body of reductive physicalism is a *corpse*, animated by a metaphysic of efficient causation. The body seems at best to be thought of as a carefully coordinated instrument that performs certain tasks and achieves a certain level of growth.

In contrast, Aquinas provides a holistic account of a living, rational animal that exhibits an essential unity as a particular kind of informed matter in which the necessary capacities for sensitive and intellectual activity is contained within what "human nature" makes possible. Being a living human person requires, for Aquinas, a holism in relation to the capacities of the material body and the soul. That is, the activities of specific parts of the body are meaningful activities for the whole body, indeed, for the entire life of the person. Specific organs, for example, can be examined and understood in relation to their function and health, just as, today, specific neurotransmitters can be analyzed in relation to neural activity, but these operations *in themselves* are fundamentally significant in that they are operations of a *whole* living body, a body with a certain kind of life (or soul). The living body cannot be reduced to the operations of its constituent parts, Aquinas's anthropology makes clear, for no one part, no one operation of one part, is sufficient when accounting for what makes a body a living human body.

Beyond such attention to the relation of parts to the whole, using the category of form, Aquinas's attention to the intrinsic teleology of human bodily life provides an alternative to the body of physicalism, a body that might be said to *act* for a purpose due to its biological programming, but it does not *exist* for a purpose. Fundamental to Aquinas's description is that human persons are teleological as rational animals (i.e., a particular kind of animal, one with a rational soul), with inclinations that include the natural desire to seek what is considered good for human thriving. With the benefit of divine aid (i.e., grace), this inclination includes, for human beings as ordered to God, as the *beatitudo perfecta*.

The conceptual work that Aquinas accomplishes in his anthropology presumes his earlier account of God and creation, and anticipates his discussion of the incarnation of Jesus and the subsequent signs of grace developed through attention to the sacraments and the church. As such, the story of human beings is placed within an account of divine life and activity that includes the perfecting of all creation through the merits of Jesus, son of Mary, Son of God.[84]

When applied to ecclesiology, with this sense of the embodiment of the church as the body of Christ, this description of a Thomistic anthropology shifts the conceptual center in matters of church decline and the promise of managerial thought and practice to more theologically rich ground. Such a shift restores questions of human identity and purpose, and subsequent questions of ecclesial identity and purpose, to the foreground. Under such conceptualization, church decline is not addressed through pragmatic appeals to managerial techniques or the reduction of ecclesial existence to missional practices; rather, the notion of ecclesial life is framed by the destiny of human persons as ensouled bodies that informs the identity and purpose of the church as a particular social body, and the unifying provision of God manifest in the concrete existence and sacramental ministry of the church. The preceding analysis has attended to human persons as particular living animals. It is now to the unifying provision through the sacramental life of the church that this work turns.

---

84. Wawrykow, *Gods Grace Human Action*, 242–47.

5

What Difference Does a Social Body Make? A *Unifying* Alternative according to a Thomistic Sacramental Theology

W ITHIN CHRISTIAN THEOLOGY THE church is understood to be a particular social body, the "body of Christ," which is none other than the living body of the raised and ascended Jesus made sacramentally present through the grace of the Holy Spirit.[1] The church is the community "in Christ," where membership in Christ's body and with each other creates a sustainable and loving community. This book contends that managerialism, resting on the assumptions of a physicalist account of the body, falls short of providing a description of the social body adequate to

---

1. A number of recent studies question the status of "body of Christ" language in relation to the church. Ian McFarland, for example, is concerned to define the absolute difference between Christ's risen body and the church in order, he maintains, to overcome any sense of an "intrinsic or automatic correspondence" between the living presence of Christ and the church that is called to follow Christ. For McFarland, it is "epistemically empty" to ally the "will of Christ" with the "will of his follows," for as the second person of the Trinity, Christ is always prior and other to the church, even as members of the church can share in Christ's ministry of reconciliation by means of divine grace that overcomes the divide between Christ and God's people. See McFarland, "The Body of Christ." Yung Suk Kim, in a number of publications, seeks to re-orient the notion of the body of Christ away from the organism metaphor to a description of a way of living that emphasizes "Christ's embodiment of God's gospel." According to Kim, Paul used "body" language to stress the exemplary life of Christ that his follows are meant to emulate through embodied practices of service and hospitality. To be Christ's body, therefore, is primarily an "ethic of Christian life," and secondarily, a description of the community that practices this ethic. See Kim, "Reclaiming Christ's Body (*soma Christou*)"; Kim, *Christ's Body in Corinth*.

the identity and purpose of the church. It falls short, in other words, in providing an adequate vision of the church as an essential *unity* whose material life cannot be extricated from a proper account of what is logically involved in the church's identity as the "body of Christ."[2]

In place of a physicalist-inspired, managerialist account, where the goals of efficiency, effectiveness, predictability, and control shape how an organization is ordered and oriented, a description of the church is needed that attends to the particular way the church exists as a social body. Building on his anthropology, the ecclesial vision of Thomas Aquinas provides an alternative to organizational theory by countering the pre-determined ends of managerialism and its ecclesial cognates with an understanding of human life as having a proper end as friends of God who share in the life of divine joy and love as members of Christ's divine humanity.

To appeal to the "body of Christ" in relation to the church requires attention to the use of this term within Aquinas's theological project, and an exploration of how its use opens a line of thinking to an alternative to the logic of managerialism and physicalism by means of his anthropology and sacramental theology. By relating his sacramental theology on the unifying character of the Eucharistic and ecclesial presence of Christ's body to his theological anthropology, where the human person is defined as a holistic unity of material body and immaterial soul, Aquinas provides an account of the church as a living body in whom all who are members share in the life of Christ, and his benefits. Such an account is an alternative to the instrumentalizing tendency within modern ecclesiologies that are concerned to demonstrate that church survival and growth are best explored by means of a managerialist logic.

This chapter draws on the Christology, sacramental theology, and ecclesiology of Aquinas to provide a corrective to the social body envisioned by managerialist logic. Aquinas's metaphysics and anthropology provides the basis for his account of the incarnation of Christ and of

---

2. In his classic study on Paul's use of "body," John Robinson defends the notion that "body of Christ" language is more than metaphorical. To say that the church is the body of Christ, Robinson contends,

> is no more of a metaphor than to say that the flesh of the incarnate Jesus or the bread of the Eucharist is the body of Christ. None of them is "like" his body (Paul never says this): each of them is the body of Christ, in that each is the physical complement and extension of the one and the same Person and Life. They are all expressions of a single Christology.

Robinson, *The Body*, 51.

sacramental theology, and together they set the conditions for a vision of the church as the body of Christ enlivened by the Holy Spirit and ordered to *beatitudo perfecta* in God.[3] Like the human body on which the church is analogically modeled, for it to be considered alive and able to exist as a particular kind of thing in the world, requires not only the material by which the church is distinguished from other organizations, but also, it requires a particular animating source. For Aquinas, the church is animated by God's very life by the Holy Spirit, through the merits and body of Christ.[4]

"Born of the Virgin Mary": Incarnation Matters

In his opening question to the treatise *On the Union of the Incarnate Word*, Aquinas stipulates that the coherence of the incarnation begins with understanding, first, how the word "nature" is used; second, what it means to call someone a person; and finally, how the proper description of Christ as human and divine requires attention to the grammar by which we speak of Jesus as man, and Jesus as the second person of the Trinity. To attend to these matters will, Aquinas states, clarify what it means to declare that in Christ "human nature is united to the Word neither accidentally nor essentially, but substantially in the sense that substance signifies a rational single substance."[5] The incarnation, Aquinas maintains, is to be approached by drawing on the anthropology analyzed in the previous chapter and applying the same logic to the one person, Jesus of Nazareth. In virtue of his human nature, therefore, Christ can be spoken of in exactly the same way to that of any human being. In virtue of his divine nature, such things as that he forgives sins, or is the redeemer, are also authorized to be said. In being able to say both of a "rational single substance," Aquinas contends, is the basis for understanding the identity and purpose of Christ.

3. Eleonore Stump cautions that attention to Aquinas's theological explication of doctrine, without taking seriously his anthropology and metaphysics, limits the clarity and overall coherence of Aquinas's project. See Stump, "Aquinas's Metaphysics of the Incarnation."

4. In his commentary of the Apostles Creed, Aquinas speaks of the church as one body with many members, the soul of which is the Holy Spirit. See Aquinas, *The Catechetical Instructions of St. Thomas Aquinas*.

5. Aquinas, "On the Union of the Incarnate Word," 460.

Aquinas takes the incarnation to amount to God becoming human, following the Chalcedonian formula that defined Christ as one person with two natures. Given his view that God is immutable, he does not take the incarnation to amount to a change in God.[6] Instead, he views it as a change on the side of what is created and thinks that God became human insofar as there came to birth in the world one who, though human, was also divine. For Aquinas, the incarnation amounts to there being a divine subject (God the Son) united with what is human in a way that allows a human being to be both human and divine.[7]

The second person of the Trinity, Aquinas maintains, assumed a human nature. That is to say, the second person added to himself another nature, in addition to the divine nature already his own, a point Aquinas stresses as a *union*, and not a wholesale assumption by which nothing identifiably human remains.[8] As noted above, for Aquinas, the nature of a material substance is conferred by a substantial form that is an individual; and a substantial form is an individual in virtue of configuring or informed matter. Consequently, when the second person of the Trinity assumes human nature, he assumes a particular human substantial form and the matter it informs.[9] Like every other human substantial form, the substantial form assumed by Christ configures matter into a human body and confers those properties essential to human beings, including understanding. In virtue of having two natures, Christ therefore has two operations. In his divine nature, he has the operation proper to the deity. In his human nature, Christ has a complete and fully human mind and rational appetite, that is to say, a complete and fully human will. Since intellect and will also characterize the divine nature, in virtue of having two natures, Christ also has two intellects[10] and two wills,[11] one human

---

6. See *ST* 1a.3.1.

7. Gorman, "Incarnation," 430.

8 *ST* 3a.2.8. In like manner, Eric Mascall refers to the union of the incarnation as "entirely concrete and particular" in the man, Jesus of Nazareth. See Mascall, *Christ, the Christian and the Church*, 19.

9. *ST* 3a.2.5. Here Thomas stands with the ecumenical councils that resisted the Apolinarian impulse to replace the rational soul with the Word, thus leaving Christ without the nature that defines humans as humans; and the Nestorian impulse to restrict any unity with the divine nature, thus effectively undermining the notion that Christ is the second person of the Trinity.

10. *ST* 3a.9.1.

11. *ST* 3a.18.1. Also, Stump, "Aquinas's Metaphysics of the Incarnation," 207–8.

and one divine. Otherwise, Aquinas notes, "the soul of Christ would have been more imperfect than the souls of the rest of men."[12]

Aquinas holds that it was fitting (*conveniens*) for God to become human because of the particular way humans understand, which proceeds by means of bodily (or sense) experience.[13] Furthermore, the fittingness extends into the need for human nature to be restored. "The Incarnation," he says, was "not necessary for the restoration of human nature since by his infinite power God had many other ways to accomplish this end."[14] On the other hand, however, Aquinas regards the incarnation as suitable for salvation since he takes it to bring about salvation in an especially good way since, among other things, it involves God addressing humanity as a human person. "Christ, as man (*secundum quod homo*)," Aquinas maintains, "is our way to God."[15] As incarnate for our "furtherance in good," Aquinas notes, God brings faith, hope, and charity to address sufficiently (*sufficiens*) human imperfection manifest in human evil, loss of dignity, and pride.[16] In the union of human and divine natures in Christ, the grace for humans to share in God's beatitude was made fittingly and sufficiently available.[17] In other words, what Christ accomplished as human becomes the "fruit" for people to obtain.[18]

His focus on the incarnation as fitting for human salvation allows Aquinas to maintain an anthropological perspective when his analysis turns to the question of how membership in Christ's body orients human life to its final end in the beatitude of God. The image of the living human body as a particular composite of matter and form with an implicit *telos* that is fitting for human life remains an enduring alternative to the non-teleological reductionism of physicalism and the rationalization that shapes the managed body. Instead of a corpse-like body that operates by means of neurobiological forces, or the atomized operations of the managed organization, Aquinas's account of the human body and the social body of the church proceeds along a path that shows how, through divine

---

12. *ST* 3a.9.1c. Again, Thomas keeps the tradition of the councils through avoiding the monophysite positions wherein the divine nature "absorbs" the human nature, or likewise, the human absorbs the divine nature.

13. *ST* 3a.1.1.

14. *ST* 3a.1.2c.

15. *ST* 1a.2.*Prooemium*.

16. *ST* 3a.1.2c & *ad.* 3.

17. Adams, *What Sort of Human Nature?* 51.

18. Levering, "Does the Paschal Mystery Reveal the Trinity?" 90.

help, human life is best ordered to sharing in fellowship animated by the gift of grace.

The Grace of Christ as Head of the Body

In the union of natures in Christ, Aquinas recognized the accompanying grace to be the means by which the benefits and merits of Christ's incarnation could be extended to include all people. Such is the role of grace in Aquinas's theological account. In general, grace, for Aquinas, is the elevating (*elevans*) and healing (*sanans*) action of God in humans leading them to union with God.[19] In the incarnation, Aquinas argues, the humanity of Christ was the instrument of the divinity (*instrumentum divinitatis*),[20] and as a result, what was accomplished in Christ had effects beyond Christ alone. Given that "no being can act beyond the limits of its specific nature," the grace enacted in the incarnation is understood by Aquinas to be a gift that "surpasses every capacity of created nature, since it is nothing other than a certain participation in the divine nature, which surpasses every other nature."[21] Like any human being, Aquinas thinks Christ can receive grace from God insofar as he is human. As the divine subject with two natures, Aquinas continues, Christ is understood to be supremely graced.[22]

Aquinas's discussion on the grace of Christ includes the claim that Christ's human soul was filled with sanctifying grace and that this grace came to be imparted to others inasmuch as Christ was God and, therefore, the source of grace.[23] As God incarnate, thinks Aquinas, Christ must have had the fullness of grace considered as something uniting humans to God. Aquinas also thinks that "since grace was at its best in Christ, it gave rise to virtues which perfected each of the faculties of the soul and all its activities" and that "in this way Christ had all the virtues."[24] In making this claim, Aquinas is asserting that Christ had all the *moral* virtues, not all possible virtues.

19. *ST* 1a2ae.109.1. Also, the discussion on habitual grace in Wawrykow, *God's Grace and Human Action*, 164f.

20. *ST* 3a.1.18.*ad*.2.

21. *ST* 1a2ae.112.1c.

22. *ST* 3a.8.5.

23. *ST* 3a.7.1.

24. *ST* 3a.7.2.

Aquinas denies that Christ had all the theological virtues since he thinks that Christ could not have had faith or hope. In that Aquinas regards faith and hope as virtues possessed only by people who do not enjoy the knowledge of God that comes through enjoying the beatific vision, he contends that faith and hope are not appropriate for Christ as one who shares in the knowledge and vision of God naturally (i.e., by nature).[25] On the other hand, Aquinas insists that Christ must have had all of the gifts of the Holy Spirit. "Clearly," he says, "the soul of Christ was perfectly subject to the movement of the Holy Spirit. . . . Obviously then he was outstandingly endowed with the gifts."[26] Another conclusion drawn by Aquinas from his teaching that Christ has the fullness of grace is that in him were to be found the effects of "grace freely bestowed" (*gratia gratis datae*). He observes: a teacher must have the means to present his doctrine;

> Now Christ is the first and chief teacher of spiritual doctrine and faith, according to Heb. 2:3,4: "Which having begun to be declared by the Lord was confirmed unto us by them that heard Him, God also bearing them witness by signs and wonders." Hence, it is clear that all the gratuitous graces were most excellently in Christ, as in the first and chief teacher of the faith.[27]

The discussion of grace in relation to Christ as an individual shifts in 3a.8 to how Christ's grace is understood in reference to others, including members of the church. Drawing on the biblical imaginary of Christ as "head of the body,"[28] Aquinas enriches the benefits of Christ's grace with particular precision by aligning the vital influence of the head on the entire body with his account of humanity in its various degrees of a graced state.[29] Just as God is source of existence (*esse*) and goodness in all creatures, so Aquinas envisions a cascading flow of grace: from Godhead into the human soul hypostatically united to it; from the soul of Christ into all the members of the "body" of which he is the head.[30] Indeed,

25. *ST* 3a.7.3–4.

26. *ST* 3a.7.5.

27. *ST* 3a.7.7c.

28. Col 1:18; Eph 1:22. These texts along with other pivotal Pauline references are explored with more depth in the following section.

29. Radcliffe, "The Body of Christ," 37.

30. *ST* 3a.8.1.

Marilyn McCord Adams maintains, for Aquinas, the "body" includes the entire human race in all times and all places,

> whose members themselves form a descending hierarchy in proportion to their union with Christ—from the closest (the blessed angels and saints) who are united to him through glory; to those who are actually united to him through *caritas*; down to those who are actually united through faith; and further to those who are as yet only potentially united because Divine predestination certifies their future actual union; and finally to humans created but not predestined by God, whose potential for union with Christ will never be actualized.[31]

The idea of Christ as the "head of the body" is given particular attention by Aquinas in relation to Christ's headship of "the body of the church." This focus helps maintain the overall image of the living body while also accounting for how Christ's grace extends to others. The church plays a particularly important role in Aquinas's overall account of Christ's grace since he thinks that all grace derives from Christ as the Son of God in whom the fullness of grace is present.[32] As head of the church (*caput Ecclesiae*), says Aquinas, Christ holds the highest place in the body of Christ that is the church, and Christ's humanity "acts upon people, on their bodies as well as on their souls."[33] In keeping with the analogy of the human body, he writes in his treatise *On Truth*, "The head in a physical body works not only for itself but also for all the members. Now Christ is the head of His body, the church. His activity was therefore meritorious for His members." Aquinas concludes, "Christ and the Church are in a sense one person."[34]

---

31. Adams, *What Sort of Human Nature?* 52–53. See , *ST* 3a.8.3c.

32. Davies, *The Thought of Thomas Aquinas*, 312–13. Also, Sabra, *Thomas Aquinas' Vision of the Church*, 58–68.

33. *ST* 3a.8.3–4. Fabian Radcliffe notes that, for Aquinas, Christ as "head" is where the body analogy begins. In other words, *Christus caput* rather than *corpus Christi* is the starting point for Aquinas's ecclesiology. See Radcliffe, "The Body of Christ," 38.

34. Aquinas, *On Truth*. George Sabra notes that Aquinas's use of *corpus* in relation to Christ and the church is too fluid to define it exclusively as an ecclesiological statement. Following Henri de Lubac, Sabra maintains that *corpus Christi* in the time of Aquinas is associated predominantly in an ecclesial sense, while earlier usage favored a Eucharistic sense. The earlier Eucharistic sense is evident in Aquinas's sacramental theology, while the ecclesial sense comes out clearer in reference to Christ as "head" of the body. See Sabra, *Thomas Aquinas' Vision of the Church*, 61–62.

Aquinas's use of *corpus* is not the only description he uses for the church,[35] but it is the most frequent and, more importantly, it communicates the unifying characteristic between Christ, as head, and the members, who as a body (*corpus Christi*) exist as a whole in relation to Christ. As the whole church is termed one mystic body or person (*una mystica persona*) from its likeness to the natural body of a person, Aquinas reasons,

> so likewise Christ is called the Head of the Church from a likeness with the human head, in which we may consider three things, viz. order, perfection, and power: "Order," indeed; for the head is the first part of man, beginning from the higher part, . . . "Perfection," inasmuch as in the head dwell all the senses, both interior and exterior, whereas in the other members there is only touch, . . . "Power," because the power and movement of the other members, together with the direction of them in their acts, is from the head, by reason of the sensitive and motive power there ruling.[36]

The threefold rationale of order, perfection, and power are, for Aquinas, perfections associated with the operations of the head of a rational person through which the entire body is organized and operates. Aquinas's understanding of body functions and organs lacks the accuracy of modern biological and neurological standards, but when considering the particular relations of the head and the body, his primary concern is to remain consistent to his anthropology. Accordingly, for Aquinas, a living person is such due to the union of a subsiding substantial form and matter, a *compositio* of soul and body. Hence, it is the entire humanity of Christ, as the "instrument" of his divine nature, which serves as the head of all people, and as such, through divine grace, the fullness of Christ's life[37] "acts upon" the whole human person, both body and soul, though "primarily on their souls and secondarily their bodies."[38] This notion of a composite human body is deeply linked, analogically, to the notion of a unified social body, as Aquinas understands the church, so that both fall

35. Sabra refers to *Congregatio fidelium* as the next frequently used term for the church, but Aquinas also uses *Populus*, *Domus* and *Civitas* at various times. See Sabra, *Thomas Aquinas' Vision of the Church*, 34–68.

36. *ST* 3a.8.1c.

37. This, for Aquinas, includes Christ's ministry, and most importantly, his passion and resurrection.

38. *ST* 3a.8.2c.

within the description of a body as a "multitude ordained or organized together (*multitudo ordinata in unum*)"; that is, a body that is essentially a unity *teleologically* ordered to God.[39]

In sum, Aquinas, in ascribing headship to Christ and participation in his body to those who receive his grace, maintains the logic of his anthropology even as his Christology stretches the analogy of the body to include the notion of a social body that shares the essential goal of the individual human person: divine beatitude. As God incarnate, Jesus shared in this beatitude even in his earthly life.[40] Through the merits of the incarnation, and Christ's eventual death and resurrection, the same life of grace that sourced in God and manifest in Christ's humanity becomes the foundation for a community who lives by means of divine grace. In the assumed flesh of the Son is the way that leads to God and also, therefore, the means to humanity's final supernatural fulfillment in face-to-face vision of God, for "men are brought to this end of beatitude by the humanity of Christ."[41]

Unlike physicalism (which restricts the human body to the goals of survival and growth) and managerialism (which treats all social bodies as in need of managing), as a fundamental principle in his Christology, Aquinas maintains that the graced community formed as *corpus Christi* has a life, purpose, and unity. Such a body includes Christ as the head, and through grace, human persons as members, that as a mystical unity has a life that is fitting for human bodily life as a community ordered to human wellbeing and oriented to divine happiness. Like the soul that gives life to a body, Christ's grace gives form to those who are members of his body.[42]

The Whole Body: Head, Members, and Unity in Aquinas's Commentaries on the Pauline Epistles

The analogical use of the human body as a definition and description of the social body, the church, is principally a development by Aquinas on

39. *ST* 3a.8.4c. Also, Sabra, *Thomas Aquinas' Vision of the Church*, 65. Yves Congar strikes a similar tone when he describes the church in the vision of Aquinas as, "humanity vitalized Godwards". See Congar, "The Idea of the Church in St. Thomas Aquinas," 337.

40. *ST* 3a.9.2.

41. *ST* 3a.9.2c.

42. Radcliffe, "The Body of Christ," 42.

the scriptural usage of that image, specifically in the Pauline epistles. It is ultimately from the teachings of these epistles that Aquinas explores questions of Christ's relationship to the church as a social body, and each member to Christ in their individual bodies. In one respect, his commentaries on Paul are one long exercise in ecclesiology, wherein his arguments from his longer treatises, especially the *Summa*, are tested and refined in light of Paul's letters.

In the Prologue to his *Commentary on Romans*, Aquinas states that the fourteen letters of Paul (Aquinas included Hebrews in this number) present teaching that bears entirely on Christ's grace: first, as grace appears in the head who is Christ (Hebrews); second, as it appears it its principal members (1–2 Timothy, Titus, Philemon); and finally, as it appears in the mystical body, the church (the remainder of the letters). The final category is further divided into a consideration of grace itself (Romans); the sacraments of grace (1–2 Corinthians, Galatians); and the work of unity that grace realizes in the church (Ephesians, Philippians, Colossians, 1–2 Thessalonians.).[43] This final category is principally where Paul develops his thinking on "the body of Christ," and therefore provides the appropriate starting point for an examination of how Aquinas reads Paul on matters pertaining to the identity and purpose of *corpus Christi*.

Paul's first letter to the church in Corinth includes the following verse: "Do you not know that your bodies are members of Christ? Should I therefore take the members of Christ and make them members of a prostitute? Never!"[44] The later reference to prostitutes speaks to the contrast Paul is raising between a person and a prostitute, and the Corinthian Christians with Christ. Paul's thought seems to be this: the body is for the Lord; not just the physicality of the bodily form but the whole person in their present bodily reality. The whole person is for the Lord, not for immorality; and this destiny is to be glorified like the body of Christ. In his commentary, Aquinas makes a number of points that highlight and develop the general thrust of Paul's concern. First, Aquinas speaks to the *role* of the body in relation to being a "member" of Christ. The body, Aquinas writes,

> is not meant for fornication but for the Lord, i.e., it had been ordained to this, namely, that it be for the Lord Jesus Christ and the Lord for the body, i.e., Jesus Christ was given to us in order

43. Baglow, *Modus et Forma*, 124–25.

44. 1 Cor 6:15.

that human bodies be conformed to His glory, as it says in Phil (3:21): "He will change our lowly body to be like His glorious body.[45]

Second, Aquinas emphasizes the human body's *affinity* to Christ.

> Do you not know that your bodies are members of Christ? As if to say: you should not be unaware of this, because all of you reborn in Christ have become members of Christ, as it says below (12:27): "Now you are the body of Christ and individually members of it," and this not only as to souls justified by him but also as to bodies, which will be raised up by him, as has been stated.[46]

The contrast Paul employs between a person and a prostitute, and the Corinthian Christians with Christ becomes the basis of an understanding of the *body* as an expression of unity with Christ and his members. The unity of Christ and his members, the church, suggests something more than a simple metaphor allows. Just as the union with a prostitute is a real union of bodies, so human bodies become members of Christ's body through *caritas*, which is the agency of the Holy Spirit.[47]

The question of how this unity of *caritas* is established and maintained leads Aquinas to address the role of the sacraments in Paul's, and his own, understanding of the church. The shift to the reality and effects of the sacraments, particularly the Eucharist, as constituting the unity of Christ's body, places Aquinas's anthropology in service to his ecclesiology. What is at stake is the living body, not the mechanistic corpse portrayed by physicalism, but the animated social body that incorporates the identity and purpose of individuals as it orients them, by grace, to a divine end.

The portion of Aquinas's commentary on 1 Corinthians 7:15—10:33, which includes the verses associated with Paul's initial instructions on the practice of the Eucharist, are lost and therefore not available for consideration.[48] This lacuna is disappointing, not least for our concerns, but the theme of the body as expressing unity, in particular, ecclesial unity, is

45. *In I Cor.* 5 lect. 3.

46. *In I Cor.* 5 lect. 3.

47. *In I Cor.* 5 lect. 3.

48. For more on the discussion by Daniel Keating on the missing portion of the commentary, see, Keating, "Aquinas on 1 and 2 Corinthians: The Sacraments and Their Ministers," 127.

picked up in the following chapters. In his commentary on chapters 11 and 12 of 1 Corinthians, we see developed Aquinas's contention that "the Eucharist is the sacrament of love and ecclesial unity."[49]

The fifth lecture of Aquinas's commentary of 1 Corinthians 11 focuses on Christ's institution of the Eucharist. This lecture provides at least three points of interest on Aquinas's teaching on the *corpus Christi*. First, he addresses the question of the appropriateness of sacraments to bodily human life. The sacraments,

> were instituted on account of a need in the spiritual life. And because bodily things are likenesses of spiritual things, it is fitting that the sacrament be proportionate to things which are necessary to bodily life . . . for the spiritual life is required food, by which man's body is sustained, and likewise the spiritual life is fed by the sacrament of the Eucharist, as it says in Ps 23 (v. 2): "He make me lie down in green pastures. He leads me beside still waters."[50]

Second, Aquinas argues that since "bodily refreshment is not complete without food and drink,"[51] so Christ's words of institution, "This is my body," is an invitation to share in the spiritual refreshment communicated to us through Christ's body and blood. Therefore, "in the sacrament of the Eucharist, which is spiritual food, Christ is there according to his substance."[52] In the other sacraments, the consecrated matter (e.g., water and oil) needs to be put to effective use if the sacrament is to affect the work of grace. In the Eucharist it is different. The Eucharist,

> is completed in the very consecration of the matter, in which Christ Himself is contained, Who is the end of all sanctifying grace. Therefore, the words which pertain to the use of the sacrament are not of the substance of the form, but only those containing the truth and content of the sacrament, which he mentions last, adding: This is my body.[53]

Third, the manner by which the body of Christ is present under the appearance of bread and wine is related to the way God creates. Contrary to those who hold the position that Christ is present in the bread and

49. *In I Cor.* 11 lect. 7.
50. *In I Cor.* 11 lect. 5.
51. *In I Cor.* 11 lect. 5.
52. *In I Cor.* 11 lect. 5.
53. *In I Cor.* 11 lect. 5.

wine *only* as a sign, or in disguise as bread and wine, Aquinas counters that something of God's creative action is at work in the Eucharist; an action of *conversion* that differs from all conversions that occur in nature.

> For the action of nature presupposes matter, and therefore its action does not extend beyond changing something according to its form, either substantial or accidental. Hence every natural conversion is said to be formal. But God, Who makes this conversion is the author of form and of matter, and therefore the entire substance of bread, the matter not remaining, can be converted into the entire substance of the body of Christ. And because matter is the principle of individuation, this whole signated individual, which is a particular substance, is converted into another particular substance. For this reason it is called a substantial conversion or transubstantiation.[54]

Transubstantiation does not mean that Christ takes on the *dimensions* of the bread and wine (as if Christ was trapped in the bread or wine), nor does it mean that the consecrated matter simply receives some spiritual power. As Aquinas states, the forms of the sacraments (i.e., the words and associated actions),

> not only signify, but also make: for *by signifying they make*. But in every instance of making, something common must be subject as a principle. But in this conversion the common factor is not a substance but the accidents, which were present in the beginning and continue to remain. Therefore, on the part of the subject in this statement no noun is used, which signifies a definite species of substance, but a pronoun, which signifies a substance without naming its species. The sense, therefore, is *this*, i.e., which is contained under these accidents, *is my body*. And this is what occurs through the words of consecration. For before the consecration that which was contained under these accidents was not the body of Christ, but *it is made the body of Christ through consecration*.[55] (Emphasis added)

The place of the Eucharist in Aquinas's understanding of the church as *corpus Christi* is neatly summarized in lecture 6 of his commentary on 1 Corinthians. Commenting on Paul's words, "For anyone who eats and drinks without discerning the body eats and drinks judgment upon

54. *In I Cor.* 11 lect. 5.
55. *In I Cor.* 11 lect. 5.

himself,"[56] Aquinas contends that the reality (*res*) of the Eucharist—namely, *caritas*—is the instrument by which ecclesial unity exists.[57] To share in the bread and wine of the Eucharist is to share in the one body of Christ, who is the source of charity and of our unity. Through the Eucharistic communion, therefore, we become one with Christ and we all become one in his mystical body.[58]

The sacramental joining of the Christian to Christ is the basic reason why Paul can, in 1 Corinthians 12, go on to speak of them in terms of a natural body: "For just as the body is one and has many members, and all the members of the body, though many, are one body, so it is with Christ."[59] Aquinas's commentary on this and the following verses elucidates what is at stake in affirming unity in the *corpus Christi*. Several points are worth noting.

First, stressing the classical metaphor that as the body is one and has many members, and all the members, though they are many, yet is the body one, Aquinas affirms,

> In the same way the body of a man or of any other animal is one, because its perfection is made up of various members as of diverse instruments of the soul; hence the soul is said to be the act of an organic body, i.e., one made up of various organs.[60]

In other words, the many parts and functions of the human body do not take away from the wholeness or unity of the body. Aquinas uses the example of a house as being one thing composed of various stones and wood to stress that the particular wholeness of the body necessitates a diversity of parts and functions.

Second, the unity of the body is taken to be the condition by which we understand how many different people can still be considered *one* in reference to the body of Christ. The metaphor of "one body, many members" is adapted (Aquinas speaks of *adaptat similitudinem*—an adaptation that resembles, or shares in similitude with) to our understanding of our unity in Christ. Just as the human body has many parts that function together for the unity of the whole, so it is when considering the one body of Christ: "he has many and diverse members, namely, all

56. 1 Cor. 11:29.

57. *In I Cor.* 11 lect. 7.

58. Swierzawski, "Christ and the Church," 247.

59. 1 Cor. 12:12.

60. *In I Cor.* 12 lect. 3.

the faithful, as it says in Romans (12:5): 'Though many we are one body in Christ.'"[61] The emphasis on the one body of Christ being the place of unity stresses a point that Aquinas finds in Paul: not, you are a body of Christians, or you form a body in Christ; but simply "you are the body of Christ, and members individually."

Third, the verses associated with the diversity of gifts or *charisms* in the Corinthian church allows Aquinas to show that since Christians are the body of Christ this diversity is what one would expect, and is indeed necessary. In other words, the completeness of a human body is only coherent in light of the relations of the members to each other. If all the church were of one state and grade (e.g., all kings and no subjects, or all teachers and no prophets), it would destroy, Aquinas says, the "perfection and beauty of the church."[62] As such, the body of Christ is diverse yet dependent on Christ in virtue of his human nature, who is the head of the church, and therefore the unifying organ of the entire body. As head, Christ is the one in whom the diversity of members find unity and by whom each Christian is a member of a member, i.e., "distinguished and arranged in such a way that to one another, as one member to another."[63]

Aquinas's commentary on Paul's letter to the Romans provides an additional context with which to investigate and elucidate the significance of *corpus Christi* in relation to the church and the unity of its members in Christ. In particular, Romans 12:4–5, returns Aquinas to the classical metaphor of "one body, many members": "For as in one body we have many members, and all the members do not have the same function, so we, though many, are one body in Christ, and individually members one of another." Here Paul gives emphasis first of all on the one body in which the individual finds themselves, and within which they must exercise their gifts. Though similar to the Corinthian passages already examined, Aquinas uses the verses in Romans to emphasis the *spiritual* unity that results from unity with the mystical body of Christ. He notes,

> [Paul] touches on the unity of the mystical body when he says we are one body: "that he might reconcile us both to God in one body through the cross" (Eph 2:16). *This mystical body has a spiritual unity through which we are united to one another and to God by faith and love*: "There is one body and one spirit" (Eph 4:4). And because the Spirit of unity flows into us from

61. *In I Cor.* 12 lect. 3.
62. *In I Cor.* 12 lect. 3.
63. *In I Cor.* 12 lect. 3.

Christ—"Anyone who does not have the Spirit of Christ does not belong to him" (Rom 8:9)—he adds in Christ, *who unites us to one another and to God by his Spirit whom he gives us*: "That they may be one even as we are one" (John 18:22).[64] (Emphasis added)

Whereas in his work on 1 Corinthians, Aquinas starts with the thought of diversity in matters of members and *charisms,* and shows that diversity in the body is proper and necessary, in his lectures on Romans, Aquinas focuses on the means by which unity in the body of Christ is understood: namely through the divine gift of faith and love which are given to us by the Spirit on account of the merits of Christ. It is his *mystical* body through which we are united with God.[65]

The principle of "one body, many members" receives further definition in Paul's letters to the Colossians and the Ephesians. In particular, the notion of Christ's headship and Christ's relationship to the body, the church, is developed by Paul and correspondingly, explored by Aquinas in his commentaries.

The attention Aquinas gives to Christ as "head of the church" in his commentary on Colossians proceeds from his analysis of Paul's assertion that "[Christ] is the image of the invisible God, the first-born of all creation; . . . all things were created through him and for him."[66] The relation of Jesus to God and to all creation forms that basis on which Paul will speak of Jesus's relation to the church. As such, before Aquinas turns to the *corpus Christi*, he first sets the scene by addressing the broader questions of how we might understand the more fundamental connection between Christ and creation. There are two points worth noting.

First, Aquinas accounts for the way in which Christ is said to be the *image* of the invisible God. If, as Aquinas argues, "[God] exceeds the capacity of vision of any created intellect, so that no created intellect, by its natural knowledge, can attain His essence,"[67] in what way can we speak of Christ being an image? Following Dionysius, Aquinas remarks:

> all knowledge terminates at something which exists, that is, at some nature that participates in the act of existence (*esse*); but God is the very act of existence (*ipsum esse*), not participating

64. *In Rom.* 12 lect. 2.

65. Rikhof, "Corpus Christi Mysticum," 159.

66. Col 1:15–16.

67. *In Col.* 1 lect. 4.

in the act of existence, but participated in; and thus he is not known. It is of this invisible God that the Son is the image.[68]

In other words, the Son is not a reproduction, mode, or form of the Father, as was held by the schools of modalistic monarchianism,[69] the point is that Christ can image God because the Son participates fully in God, as the very act of existence (*ipsum esse*). Concerned to quell the idea that the Son and the Father are identical, or conversely that the Son and Father are of different natures, Aquinas retorts,

> Now the Son is like the Father, and the Father is like the Son. But because the Son has this likeness from the Father, and not the Father from the Son, we, properly speaking, say that the Son is the image of the Father, and not conversely: for this likeness is drawn and derived from the Father.[70]

The second and related point Aquinas makes prior to the discussion of Christ's relationship to the church focuses on what it means that Christ is the firstborn of all creation. Aquinas observes that God knows himself, and consequently all creation, in the Son. He explains,

> inasmuch as the Son is begotten, he is seen as a *word representing every creature, and he is the principle of every creature.* For if he were not begotten in that way, the Word of the Father would be the first-born of the Father only, and not of creatures; . . . the Son is the first-born because he was generated as the principle of creatures (*principium creaturae*).[71] (Emphasis added)

It is Aquinas's assertion that confessing Christ as the "firstborn" of creation leads to two conclusions. In relation to the created order, Christ is the "firstborn" for no other reason than that he is its creator and sustaining cause of everything within it. In relation to humanity Christ is "firstborn" because he took our human condition upon himself and went so far as to suffer, die, and rise from the grave as the first-born of the dead.[72] The creation of humankind in God's image and our redemption

---

68. *In Col.* 1 lect. 4.

69. See Dünzl, *Brief History of the Doctrine of the Trinity in the Early Church*, 25–35.

70. *In Col.* 1 lect. 4. For Thomas, this non-transitive relationship is not odd, for to use a contemporary analogy, it is clear that a photograph of someone is like the person, but it would be perverse to say that the person is like the photograph. Thanks to Andrew Davison for this insight.

71. *In Col.* 1 lect. 4.

72. Edwards, "Aquinas on Ephesians and Colossians," 158.

are linked by the fact that as Christ has assumed human form, he is able to lead humanity towards resurrection. Having established the relation of Christ to the Father, and to creation as the *principium creaturae*, Aquinas's next move is to address Christ's relation to the church.

"He is the head of the body, the church," Paul contends in Colossians 1:18, "he is the beginning, the first-born from the dead, that in everything he might be pre-eminent." In what sense is Christ the head of the church? Aquinas develops his response to this question through attending to the following lines of inquiry: first, church as a body; and secondly, Christ as its head.

In parallel to his analysis of passages in 1 Corinthians and Romans that have already been addressed, the church, Aquinas contends, is called a body because of its likeness (*similitudinem*) to an individual human being.[73] Like the human body, the church has distinct limbs or members (understood through the distinctive gifts of *charisms*), and just as in the body each member operates in mutual service for the good of the whole, so in the church, each member serves one another in ways that are different from each other, yet they do so *as one*. "Again, just as a body is one because its soul is one, so the Church is one because the Spirit is one: 'There is one body and one Spirit' (Eph 4:4)."[74] Or, as Aquinas says later in his commentary, "we should understand that Christ and the Church are one mystical person, whose head is Christ, and whose body is all the just, for every just person is a member of this head: 'individually members' (1 Cor. 12:27)."[75]

The particular privileges of Christ as head of the body, the church, are explored by Aquinas in three points. First, he attends to the dignity of the head in relation to the body. As head of the church (and as previously argued, as the image of God, and the firstborn of all creation), Christ is the source or principle (*principium*) of justification and the beginning of beatitude, which will come after the resurrection. In other words, the grace of the present, and the glory in the future, are both to be found in the church, for Christ is her head now and forever.[76]

The second privilege of Christ as head is understood in light of Aquinas's understanding of the head as being *plenitudine sensuum*, that

73. *In Col.* 1 lect. 5.
74. *In Col.* 1 lect. 5.
75. *In Col.* 1 lect. 6.
76. *In Col.* 1 lect. 5.

is, having an abundance or fullness of all the physical senses needed to live humanly well. Likewise, Christ as head has the fullness of all graces and gifts which he distributes in the church. "For some saints had particular graces, but Christ had all graces."[77]

Finally, Aquinas argues that just as the head has a causal influence on the rest of the body as the source of an inflow of sense and movement (*influxu sensus et motus*), so too in the body of Christ, where grace *flows* from Christ and into the body, the church. The benefit of this inflow of grace is reconciliation: through his mortal and now gloried body; through making us holy; and through the cleansing of our sin.[78] In sum, Christ as head brings about the reconciliation of the membership of the body through reconciling grace working in the members themselves. Though the head benefits the rest of the body, and this might lead to the conclusion that the body is not unified, the realization of the unity is precisely in the role of Christ as head: the source of divine grace, and the one by whom all the members operate.[79]

Aquinas frames his attention to Christ as head in his commentary on Ephesians by stressing a key Christological point: "The divine activity in Christ is the form and exemplar (*formam et exemplar*) of the divine activity in us."[80] That Christ is referred to as "form" and "exemplar" is suggestive of the distinct yet related relation Christ shares with those who are members of his body. Like the emphasis we find in his lectures on Colossians, the theme of Christ's "headship" in the lectures on Ephesians focuses on the "relation" (*habitudo*) Christ as head shares with the rest of the body, the church.[81] Commenting on Paul's assertion that "[God] has subjected all things under [Christ's] feet and has made him head over all the church, which is his body," Aquinas emphasizes the quality of this relation between Christ and the church:

> Concerning the first, he says God the Father hath made him head over all the Church (*caput super omnem Ecclesiam*), both of the Church militant, composed of men living in the present, and of the Church triumphant, made up of the men and angels in the fatherland. On account of certain general reasons, Christ is even the head of the angels—"who is the head of all

77. *In Col.* 1 lect. 5.
78. *In Col.* 1 lect. 5.
79. Rikhof, "Corpus Christi Mysticum," 167.
80. *In Eph.* 1 lect. 7.
81. Baglow, *Modus et Forma*, 180.

principality and power" (Col. 2:10)—whereas Christ is spiritually the head of mankind for special reasons. For the head has
a threefold relationship (*habitudinem*) with the other members.
First, it has a preeminent position; secondly, its powers are dif-
fused [throughout the body] since all the senses in the members
are derived from it; thirdly, it is of the same nature [as the other
members].[82]

The manner in which Christ as head is explored here has several
parallels to Aquinas's commentary on Colossians.[83] In fact, the basic idea
of the church as being "one body, many members" that was articulated
in Aquinas's work on Romans and 1 Corinthians has been expanded and
more clearly defined in Colossians and Ephesians by the use of the natural units of the human body: head and limbs (members). What is new in
Aquinas's lectures on Ephesians is fleshed out with his identification of
the church as, in Paul's words, "the fullness of him who is filled all in all."[84]

Whereas the head/body language has proven to be a stable metaphor for Aquinas, the idea that Christ's activity in the church is explicated
with the term "fullness" (*plenitudo*) gestures toward something more
than metaphor in considering how Christ and the church are related.[85]
Aquinas's own understanding of the church as the fullness of Christ is
considered in a key passage which is worth quoting at length.

> [Paul] explains *which is his body* by adding the *fullness of him*. To
> one asking why there are so many members in a natural body—
> hands, feet, mouth, and the like—it could be replied that they
> are to serve the soul's variety of activities. [The soul] itself is the
> cause and principle of these [members], and what they are, the
> soul is virtually. For the body is made for the soul, and not the
> other way around. From this perspective, the natural body is a
> certain fullness of the soul; unless the members exist with an
> integral body, the soul cannot exercise fully its activities.
>
> This is similar in the relation of Christ and the Church.
> Since the Church was instituted on account of Christ, the

82. *In Eph.* 1 lect. 8.

83. See *In Col.* 1 lect. 5.

84. Eph. 1:23b. Aquinas wrote his commentaries on Paul between 1265 and 1273.
Though the dates are difficult to verify for any one of the works, it is thought that his
commentary on Ephesians was one of his last. For detailed discussions concerning the
dating of Aquinas's writings, see Torrell, *Saint Thomas Aquinas*.

85. For a summary of differing interpretations on this matter, see Baglow, *Modus
et Forma*, 182.

Church is called the fullness of Christ. *Everything which is virtually* [or, *truly*][86] *in Christ is, as it were, filled out in some way in the members of the Church.* For all spiritual understanding, gifts, and whatever can be present in the Church—all of which Christ possesses superabundantly—flow from him into the members of the Church, and they are perfected in them.[87] (Emphasis added)

This passage is significant for a number of reasons. First, Aquinas links his understanding of the relationship between the soul and body with the more familiar head/body similitude. His identification between body and soul was addressed already,[88] but for the purposes here, it is worth noting that for Aquinas, the identification between body and soul is so inseparable (without ever becoming one and the same) that he can offer the formula: "The soul is the form of the body."[89] When applied by Aquinas to the relation of Christ to the church, he notes that in a similar (*similiter*) way, Christ has given himself in fullness (*plenitudo*) and as the source of life (i.e., *anima*) to the church, such that "the body" "becomes his manifestation, and not just any manifestation, but the one proper to him."[90]

The second point of this passage follows on the first. As the fullness of Christ, the members of the church are perfected in him (*membra Ecclesiae et perficiantur in eis*). Aquinas continues with his use of "members" with reference to the church to emphasize that as a complete body the church in her parts is destined for glory, as in fact, Christ's human body was glorified by God in the resurrection and ascension. In sum, the relation Christ shares with the church not only animates the church with the fullness of Christ's grace and gifts, but also defines the depth of hope for all who are members of the *corpus Christi*.

The Pauline commentaries of Aquinas articulate a vision of the church as ordered and oriented by the body in which it has life, the body of Christ. Aquinas finds repeated attention in the epistles to the unity and related benefits that animates the church by means of the grace of Christ: the divine power that "flows" into the *corpus Christi* as a result of

86. Baglow prefers "truly" over "virtually" as a more contemporary translation of *virtute*. See ibid., 183, n. 97.

87. *In Eph.* 1 lect. 8

88. See chapter 6.

89. *ST* 1a.76.1

90. Baglow, *Modus et Forma*, 184.

the incarnation, death, and resurrection of Christ. Such grace is fitting and given in fullness so that with Christ as head, the church can be said to be a *una mystica persona*, which neither confuses nor conflates whose grace, or whose body, the church is said to have unity through. Such is Aquinas's use and understanding of what a human body is, and how a human person operates, that the church is only intelligible as a particular kind of social body that has life in and through the human nature of Christ employed instrumentally by God for the healing of humanity and the raising of this same humanity to a vision of God. For the church is nothing but the community that sacramentally foreshadows the life for which God has destined humanity.[91]

The intelligibility of the church as *corpus Christi* assumes, for Aquinas, that the social body of the church is a unified body. This has implications when considering the church in light of the claims of physicalism and managerialism. First, in contrast to the rationalization of the managed body that privileges the control and manipulating of the parts, Aquinas, following his reading of Paul, understands that Christ as head of the church brings about the reconciliation of the membership of the body through reconciling grace working in the members themselves. Like a human body where each part's activity is understood to be an activity of a whole living organism, the members of the church share in the fruit of Christ's reconciling grace as incorporated members into the unifying body of Christ.

Second, in place of the dissected social body of coordinated parts all operating to serve instrumentalized ends, the ecclesial body and her members operate by means of a logic that orders the purpose of the body to the fulfillment of divine happiness. Where the managed body is a generic body without purpose other than growth and survival, the ecclesial body, animated by the Holy Spirit, is oriented in worship to such things as praise, service, thanksgiving, and reconciliation. Through the sacramental life of the church, and the Eucharist in particular, people reach living union with the humanity of Christ, which as the instrument of his divinity, makes people members of his body church and opens the way for people to share in the beatitude of God.

91. McCabe, *The New Creation*.

"This is my Body": The Eucharist as Sign of Unity

In the prologue of 3a.60, Aquinas writes: "Now that we have completed our consideration of the mysteries of the Incarnate Word, our next field of investigation is the sacraments of the Church, seeing that it is from this same Incarnate Word that these derive their efficacy."[92] For him, the sacraments are particular rites or rituals celebrated by believers within the church. More specifically, they are rites by which Christ's followers are conformed to Christ and benefit from his life, death, and resurrection. By means of them, thinks Aquinas, people grow in grace. Through the sacraments, people enjoy the presence of the Holy Spirit given to dwell in them. In short, sacraments are physical rites or actions of worship by which the saving work of Christ is applied to or bears fruit in the lives of his followers considered as members of a society established by Christ.

Aquinas frequently refers to sacraments as "signs" (*signa*). He does not think that sacraments are signs in the sense that they merely symbolize or represent something or other. He takes sacraments to be signs insofar as they are physical processes that actually *effect* or *bring about* the union of people with God, the presence in them of the Holy Spirit.[93] At one level, Aquinas thinks, sacraments certainly symbolize and do so because of the natural symbolic meaning of the rituals associated with them. Hence, for example, he takes baptism with water to symbolize coming to be cleansed from sin because of the connection commonly made between water and cleansing. At the same time, however, he also thinks that baptism actually does cleanse people from (original) sin, that the rite of baptism is efficacious in releasing people from the sin of Adam. And he thinks something similar when it comes to all the sacraments. His view is that in the sacraments God shows us what he does and *does what he shows us*. So, he observes, "The very fact that the term 'sacrament' signifies the reality which sanctifies means that it should signify the effect

---

92. *ST* 3a.60.*Prooemium*.

93. Aquinas, drawing on Augustine, Hugh of St. Victor, and Peter Lombard, deploys a threefold "level" to the sacraments: First, the sacramental rite (*sacramentum tantum*), something that is visible to believer and unbeliever alike. Second, the sacramental reality or ecclesial reality (*sacramentum et res*), a reality known only by faith and inaccessible to the unbeliever; the level at which the church has her being. Third, the final reality (*res tantum*) for the sake of which the church exists, the personal sharing in the divine life of grace. See for example, these levels described in relation to baptism in *ST* 3a.66.1. For a concise summary of these levels, see, McCabe, *The New Creation*, 88f.

produced."[94] Standing behind this idea is the view that the primary sacrament (though not one of the seven usually prescribed) is Christ as the incarnate Son of God.[95] In that Christ is divine and not something that just reflects what God is in some way, Aquinas will say that "the sacraments derive their power from Christ" and that their being able to play a role in human salvation should be thought to "flow from the divinity of Christ through his humanity into the actual sacraments."[96] The Incarnate Word is, for Aquinas, part of the physical world drawing people to union with God. In a similar way, thinks Aquinas, sacraments (physical goings on) are processes by which people are truly brought closer to God, processes through which they acquire grace and are ordered to the beatific vision.[97]

Aquinas is quite clear that one can receive grace without getting involved with the rituals involved in the celebration of sacraments. "The Passion of Christ," he notes, "is the sufficient cause of the salvation of people." "But," Aquinas continues,

> It does not follow on this account, that the sacraments are not necessary for human salvation, for they produce their effects in virtue of the Passion of Christ, and it is the Passion of Christ that is, in a certain manner, applied to people through the sacraments.[98]

Aquinas is aware that, though the saving work of Christ took place in the past, Christ's followers live after his ascension. He thinks, therefore, that God has provided them with means to render his saving work effective in them as time goes on. As Timothy McDermott puts it, Aquinas's view is that "each sacrament is a moment in my human life on this earth, a moment which develops the identification of my individual life with the

94. *ST* 3a.60.3.*ad*.2.

95. Edward Schillebeeckx refers to Christ as the "primordial sacrament." By that, he means, insofar as Christ's human activity as an instrument of his divinity, Christ himself is the source of the efficacy of all other sacraments. See Schillebeeckx, *Christ the Sacrament of the Encounter with God*. Likewise, Colman O'Neill notes that Christ's body "constitutes the foundational sacrament. . . . Christ's body in its human activity finds its true significance beyond the sacred humanity in the divine mystery of redemption". O'Neill, *Meeting Christ in the Sacraments*, 80.

96. *ST* 3a.62.5.

97. As Liam Walsh notes, "Thomas's discussion of the sacraments falls within a theological effort that always has God for its subject, God in himself and as he is the beginning and end of creation". Walsh, "The Divine and the Human in St. Thomas's Theology of Sacraments," 326.

98. *ST* 3a.61.1.*ad*.3

saving life of Christ, and so at the same time marks my individual life as a continuation of that saving life."[99]

Aquinas understands the sacraments to be fitting to human anthropology, as appropriate items and actions that correspond to the kind of things people are, and the kind of existence people have. In 3a.61.1, he provides three reasons that reflect his understanding of human life as bodily, social, and as the site of divine grace. In the first place, it belongs to humans to use signs to express the transcendent, not in itself, but through that which it transcends, through using natural things as pointing beyond themselves, as significant. "The condition of human nature," Aquinas maintains, "is such that it has to be led by things corporeal and sensible to things spiritual and intelligible."[100] A second reason pertains to how the sacraments are connected with the sinfulness of humanity. By sin, people have subjected themselves to material things and therefore it is appropriate that through material things they should be cured of sin. Reflecting his earlier teaching on divine grace as elevating and healing, Aquinas argues,

> Now the healing remedy should be given to a man so as to reach the part affected by disease. Consequently, it was fitting that God should provide man with a spiritual medicine by means of certain corporeal signs; for if man were offered spiritual things without a veil, his mind being taken up with the material world would be unable to apply itself to them.[101]

The third reason reflects the notion that people are prone to direct their activity chiefly towards material things. In other words, human life is a certain kind of material life that finds purpose and meaning in a world of material things. In order to avoid the idea that God gives grace in any other way than what is appropriate to the kind of things people are,[102] material symbols were offered to humanity in the sacraments, "by which people might be trained to avoid superstitious practices" and instead, participate in the "healthy exercise of the sacraments."[103] In other words, the sacraments help satisfy the human desire to deploy material

99. Aquinas, *Summa Theologiae*, 543.

100. *ST* 3a.61.1c.

101. *ST* 3a.61.1c.

102. *ST* 3a.61.1.*ad.2*.

103. *ST* 3a.61.1c.

means to communicate what lies beyond human material life, namely, the divine life of God.[104]

Aquinas takes grace to be God drawing people to share in the divine life. As the incarnation is the basis for the instrumentality of Christ's humanity by means of his divine nature, Aquinas can speak of first, the grace of Christ's headship and, second, of the sacraments as instruments of this grace.[105] The way sacraments operate in the economy of salvation is through being instituted by Christ as means by which his followers can come to share in his life and death. The purpose of the sacraments is therefore aligned to God's scheme for drawing people into divine beatitude. "Through the sacraments of the New Law," Aquinas maintains, "people are incorporated into Christ. . . . But people are not made members of Christ except through grace."[106] Hence, Aquinas will deny that the sacraments are mere *signs of grace* that simply gesture toward divine activity; rather, appealing to the notion of instrumental causality, the sacraments can be thought of as *causing grace* by particular means that God has decreed. Aquinas reasons: (1) God can cause someone to have grace just because God is God and intrinsically has the power to do so, but (2) God can also cause grace by means of the sacraments considered as instruments of God in causing grace. He writes:

> The principal cause produces its effect in virtue of its form, to which that effect is assimilated, as fire warms in virtue of its own heat. Now it belongs to God to produce grace in this way as its principal cause. . . . *An instrumental cause, on the other hand, acts not in virtue of its own form, but solely in virtue of the impetus imparted to it by the principal agent.* Hence, the effect has a likeness not to the instrument, but rather to that principal agent. . . . And it is in this way that the sacraments of the New Law cause grace. *For it is by divine institution that they are conferred upon man for the precise purpose of causing grace in and through them.*[107] (Emphasis added)

104. *ST* 3a.62.1.

105. According to Timothy Kelly, the "doctrine of instrumentality" that Aquinas employs in the *ST* displays a maturity in thought from Aquinas's earlier words, specifically the *Sentences* and his scriptural commentaries. Kelly contends that the shift in Aquinas's doctrine allies with the later influence of Cyril of Alexandria on Aquinas's thought. For a discussion on the shift, see, Kelly, "Christ and the Church," 128–35.

106. *ST* 3a.62.1.

107. *ST* 3a.62.1c. Also, *ST* 3a.62.4.

Like a sculptor raising a sharp chisel to the marble, "the Divine Nature makes use of (*utitur*) the operation of the human nature, as of the operation of its instrument."[108] Sacramental rites, therefore, cannot on their own bring about grace, yet such rites have causal efficacy when considered as instruments of God. As such, Aquinas takes the rites to be appropriate to conferring of grace "in some manner" (*per aliquem modum*) "inasmuch as they are ordained by God unto the production of a spiritual effect."[109] This means of conferring grace, Aquinas maintains, is due to the union of humanity and divinity in the person of Christ. "Now the principal efficient cause of grace is God Himself, in comparison with Whom Christ's humanity is as a united instrument," Aquinas states, "whereas the sacrament is as a separate instrument. Consequently, the saving power must be derived by the sacraments from Christ's Godhead through His humanity."[110] On this account, the sacraments are neither merely symbolic nor redundant. They are "causes and signs at the same time" (*simul sunt causae et signa*),[111] by which the "Church receives power specially from Christ's Passion, the virtue of which is in a manner united to us by our receiving the sacraments."[112]

Sacraments impart grace over and above the grace that is had by those with the so-called theological virtues (i.e., faith, hope, and love) and the gifts of the Holy Spirit.[113] Christ instituted the sacraments, he thinks, for a purpose given that people live in time and live as graced in God's church. "The sacraments," he says, "are designed to achieve certain special effects which are necessary in the Christian life." As such, he continues, "Sacramental grace adds something over and above grace as

---

108. *ST* 3a.19.1c.

109. *ST* 3a.62.4.*ad*.1.

110. *ST* 3a.62.5c.

111. *ST* 3a.62.1.*ad*.1.

112. *ST* 3a.62.5c. Louis-Marie Chauvet, drawing on the critique of "onto-theology" in Heidegger, questions the instrumental causality that Aquinas assumes in relation to the sacraments. According to Chauvet, Aquinas deploys a notion of grace that inevitably leads to grace as kind of *producing* power whereby something (e.g., a word, something of value, an idea) is crafted. Yet, grace is not a product of any kind, Chauvet argues, for it cannot be calculated or measured. A second critique judges Aquinas's logic of the hypostatic union as the basis for sacramental efficacy. Such reliance, Chauvet argues, suggests that the sacraments are a continuation of the union rather than the mystery of human unity. For an overview of Chauvet's position in relation to Aquinas's, see Blankenhorn, "The Instrumental Causality of the Sacraments," 257–61.

113. For his discussion on the gifts of the Holy Spirit, see, *ST* 1a2ae.70.1–4.

commonly defined, and also about the virtues and the Gifts, namely a special kind of divine assistance to help in attaining the end of the sacrament concerned."[114] In Aquinas's view, the grace that people acquire by celebrating the sacraments is not just the dispositional virtue to live well. It is the actual appropriation of the effects of Christ's specific work—not just virtue or good living in general, but that which Christ uniquely came to bring.[115]

In the estimation of Aquinas, the pivotal sacrament to understanding sacramental efficacy in light of the incarnation of Christ, his grace, and the union in love that grace makes possible, is that of the Eucharist. The causal relation between the sacred humanity and the Eucharist indicates, for Aquinas, the continuity between the time-bound episodes of Jesus's ministry and the subsequent communication of grace through sacramental rites in general. This relation, evidenced in the Eucharist, provides the basis for Aquinas to call it "the summit of the spiritual life and all the sacraments are ordered to it."[116] Moreover, he states, "In this sacrament, is included the whole mystery of our salvation."[117] Just as baptism and confirmation bring people to Christian birth and to maturity as Christians, so the Eucharist, thinks Aquinas, nourishes people as members of the church.[118]

The pre-eminence of the Eucharist, Aquinas maintains, is in virtue of the conversion of the substances of bread and wine into the substances of Christ's body and blood. Under the mode of conversion, the Eucharist "contains Christ Himself substantially, whereas the other sacraments contain a certain instrumental power which is a participation of Christ's

---

114. *ST* 3a.62.2c. Also, Blankenhorn, "The Instrumental Causality of the Sacraments," 289–90.

115. Davies, *The Thought of Thomas Aquinas*, 353.

116. *ST* 3a.73.3c.

117. *ST* 3a.83.4c. Colman O'Neill speaks of the "continuity of efficient causality" that exists between the glorified body of Christ and the sacraments of the church that lends to a "new realism" to the denomination of the church as the body of Christ. See O'Neill, "St. Thomas on the Membership of the Church," 111.

118. Paul McPartlen, following de Lubac, speaks of the Eucharist as that which makes the church. As de Lubac himself notes, "The Church, like the Eucharist, is a mystery of unity—the same mystery and one with inexhaustible riches. Both are the body of Christ—the same body." Lubac, *Splendor of the Church*, 156. For McPartlen's use of de Lubac in articulating a view of the church that is Eucharistically centered, see, McPartlan, *Sacrament of Salvation*.

power."[119] In other words, the Eucharist is not, therefore, an *instrumentum separatum* but an *instrumentum coniunctum*, the very body hypostatically united to the Word.[120] It does not convey Christ as an action conveys his power; rather, under its sacramental species, it conveys him *directly*, as the hypostatically united body conveys the divine person. Consequently, in distinction from all the other sacraments, in being the personal body of the Word, the Eucharist "has of itself (*ex seipso*) the power of bestowing grace."[121] It does not participate in the power of the united instrument, but rather is that very united instrument in its sacramental mode. Whereas baptism brings people to be united to Christ, the faith by which people are said to be one with him, Eucharist brings people to Christ himself. This is what Aquinas means by putting the Eucharist at the center of the sacramental life—in the Eucharist *is Christ*, who as incarnate Word is what all sacramental activity is about. He goes on:

> The sacrament of the Eucharist comes to completion (*perficitur*)
> in the consecration of the matter, the bread and wine, whereas
> the other sacraments come to completion in the use (*applicatio*)
> of the matter for our sanctification.[122]

In approaching the Eucharist in this way, Aquinas is working from the view that Christ is truly present in the Eucharist and truly received by people who consume it. In his view, in this sacrament "we have the reality of Christ's body; . . . the complete substance of the bread is converted into the complete substance of Christ's body, and the complete substance of the wine into the complete substance of Christ's blood."[123] This immediacy of bodily presence is illuminated by what he has to say

119. *ST* 3a.65.3c. The "participation" that Aquinas refers to can, in an important sense, be the basis for understanding the incorporation of human nature into the divine life of God. Human beings become what they are meant to be only in union with God; and the specifically human activities associated with the sacraments are a form of participation in divine beatitude in this life. Catherine Pickstock argues that for Aquinas, "partaking of the Body and Blood of Christ under the species of bread and wine has become the means of deification." Pickstock, "Thomas Aquinas and the Quest for the Eucharist," 175.

120. Kelly, "Christ and the Church," 152.

121. *ST* 3a.79.1.*ad*.1.

122. *ST* 3a.73.1.*ad*.1. Also O'Neill, *Meeting Christ in the Sacraments*, 74.

123. *ST* 3a.75.5c. On this point, Herbert McCabe notes that "The bread does not turn into the body by acquiring a new form in its matter; the whole existence of the bread becomes the existence of the living body of Christ." McCabe, *God Still Matters*, 119.

about the role of the matter in the Eucharist, in relation to the matter of the other sacraments. If the latter convey, momentarily, the divine power that goes forth from his ascended body, the matter of the former does not participate in his grace, but itself *becomes* that very body from which grace proceeds. The principle of sacramental mediation is thereby intensified, since the instrumental conveying of grace through sensible matter (which characterizes the other sacraments) is here replaced by a substantial containing under the sacrament's material species:

> A sacrament is so termed because it contains something sacred. Now a thing can be considered sacred from two causes: either absolutely, or in relation to something else. The difference between the Eucharist and other sacraments having sensible matter is that whereas the Eucharist contains something which is sacred absolutely, namely, Christ's own body; the baptismal water contains something which is sacred in relation to something else, namely, the sanctifying power: and the same holds good of chrism and such like. Consequently, the sacrament of the Eucharist is completed in the very consecration of the matter, whereas the other sacraments are completed in the application of the matter for the sanctifying of the individual. And from this follows another difference. *For, in the sacrament of the Eucharist, what is both reality and sacrament is in the matter itself.*[124] (Emphasis added)

Aquinas's position subtly shows how the Eucharist both transcends the lines of communication essential to the others, and perfects the entire sacramental order and therefore perfects the sacramental prolongation of the incarnate mission of the Word. For, according to his understanding of the matter of the Eucharist, in this sacrament the ascended body of Christ is not acting upon people through an extraneous and momentarily raised agent of his power, but is itself substantially present under edible species.[125] In other words, the sacrament of Christ's body is the direct sacrament of the incarnation, rather than a specific application of the power that proceeds from it. The consecrated species is not temporarily raised to be a separated instrument of Christ's power but is his permanent sensible sign and bearer, containing the very body from which the sacramental power of all the other sacraments proceeds. Hence, "this sacrament is accomplished by the consecration of the matter, while the

124. *ST* 3a.73.1.*ad*.3.
125. Kelly, "Christ and the Church," 154.

rest are perfected in the use of the consecrated matter (*in usu materiae consecratae*)."[126]

Insofar as the Eucharist is the direct sacrament of the incarnation and accordingly, the very instrument of divine grace as Christ's body, Aquinas recognizes the Eucharist to be the basis for "the unity of the Church," into which people are drawn together.[127] To posit unity of the church in Christ through the Eucharist, a graced unity, supposes a previous natural unity, the unity implicit in the shared nature that defines humanness.[128] For Aquinas, human existence (*esse*) as ensouled bodies and as such, individuated members of the nature humanity, provides the basis for understanding the fittingness of the incarnation for humanity's healing and elevation to the divine life. In other words, just as there is one humanity because ultimately human bodies are linked with those of their common ancestors, likewise, people belong to the graced humanity because their bodies are linked by the Eucharist with the risen body of Christ.[129] As was previously observed, with a living body, the principle of life is united to the body as form to matter, act to potency.[130] The human body is only "one," teaches Aquinas, because of that principle of life that unites all its parts.[131] Now, "by coming sacramentally into man (*in hominem sacramentaliter veniens*),"[132] the true body of Christ is able to form a new bond with the communicant's body precisely through being food for the body's own form, the soul. Hence, the Eucharist, for Aquinas, provides the basis of the substantial presence of Christ, his very body being present as the sacrament of human unity through divine *caritas*. This is the ultimate meaning and purpose of the Eucharist.[133] In sum, as *corpus Christi*, the Eucharist is the sacrament of the unity of the church, the *corpus Christi mysticum*; it signifies and effects the unity.[134] Moreover,

126. *ST* 3a.78.1c.

127. *ST* 3a.73.2 & 4.

128. Lubac, *Catholicism*, 25.

129. McCabe, *The New Creation*, 78.

130. *ST* 1a.75.1 and 76.1.

131. *ST* 1a.76.1.

132. *ST* 3a.79.1.

133. For an account of the implications of Thomas's hylomorphic anthropology on his understanding of the glorious resurrection of the Christian's body, see, Bynum, *The Resurrection of the Body in Western Christianity, 200–1336*, 256–71.

134. As Henri de Lubac demonstrated in his seminal work, *Corpus Mysticum*, before the middle of the twelfth century, the expression "*corpus Christi*" referred either to the

as George Sabra contends, for Aquinas, Christ's relationship to, and influence on,

> his members would be impossible without unity with him.
> Christ redeems his members insofar as they are united to him.
> The members of the church would not really be its members if
> they were not united to each other through love, faith and peace;
> they are baptized into one mystical body.[135]

The Body of Christ is like a "natural body" in that it is one living reality made up of many members. However, unlike a natural body, it is supernatural; that is, Christ, as the head of the body, enlivens it through the divine life of his Holy Spirit and so simultaneously, through the same Spirit, makes it one living reality in union with himself. The church, posits Herbert McCabe, is not present merely because her members are together in one room. "It is not their bodily presence to each other that fundamentally links them, but their common bodily presence to the risen body of Christ."[136] The Eucharist and the sacraments in general make Christ present, but they do this in the act of making the church present. Thus, while the body of Christ differs from a natural body, it equally must not be thought of as simply an accidental or merely constructed body—a group of loosely knit individuals united by some common purpose. For Aquinas, the unity of the mystical body of Christ that is the church is nothing less than *caritas*, the love that is a sharing *into* the Holy Spirit. To speak of the purpose of the church, therefore, is not to address first its functionality,[137] rather, it is to address that to which the church is ordered, namely, the beatitude of God.

---

historical body of Christ or to the church, while the Eucharistic body of Christ was designated *corpus Christi mysticum*. From that time onwards, the reference shifted and *corpus Christi mysticum* came to designate the church, while the Eucharist came to be called *corpus Christi* or *corpus verum*. See de Lubac, *Corpus Mysticum*, 75–100.

135. Sabra, *Thomas Aquinas' Vision of the Church*, 65. See *ST* 2a2ae.39.1 and 2a2ae.183.2c.

136. McCabe, *The New Creation*, 83.

137. George Sabra maintains that *functionality* is precisely what the church has in Aquinas's theological project. In his explanation of this, Sabra refers to the "common good" (*utilitas*) that defines the service of the church's members, including the clergy. However, as Sabra concedes, *utilitas* for Aquinas is not on parity with the functionalism of utilitarianism whereby the pragmatic usefulness of something determines its ultimate worth. See Sabra, *Thomas Aquinas' Vision of the Church*, 115–21. This notion is examined in the final chapter.

The supernatural unity of the church as Christ's body is the basis for understanding how the efficacy of the sacraments draws members more deeply into the divine life, and a deeper life with others. Appeals to the need for each individual community to have a "comprehensive statement of identity" that gives reference to the particular values and interests of that community are mere managerial techniques in light of the unifying and purpose-filled vision of the church as a body whose life is sourced in divine *caritas*. The perception that each church needs its own purpose and mission, therefore, fails to account for how the sacraments signify and effect the identification of all church members with the saving life of Christ. For the church, the goal is always divine beatitude.

Subsequently, when viewed in light of the *caritas* of Christ, who, in all the sacraments is made present as the source of human unity, appeals to the efficiencies or effectiveness of a managerial logic simply lose their status as techniques designed to bring about a sustainable community. In contrast to the objectives of the missional-approach to the church, which seeks to orient all ecclesial activity around one organizing principle, the ecclesiology of Aquinas assists in promoting an account of the church where the divine humanity of Christ through sacramental signs provides sufficient order for how the church operates as a living unity. How this unity can be thought of as organizing and orientating the church as something more than an institution in need of management, is the question for the final chapter of this study.

6

To What End?
Organizing the Ecclesial Body

THE CHURCH IS A social body oriented and ordered to the beatitude of God. This notion reflects one of the fundamental themes in Aquinas's theology: people are ordained to the perfect knowledge of God in which consists eternal bliss.[1] To affirm Aquinas's vision of the church as within a God-oriented vision of all things means accepting the governing principle in his ecclesiology: that the church is a social body that has its beginning and end in God's divine economy of grace. Moreover, within this economy, the Eucharist is the sacrament of the unity of the church in that it signifies and effects the unity and as such, orders the church as a social body to a goal suitable to the kind of body it is. For the church is nothing but the *corpus Christi mysticum,* a community that sacramentally foreshadows the life for which God has destined humanity.

Renewing an ecclesial vision that gives proper attention to the church as Christ's body as a constructive alternative to the technique and missional responses to church decline has required attention by this book to the particular definition and description of the individual and social body as it is assumed by physicalism and adopted by managerialism. Conceptually, the reductive account of physicalism provides the metaphysics for an understanding of organizational life as the privileging of managerial practices that give priority to the rationalized goals of efficiency, calculability, predictability, and control. In contrast, in having as its basis an anthropology concerned with the material and immaterial aspects of human life, and a sacramental theology that orders the social

1. *ST* 1a.1.4c.

body of the church to divine beatitude, the ecclesial vision of Aquinas challenges managerial-inspired ecclesiologies while promoting the hope of human bodily redemption through union with Christ in the sacraments. The happiness that is a sharing in God's life is not some interior mental state. As Timothy Radcliffe notes, it needs to find bodily expression if it is to be truly human.[2]

Aquinas's writings on the Eucharist, and the sacraments in general, reflect this general impulse to see God's grace working with and not in competition with the natural properties of creatures. The sacraments are therefore a resounding affirmation of the goodness of created things. Speaking of the outward *cultus* of worship, in which "certain blessings using sensible things are provided for human beings, whereby one is washed, or anointed, or fed, or given drink, along with the expression of sensible words," Aquinas notes that "it is not astonishing if heretics who deny that God is the author of our body condemn such manifestations." Aquinas concludes, "They have not remembered that they are human beings."[3] Living fully into our humanness, ordered as humans are to happiness, and ultimately divine beatitude, is in essence at the heart of Aquinas's theological project and basic contention of this book.

Accounts of the church, therefore, that adopt the logic of managerialism reflect a conceptual problem in attending to the interconnection of human bodily life, human purposefulness, and the promise of divine happiness and joy. Whereas a vision like that of Aquinas promotes a fully human account of life with God, all that a managerial-inspired ecclesiology can sustain is a dim picture of a machine-like body that requires the manipulation by techniques for it to appear to be alive. Managerial-oriented ecclesiologies are ultimately ill equipped to address how the body of Christ is the foundation of the ecclesial body and the one in whom Christians are incorporated through the instrumentality of his humanity by means of the sacraments. Other goals, such as growth and status, become, in lieu of this inadequacy, the principle ways through which the church is said to fulfill its task and maintain its purpose. Important as such goals might be, particularly as growth and status are thought to enhance and expand the organizational power and reach of the church, the renewal of an ecclesiology grounded in a Thomistic anthropology and sacramental theology raises doubts as to whether these goals are

2. Radcliffe, *What Is the Point of Being a Christian?* 89.

3. *SCG*, Bk. 3, chap. 119, Note 3 & 5.

sufficient and proper for the kind of body the church is and the kind of life the church has by means of the indwelling of the Holy Spirit, who is the "soul" of Christ's body.

If the church is oriented and ordered by Christ's body in which it has life, in what way can it be said also to be *organized*? According to the managerial logic of proponents of a technique or missional-based approach to ecclesiology, the church can appear as simply one more organization in need of proper management through techniques and strategies learned from organizational theory and practice. Yet, the ethos of such managerialism distorts not only the character of social relations in general, but also the purpose and identity of the church. This distortion arrives by means of the assimilation of means-ends rationality through the purposive goals of efficiency, effectiveness, predictability, and control; goals generated from the last century of organizational theory. The privileging of these ends by practitioners within Congregational Studies and related church-based theorists distracts the church from being the site of membership and union with the living God, an ecclesial body unified by the love and grace of the Holy Spirit. The church, in the case of technique and missional approaches, is restricted from living out from its implicit essence. In the place of a theological vision of the church, managerialism provides habits of thought and practice that display the kind of instrumentalizing reason that seeks to organize all social, political, and economic spaces into managed units that serve pragmatic ends.[4]

In place of carefully crafted techniques and strategies to help humanize the mechanized ecclesial body, the central argument of this book is that the church is a specific kind of social body capable of resisting the adoption of managerialism in favor of an identity as a holistic and unifying body where sacramental participation by individuals entails connection and membership in the glorified humanity of Christ. The form of this life is prescribed in this concluding chapter by means of three constructive alternatives. First, the shape and order of the church as the sacramental community whose life anticipates the consummation of God's kingdom requires a form of leadership that is non-managerial in orientation. In Thomistic thought, the virtue of *prudentia* as "right practical reason" provides an alternative basis and logic to the reductive and

4. See Parker, *Against Management*, 2–4. In light of the prevalence of a managerial-inspired approach to the church as a social body, John Milbank is surely correct to call for a form of "Christian sociology" as an analysis that adopts the concerns and agenda of the church. See Milbank, *Theology and Social Theory*, 380.

instrumentalizing habits of technique and missional-based approaches to the church. Second, an account of the church as a social body, Christ's body, provides the principle for addressing questions of human unity in a time of the ascendency of specialized ministries that adopt the logic of emotivist "lifestyle choices." Third, an understanding of the church as formed and ordered to beatitude in God contributes to matters of organization that resist the imposition of technique-oriented goals implicit to the implementation of contemporary strategic planning.

Prudentia, Leadership, and the Shape of the Church

In this section, the concern is to address how the exercise of *prudentia* or right practical reason (*recta ratio agibilium*)[5] accomplishes what managerial-based approaches to church leadership cannot. Whereas technique and missional leadership orders the church to survival and growth, the disposition of *prudentia* orders the execution of decisions to the proper end of the church as the site of human unity and wholeness in Christ. The form of leadership prescribed through the exercise of *prudentia* overcomes the reduction of leadership to the application of techniques through attending to the place of good service, proper order, and faithful activity.

The church, as a social body, maintains a visible presence through its operations, public rites, and physical structures. At one level, the visible life and shape of the church might seem sufficient to constructing an account of its organizational life. Such is the position of those who espouse the importance of organizing the church by attending to congregational uniqueness and identity, by communal-shaped planning that is effective and efficient, and by a renewal of church leaders who think strategically about the management of time, resources, and people. This approach, which displays the tenets of managerialism, justifies its claim to authority and the requisite organizational power by maintaining expertise in effecting and controlling change, and doing so with law-like generalizations that possess strong predictive powers. With these conditions in place, concerns like declining church membership are attended to through various forms of organizational manipulation that are designed to *realign* the church toward the direction dictated by the particular "mission" and "purpose" the individual church believes will lead to renewal and growth.

5. *ST* 2a2ae.47.2.

The church, in this case, is oriented and ordered; the questions are, to what and by whom?

The operations of organizational manipulation meant to realign the church are evident particularly in the promotion and exercise of managerial forms of leadership in the church. This is not, as might be argued, an issue only for churches where there is a significant membership of "professionals" and others who function as leaders in the church as those used to managerial practices in their workplaces. Churches of all sizes and makeup require levels of organization and oversight that are vulnerable to the promises of a more managed condition, particularly when the community faces declining membership. The attractiveness of the "managerial-leadership" model is that it promotes some people to positions of power in order that they can "get things done" in the most efficient and effective way. Most church boards, no doubt, would be pleased to have such leaders in their ranks. When there are budgets to create and maintain, staff to hire and fire, and buildings that require appropriate attention, the more managerial-inspired leadership may seem the most appropriate form. It is as though only a certain kind of leader can actually lead, one that promotes the seemingly rational and results-oriented strategy that pervades the contemporary business culture.[6]

Such "managerial leadership," however, assumes such a level of reliance on an instrumentalized account of what constitutes *good* leadership that there remains the possibility of such leaders becoming principally animated by the assumptions of a managerial logic that attends to all aspects of an organization (e.g., in the case of the church, not simply the church governing board, but also pastoral care and liturgy) as a site of activity in need of managing. How leadership is exercised, and what shape such leadership should take in light of the church's commitments, are questions that concern every church community. As this book contends, an over-reliance on a managerial logic reduces the life of the church to that of a mechanized corpse. A mechanized model risks reducing the identity and purpose of the church to a temporary product that is formed and reformed depending on the felt-needs of the religious consumer

6. Lewis-Anthony, *You Are the Messiah, and I Should Know*, 263. The concern with an overly pragmatic approach by Christians to certain forms of leadership is addressed in the work of Tim Suttle. Suttle notes, "The word *Christian* modifies the word *leader* in ways that should make it incompatible with most of the leadership principles found in the world of business, especially when to comes to the primacy of effectiveness and success." Suttle, *Shrink*, 23–24.

by means of contemporary models of effective leadership. Under these conditions, something called "church leadership" comes to represent the only way the church is able to embody her organizational life and her practices of deliberation, for the church itself is thought to be bereft of any implicit purpose.

An account of leadership that takes seriously the implicit identity and purpose of the church requires an alternative basis than that described in contemporary manuals of church leadership. As managerialism operates as a kind of logic that sets the conditions for organizing by means of an instrumental rationality that seeks to impose a technique-based order on individuals and institutions, what is required is an account of leadership that relies on different premises to those of contemporary organizational theory while remaining *practical*, that is, while pertaining to the task of getting something done well. Such logic exists in the notion and exercise of *prudentia* as the virtue, or developed disposition, to deliberate well, to decide well, and to execute actions well.[7]

For Aquinas, *prudentia* is not some quality that is brought to deliberations in order to deploy particular law-like generalizations or accomplish predetermined goals in the most effective way. It is not a technique or strategy that is theorized to have universal applicability regardless of context.[8] What Aquinas had in mind (and took from Aristotle) was a virtue or developed ability which enables a person to make and carry out good decisions and to do so as the kind of person who would engage such activity. *Prudentia*, like all the virtues, is concerned with character, in that a virtue is that which makes its possessor good, and the work good likewise.[9] In Thomistic theory, the exercise of right practical reason is the developed ability to choose the right means that are appropriate to the goal sought, to make decisions, to consider other possibilities when

---

7. Davies, *The Thought of Thomas Aquinas*, 242.

8. Recent attempts to apply Thomistic *prudentia* (or Aristotelian, *phronesis*) to managerial practices tend to use it as a new "tool" for improving managerial effectiveness. See Kinsella and Pitman, *Phronesis as Professional Knowledge*. In an attempt to align insights from Aquinas with management practice, Wolfgang Grassl, though less tempted to simply apply *prudentia*, nevertheless creates a hybrid account of the managed organization whereby the structure of action that Aquinas uses to define "good sense" becomes a "model" for how managers can reach decisions. See Grassl, "Aquinas on Management and Its Development"; Grassl, "Mission, Vision, Strategy."

9. *ST* 2a2ae.47.4.

necessary, and to put the decision correctly into action.[10] It is, according to Herbert McCabe, the possessing and exercise of *good sense*.[11]

The rationale for where *prudentia* fits within an understanding of human identity and purpose is presented by Aquinas in *ST* 1a2ae.57.5. In the body of the article, Aquinas outlines the way the application of "good sense" contributes to the perfection and purposefulness of human beings as a particular kind of ensouled body. As rational animals, the interplay of intellect and will contributes to the ability of the human agent to see actions in relationship to a goal. A rational agent is able to see the connection between the goal and actions that may not be attractive at all in and of themselves (such as undergoing surgery), and willingly choose them for the purpose they achieve. For instance, the woman who wants to become an expert on Russian affairs chooses to spend her time on the tedium of learning Russian verbs, while the man who desires to excel on the playing field may willingly spend hours jogging and lifting weights.[12] For Aquinas, all human actions are a product of a choice that is the result of a judgment of reason.

The choosing of a course of action, notes Aquinas, requires an understanding of what constitutes a good goal or end and what means are suitable for attaining that due end. Consequently, he notes,

> an intellectual virtue is needed in the reason, to perfect the reason, and make it suitably affected towards things ordained to the end; and this virtue is *prudentia*. Consequently, *prudentia* is a virtue necessary to lead a good life.[13]

The application of *prudentia* means that a person operates with a deep sense of what is needed in a particular situation to reach a goal, and with a flexibility to discern in new situations the means to reach the desired goal. For Aquinas, "good sense" is as concerned with the overall goal of an action as it is with the particular circumstances within which deliberation and choice is exercised. The range of goals and means that are shaped through the practice of "good sense" might be considered endless, but as a perfecting of reason, that is, as the coming-to-be of an understanding of what constitutes a *good* end and appropriate means to

10. Westberg, *Right Practical Reason*, 187.

11. McCabe, "Aquinas on Good Sense," 419. McCabe draws his use of "good sense" from Jane Austin, particularly her use of the concept in her novel, *Pride and Prejudice*.

12. Westberg, *Right Practical Reason*, 74.

13. *ST* 1a2ae.57.5.

that end for a person, *prudentia* operates in light of the perfecting inclinations implicit to the human person, mainly human happiness (*felicitas*)
and through divine grace, *beatitude*, as the ultimate goal of human bodily
life.[14] In sum, while "good sense" is operative in everything from taking
a walk to learning the Russian language, the actualizing of the judgment,
deliberation, and execution associated with *prudentia* is constituent to
the goal-directedness of human life, and in particular the goal, actualized
by *caritas*, to share in the divine friendship of God.

Another benefit of the exercise of *prudentia* is that the good of the
community is assessed in terms of the means to a proper end, not simply
the benefit of the individual person whose role it is to make a decision.
The concern, in other words, is not simply with "leadership development" as a skill, but with the inhabiting of good sense by leaders who
recognize the larger good in relation to the goal. Aquinas recognized that
those who inhabit "good sense" are doing so as members and participants
of communities. In *ST* 2a2ae.47.10, Aquinas speaks of *prudentia* as pertaining "not only the private good of the individual, but also the common
good of the multitude," since right reason "judges the common good to
be better than the good of the individual."[15] In other words, and keeping
with his general metaphysical outlook, Aquinas maintains that the good
disposition of the parts depends on their relation to the whole. It is the
identity and purpose of the whole that shapes what is appropriate for the
activity of the parts.

The connection between means and ends, and individual and communal, is further clarified by Aquinas when he considers the implications
of the lack of *prudentia*. *Astutia*, that is, the careful rational pursuit of a
bad or inappropriate end,[16] employs most of the same characteristics of
"good sense" with the exception that the goal sought is "good not in truth
but in appearance."[17] The goal may seem worthy and indeed it might be
worthy (growing the church, for example), however, to assume that the

14. For Aquinas, there is a connection between *prudentia* and divine *providentia*
(providence). As he notes in *ST* 1.22.1, it belongs to *prudentia* to direct other things
towards an end whether in regard to oneself or in regard to others subject to that person. Aquinas contends that *prudentia* is suitably attributed to God, and given that the
God is the last end, the ordering in things towards an end in God is called *providentia*.

15. *ST* 2a2ae.47.10.

16. *ST* 2a2ae.55.3. Modern English translations render *astutia* as craftiness or
cunning.

17. *ST* 2a2ae.55.3c.

results of an action is all that matters is to assume that the identity and purpose of the community in question requires the imposing of goals rather than the judgment, deliberation, and execution of actions that seek to address or fulfill the implicit purpose and goals of the particular kind of community. Again, for Aquinas, different kinds of communities have different ends, so it is to risk *astutia* to assume that the goals of one kind of community (e.g., a business) are appropriate to another (e.g., a church).

What, then, is the shape *prudentia* takes in relation to leadership in the church? The possessing and exercise of "good sense" is shaped by the church being a social body animated by the indwelling of Christ's life through the grace of the Holy Spirit.[18] In this body, the sacraments are the effective signs of living contact with the humanity of Christ, through which people share in divine life. The church, therefore, is understood as a community of graced people who form the body of Christ: a body that is strengthened and transformed by the sacraments, in particular, baptism and the Eucharist. Given this, the notion that the definition of a church leader is one who efficiently leads by way of a rationalized and re-sults-oriented strategy is proven inadequate and incoherent. Leadership, under these rationalized conditions, is the exercise of law-like precepts that have universal applicability that are limited to judicial functions. Yet, leadership in the church, specifically in the clergy, requires a closer relationship with what the church is, and what the church is for, in order for it to be *church* leadership. The possession and exercise of "right practi-cal reason" in relation to the identity and purpose of the church places church leadership on more solid foundation. In particular, there are three criteria of church leadership that serve to help order and orient the mem-bers of Christ's body to their proper end of salvation and *beatitude*.

The first criterion is that of *good service*. The exercise of "good sense" church leadership is understood in terms of its operation or function, "whereby the good of our neighbor is intended."[19] Its function is its principal and final goal of divine *beatitude*, and that function is always oriented to serving others. Aquinas gives the example of bishops: "The perfection of the episcopal state consists in this: that for love of God a

18. *ST* 1a.92.3. According to Frederick Bauerschmidt, Aquinas conceived of the goal of John's Gospel to be the formation of the church as a community of disciples, a goal that is achieved through the proclamation of the humanity and divinity of Jesus. See Bauerschmidt, "That the Faithful Become the Temple of God," 296.

19. *ST* 2a2ae.185.1.

man binds himself to work for the salvation of his neighbor."[20] The vocation of service in reference to ordained leadership is present in Aquinas's use of *utilitas*, ("good service"). Ordained leaders are there for the
utilitas, the "good of their subjects," the "good of the church," the "good
of their neighbor."[21] Such service is not the pragmatic utility or practical usefulness that is oriented principally to efficient and effective means
to complete tasks and functions. What *utilitas* defines is the exercise of
practical wisdom that is oriented to the goal of the church as the site of
the unifying and salvific good of all human beings.[22] As such, the service
in question is no less *practical* than managerial-inspired activity in that it
seeks to accomplish actions, and do them well. The difference resides in
the relationship of the means of service (i.e., its inner logic) to its proper
end. For church leaders, the ultimate and defining end for the church is
always the supernatural gift of unity in Christ.

The second criterion of church leadership as an exercise of "good
sense" is leadership as an *instrumentum* ("good tool or instrument").
Aquinas considered ordained leadership as an *extrinsic* instrument. That
is, when church leaders perform tasks or make decisions they act as specific agents in service to, and as an instrument of, the *intrinsic* activity
of God in and through the ministry of the entire church. As *animate*
instruments, leaders play an active role in bringing about a specific result in what they do, but the primary agency by which the purposes of
the church are obtained belongs to God.[23] Aquinas has in mind here the
role of ordained leaders in reference to the administration of the sacraments. In 3a.64.8, for example, he notes how washing with water can be
done for the purpose of bodily cleanliness and even amusement. When it
comes to washing with water for the purpose of baptism, "it needs to be
determined to one purpose, i.e., the sacramental effect, by the intention
of him who washes." The water itself as an inanimate instrument is not
implicitly intended towards a particular effect; rather, it is the motion and
intent of the priest or bishop to subject themselves as an *instrumentum*
to the goal and action of the principal agent of the sacramental activity,
that is, Christ. In so doing, the ordained leader serves for the purpose of

20. *ST* 2a2ae.185.4.

21. A few examples of this use are found in *ST* 2a2ae.63.2, 147.3, & 185.3

22. Sabra, *Thomas Aquinas' Vision of the Church,* 117.

23. *ST* 3a.64.3.3.

effecting a result that is oriented toward the final goal, the unity of people as the body of Christ.

The leader as *instrumentum* problematizes the rationalized goals of efficiency and effectiveness of managerial-shaped leadership in re-ordering the goals of the church to reflect more clearly the final reality (*res tantum*) of the sacraments, that is, the life of grace. The effect of good leadership, therefore, is measured principally in how and by what means the leader of the community acts to promote and assist in orienting the community to unity in Christ. Not every action is meant to be a sacramental action, yet in that the sacraments are the principal means to share in God's life, the general movement expressed in actions and decisions small and large is oriented to, and as an instrument of, the agency of Christ in effecting human wholeness and unity. Since the *instrumentum* of the ordained leadership is ordered to the final goal of the church, the ministry and activity of the church itself can be construed as an *instrumentum salutis*.[24]

A third criterion when considering leadership in the church, is that of *ministerium* ("having a specific office"). Whereas *utilitas* and *instrumentum* outline how leadership is exercised, the use of *ministerium* in relation to leaders acknowledges that in the life of the church there are specific roles or offices occupied by individuals. What is notable to Aquinas's understanding of these roles is that he places far greater emphasis on these offices as relating to, and receiving coherence from, the sacramental life of worship and service, more than the juridical responsibilities allied with these roles, for example, the administration of committees or parish buildings and grounds. As was discussed above, leadership in the church is specific to the *kind* of social body the church is. Hence, to emphasize the sacramental over the juridical is to acknowledge that participation in the sacraments conveys a spiritual power or ability that effects those participating in a manner that is fundamentally ordered to the true and ultimate end of human life. The administration of sacraments are, for Aquinas, immovable (*immobiles*) as to their nature and effect, whereas the juridical operations are of a "lower power," in that associated actions lack *immobiles* because juridical operations are more determined by circumstance and context.[25] Appropriate church leadership is principally the exercise of activity that is "natural" to the kind of social body where

24. Sabra, *Thomas Aquinas' Vision of the Church*, 119.

25. *ST* 2a2ae.39.3.

the leadership is manifest. And there is nothing more natural for the church than the participation and reception of the gifts of grace and love received through sacramental actions.

Leadership as *ministerium* averts the dualisms of spiritual/temporal or visible/invisible that might be assigned to particular parts of ordained office by maintaining a strongly realist position when it comes to how the church and the sacramental life are fitting (*conveniens*) to the nature of human beings and their graced final end. We can see in this position the grounds for a rationale for the church as a social body whose life is properly sourced in that of the Incarnate Word as the first and universal cause of salvation. It is fitting, therefore, that the instruments of salvation (i.e., the sacraments and those who administer them) should possess a certain similitude to their first cause. Thus, the role of church leader is not established by means of comparison to leadership in other kinds of social bodies, but through a certain similitude to Christ, who, as the invisible Word that operates through the visible signs in the sacraments, orders and orients the good sense and person of church leaders to himself. [26] There is no greater orientation for church leaders than to being the instruments of service whose purpose and activity is determined by the immovable grace of God as received in the sacraments.

Leaders in the church, therefore, participate as members of the body of which Christ is the head, and through their service, instrumentality, and office, they preserve the unity signified and effected in the sacraments, and orient the community in the day-to-day matters of the church to modes of human wholeness that are enacted through the presence and activity of the Holy Spirit. Such leadership cannot reflect the law-like imposition of goals that seek managerial efficiency or prescribed methods of planning that seek to define the church by its juridical modes of organization. As is appropriate to the kind of social body the church is, leadership is the exercise of good sense that engages in the execution of wise action that at all times is shaped by sacramental unity and oriented to divine happiness.

To summarize, as Fabian Radcliffe declares, "the Church is radically different from every other human society; its very social structure is supernatural reality, something that is given and maintained by God."[27] There could be no natural organization and no general form of leader-

26. Sabra, *Thomas Aquinas' Vision of the Church*, 112.

27. Radcliffe, "The Body of Christ," 155.

ship that could form the basis upon which the supernatural gifts of unity and grace could be superimposed. There could not be this, particularly in light of Aquinas's thought, because what something is *essentially* provides the logic for how the thing in question operates and provides the goals for the good order of the thing. Aquinas did not entertain the possibility of natural society being formed that could in any fundamental sense display the benefits of Christ's passion and resurrected life, as such an enterprise would fail to have the necessary order or orientation to operate as anything but a human institution. As the social body animated by Christ's life through the indwelling of the Holy Spirit, the church is not organized by means of some general aspect of social production, but has its end in terms of grace. In the church, the sacraments communicate the bodily presence of Christ, and this sacramental order is the presence of the risen body of Christ to the world, the source of his Spirit in the world.[28]

The Church as Christ's Body is the Principle for Human Unity

This second section is concerned with the way the church as Christ's body can serve as the source for human unity in an age when increasing specialization and "lifestyle choices" shape the landscape of ecclesial life. It is generally accepted that people form one human race because ultimately human bodies are linked with those of common ancestors who share a common nature. The unity of the church, however, is not found primarily in what people have in common with each other (e.g., interests, outlooks, or demographics); the community that is the church is unified because the bodies of the members are linked with the risen body of Christ. To inhabit the life made possible through union with God in the Eucharist, the sacrament of the unity of humanity in Christ, orders the members of Christ's body to their proper end in the beatitude of God. How the church orders and organizes its common life is fundamentally because of this ultimate end.

The church is informed by the living presence of Christ and therefore organized along an alternative logic to that of modern managed organizations. The church, in Aquinas's theological project, is a dynamic and animated entity, which as an *inclusive* and *incorporating* body welcomes members to share in the life and benefits of Christ through her

28. McCabe, *The New Creation*, 39.

sacramental life that orders the entire body to the beatitude of God.[29] As head of the church, Christ is the source (*principium*) of justification and the beginning and end of human beatitude. In him, everything human is brought into relationship. And in those depths members of Christ meet one another in a different way. The immersion into Christ through baptism becomes an immersion in and with all who share the divine life through grace. This inclusivity draws people out of their self-defining, self-contained worlds and brings them into communion in the depths of Christ's divine humanity.

The inclusive and incorporating nature of Christ's body, that draws people into the depth of Christ's divine humanity, is a characteristic missing from managerial-oriented accounts of church, especially when considering the emphasis in such accounts on "lifestyle choices" for particular demographic groups.[30] Though a shared demographic identity may appear as sufficiently inclusive for a church interested in a focused ministry, such inclusivity too narrowly defines the shape of Christian life to align with the interests of the members rather than the incorporation nature of membership in Christ's body.

Consider, for instance, the work associated with youth ministry and its struggle to be a sustainable part of a church's life. In an age of increased production of programs, manuals, and youth ministry "experts," the findings from the National Study of Youth and Religion in the U.S. suggest that attempts by church leaders to "program" youth incorporation into ecclesial life through means deemed "relevant" has given rise to a religious outlook that Christian Smith and Melinda Denton call "Moralistic Therapeutic Deism."[31] This outlook accepts as normative that the Christian life is about having one's needs met by a God who is more butler or therapist than living, present, and active Creator.[32] Moreover, this outlook has its roots, Smith and Denton note, in the tendency by church leaders to underemphasize Christian commitment, over-state theological debates, frame life situations in alarmist or fear-based terms, and latch on to simplistic answers to alleged moral and spiritual problems.[33] Unsurpris-

29. Sabra notes that for Aquinas, the "mark" of the church that occupied him the most was the question of unity. See Sabra, *Thomas Aquinas' Vision of the Church*, 70.

30. See the discussion on *Fresh Expressions* and similar programs in chapters 1 and 2 above.

31. Smith and Denton, *Soul Searching*, 171.

32. Ibid., 127.

33. Ibid., 266.

ingly, the attitude by youth towards the church is largely apprehensive. As Kendra Creasy Dean notes, the attitude of young people to religious participation is like their attitude to music or sport participation: it is an extracurricular activity that is a good thing to do but unnecessary for an integrated life.[34]

The results of the Youth and Religion study indicate that, despite the seemingly inconsequential attitude of youth to the church in general, the churches that have sustainable ministry with youth display a focus on incorporating young people into the full liturgical and formational life through fewer youth "programs" and more attention to prayer, study, and discipleship.[35] In fact, there is a general increase in interest in religious matters by youth. As Dean contends, the issue for the church is not primarily one of indifference, but an issue of replacing the instrumentalist view of faith that reduces "youth ministry" to specialized programs that promote "bland religiosity" and coordinate youth into an ecclesial *ghetto* with incorporative practices that stimulate full participation in the life of the church and the cultivation of the call "to follow Christ into the world as envoys of God's self-giving love."[36] In other words, what young people are interested in is a church that enacts the unity it has in Christ and less in a church concerned with creating the right "product" for a particular demographic subgroup.

As the example of youth ministry demonstrates, a bureaucratic rationality, wherein the social body is defined as the coordination of people and the deployment of such towards the meeting of specific and efficiently defined goals, runs the risk of reducing the church and its life to bland, religiously-inspired, specialized programs. To repeat an earlier point, managerialism is exercised explicitly by treating all social bodies as organizations that require the necessary management in order to grow, survive, or exert social influence. In all societies, managerialism assumes, every productive process that constitutes society is in need of coordination or management. In the context of managerialism, an organization is likened to a mechanized organism that behaves in particular ways to carry out certain functions in order to subsist. In the logic of managerialism, there is no social body that should not be managed, and no purpose

---

34. Dean, *Almost Christian*, 6.

35. Dean, "Faith, Nice and Easy," 26.

36. Ibid., 27.

for social bodies other than increased functionality and survival.[37] Under such conditions, the genuine identity of the church as *corpus Christi mysterium* is pushed into the background by influences of financial, cultural, political, or other interests or concerns.[38] What is lost, therefore, when managerialism guides ecclesial reflection and practice is how this particular social body is a sign (*signa*) of human unity.

To speak of the unity of the *corpus Christi* for Aquinas was not principally a comment on the pragmatic need to define the association of the church with a single descriptor (i.e., a body). As will be soon addressed more fully, it was, for Aquinas, the ordering of members to a common end that essentially formed and gave unity to a society in general, not the oneness of the leader, or the ratification by superior authority.[39] Thus, the unity of the church is not just the unity of a society with common ambitions; it is not just the unity of a society with a single recognized ultimate authority; it is not just the unity of people who share a common way of thinking or acting; it involves something like all these things, but the unity of the church is first of all the unity of one life.[40] In other words, the church is not essentially a society or community plus a divine mandate. What binds the church together is that its members share the same life, the life of Christ, which through the *caritas* of the Holy Spirit, animates the body and gifts its members for service and mission.

In Aquinas's commentary on Ephesians, the idea of gathering people to form a body is summarized. According to Aquinas, the gathered (*congregatio*) of the resurrected at the last day will coincide with the kind of things people are, ensouled bodies. Such a gathering amounts to the formation of a body *in Christ*, that is, as a corporal reality that has as its basis for gathering and staying gathered, the grace and benefits of Christ's glorified body.[41] As he discusses in the *Summa*, as sign, the body of Christ for Aquinas denotes unity. Thus, he shows the fittingness of the institution of the Eucharist through closely identifying the substantial conversion (*conversio*) of the bread and wine into the body and blood of

37. Enteman, *Managerialism*, 35f.

38. Brodd, "Church, Organisation, and Church Organisation," 259.

39. *ST* 1a.31.1.*ad*.2.

40. McCabe, *The New Creation*, 34.

41. *In Eph.* 1 lect. 8. Samuel Wells notes that any disunity within the church is fundamentally a Eucharistic matter. "If the Church cannot be one before God, it cannot fully receive everything God has to give it through the Eucharist". Wells, *God's Companions*, 197.

Christ, and through human participation, their conversion in Christ who is the end of this conversion.[42]

As the preeminent sign of union of people to God, and people to each other, the Eucharist is how the individual church overcomes the pressure to settle for appeals for uniqueness that too closely links the meaning and purpose of the church made present through the Eucharist with the particularities of one parish that are seen to "fill a niche."[43] Accounts that privilege uniqueness for the church deploy the same logic that physicalism provides for the human body: it is a unity of *operation*, not a *substantial* unity. In other words, the focus by proponents of more market-driven approaches to the church limit unity by means of atomizing the "body of Christ" into parts that "operate" as a whole due to shared traits or interests. Such an approach is evident, for example, in attempts to bolster declining parishes through encouraging "niche building" that focus the resources and purpose of a particular church to a specific area of ministry. Whether the *niche* is "young people" or "social activism," this approach assumes that specialization through a homogenized vision is the most suitable approach for churches operating in the "competitive market place."[44] Yet, such atomizing through shared traits or interests ultimately limits access to the "body."

This position receives a correction in Aquinas's account of the Eucharist. According to Aquinas, in the Eucharist the ascended body of Christ is substantially present under edible species.[45] As the direct sacrament of the incarnation and accordingly, the very instrument of divine grace as Christ's body, Aquinas recognizes the Eucharist to be the basis for "the unity of the church," into which people are drawn together.[46]

42. *ST* 3a.74.2.*ad*.2.

43. See *Mission-Shaped Church*. The report speaks of church "networks" being unified, for instance, by "leisure interest, music preference, or disability." The idea of homogeneity with regards the church is, according to Philip Lee, an extension of a market-oriented growth movement that segregates communities into particular groups in order to better market particular aspects of the church. The claim that particular sub-groups feel "more at home" with people of similar interests or background is no justification, Lee maintains, for promoting homogeneity in the church. In fact, Lee concludes, it is an "inexcusable affront" to the gospel. See Lee, *Against the Protestant Gnostics*, 265.

44. Olson, "Congregational Niche Building and Community-Based Sociopolitical Activism."

45. Kelly, "Christ and the Church," 154.

46. *ST* 3a.73.2 & 4.

To posit unity of the church in Christ through the Eucharist, a graced unity, supposes a previous natural unity, the unity implicit in the shared nature that defines humanness.[47] For Aquinas, human existence (*esse*) as ensouled bodies and as such, individuated members of the nature humanity, provides the basis for a corporal reality that truly incorporates human life into the divine life of beatitude.

The church as a whole is constituted, in Aquinas's thought, as a *unitas collectiva*, as an all-encompassing unity. Its unity is not a simple unity, but like that of many people who form one nation. The church, in other words, is one corporative society, the whole ordered and unified by a common end and activity. "A multitude of members," Aquinas maintains in his commentary on 1 Corinthians, "does not take away the unity of the body; hence (Paul) adds: and all the members of the body, though many, are one body, which is completed by all."[48] There is no precedent, therefore, for members to be of one kind of group, or interested in one kind of activity; the organizing of the church's unity is the unity of Christ's body that by divine grace incorporates and orients the members of the body. For Aquinas, the promotion of uniqueness and the development of difference in particular churches is tantamount to accepting a kind of schism in Christ's body, and consequently, permitting *disorder* to be allowed to flourish.[49]

The Church Is Formed and Ordered to Beatitude in God

The concern of this third section is with the way in which the church finds its organizing logic as a particular social body that is ordered to God's divine happiness in a time when techniques and strategies are readily offered as means to a more efficient and effective church. The church formed and ordered as the body of Christ places in doubt the logic of technique and such missional-based approaches to the church that give focus to questions of effectiveness strategies and ends-means rationality as activities that provide coherence to the mission and purpose of the church. The implicit ecclesiology of managerial accounts of the church fail to offer a vision for human wellbeing and unity due in part to the way

47. Lubac, *Catholicism*, 25.

48. *In I Cor.* 12 lect. 3.

49. *In I Cor.* 1 lect. 2.

a managerially-shaped vision of the church settles for goals and purposes that fall short of the *telos* of divine beatitude.

The managerial notion of "goals" draws on the organizational independence of "mission statements" and "congregational uniqueness," which mirrors the autonomy that private-sector organizations enjoy, and creates the conditions whereby it is unclear to whom the organization is accountable and whose interests should be served. In contrast, the teleological notion of beatitude is incorporative of specific actions that are orienting to one, final end. It is worth rehearsing here that for Aquinas, the end of humans includes two related notions.

First, human beings, by their very nature as creatures of intellect and will, desire a perfect happiness that cannot be found in this life. This perfect happiness can only be found in union with God, since there is no end to human seeking in this life, and God alone is the universal good that can entirely satisfy human desire.[50] Second, union with God, the vision of God made possible by grace, surpasses the very nature of every creature, including the human being. All creaturely knowledge falls short of this vision, "which infinitely surpasses all created substance. Consequently neither human beings, nor any creatures, can attain final happiness by their natural powers."[51] The paradox of these notions are not dissolved in Aquinas;[52] rather, like the body/soul *compositio* of human nature, and the substantial change of bread/body in the Eucharist, that humans seek happiness but also have the ability to seek after what they cannot find through their own efforts is fitting to Aquinas's anthropology and metaphysical account of things. In other words, in a world created and ordered to God, the basic premise of human fulfillment resides in the very fabric of human existence, and is brought to completion or perfection through divine grace.

The church, then, is not the kind of social body that can operate with integrity within the framework of the confluence of a "provider-customer" transactional relationship within a prescribed supply-side organizational structure. This is partly because no social body can really flourish under the primacy of transactions over the more fundamental exercise of mutual engagement. Despite appeals to notions of the church as "the body of Christ," the thrust of managerial-inspired ecclesiologies

50. *ST* 1a2ae.2.8 and 3.8.

51. *ST* 1a2ae.5.5 and 1a.12.4.

52. For an overview of recent debate on this paradox, see, Ashley, "What Is the End of the Human Person?"

assume a weak analogy to the human body and subsequently those pro-moting managerial notions rely on the modern organization as the basis for the image of the church. In the place of a body enlivened by the Holy Spirit and oriented to divine joy, the church in Congregational Studies replicates the more mechanistic and easily replicated body that remains atomized as simply the aggregation of individual elements to the embody-ing structure (i.e., the organization). Aligned with the uniqueness that some Congregational Studies proponents advocate, the technique-based approach to the church creates something close to "soul-less clones," who are going nowhere in particular.[53]

One area that exemplifies the ascendency of the managed, tech-nique-based church is the application of a results-oriented method of strategic planning. Such planning is accomplished through defining a parish-specific vision and elevating its importance, identifying the personnel and process for giving birth to vision, and giving counsel on communicating vision to the constituency. The desired result is the adop-tion of the vision, its implementation and preservation.[54] The strategic planning model, argues Aubrey Malphurs, is the answer to the problem of church decline, assuming that such planning takes place by means of leaders who can effectively lead their churches through the process. For Malphurs, strategic planning requires strategic leadership and receives its viability and hope from such leadership, and not from anything that the church intrinsically possesses as being Christ's body.[55] As a form of managerial control, however, strategic planning aims at the coordination of human energies and goals for the desired result of limiting options in favor of the chosen "vision." It envisions a unified horizon of human potential that can be made through a rational coordination of human resources and activity.

The power of predictability, through an instrumentalized process of assessment and closely defined commitment, is never far removed from the actual implementation of the plans. Against the fear of irrational-ity and randomness, strategic planning works toward possibilities that implicitly assume that right planning will produce favorable results. In

53. On this point, John Milbank maintains that "technique-based" managerial-ism in the church denotes the "meaningless but efficient manipulations which are all that is left to do with things once they have been de-sacramentalized." Milbank, "Stale Expressions," 128.

54. See the discussion on planning in chapter 1.

55. Malphurs, *Advanced Strategic Planning*, 17.

other words, the rhetoric about strategy reflects and justifies not only the responsibilities of the strategic leader for leading the church, but also the unavoidable necessity of a managerial logic to pursue the desired goals. What is lost under such deterministic conditions is confidence in the ordering of human life, and in particular, graced human life, to any goal or end other than the *imminent* goals and ends of a planning process. As the earlier section on *prudentia* and leadership demonstrated, there is no greater orientation for the church and her leaders than to inhabit a common life whereby the instruments of service whose purpose and activity is determined by the immovable grace of God as received in the sacraments is the very measure of how the church plans and executes its activity. Such use of right practical reason provides an alternative logic to the presumed dominance of managerialism and its basis in efficiency, effectiveness, predictability, and control.

It is noteworthy that Aquinas's account of the church offers a vision of the Christian life ordered to divine beatitude that takes seriously the deliberation and activity of humans in their journey to God. His vision of the church assumes the practical questions faced in the actual living out of Christian belief. A vital contribution of Aquinas in these matters is how he provides a corrective to the teleological immanence of strategic planning and the broader instrumentalized, technique-based forms of managerial-oriented ecclesiologies. As the fullness of Christ, the members of the church are *perfected* in him (*membra Ecclesiae et perficiantur in eis*).[56] Aquinas's use of "members" with reference to the church emphasizes that as a complete body the church in her parts is destined for glory, as in fact, Christ's human body was glorified by God in the resurrection and ascension. In other words, whereas managerial ecclesiologies assume that individuals participate in the life of the church through congregational-specific goals,[57] an account that follows Aquinas and the theological tradition that derives from him recognizes that membership in Christ's body is constituted through the entire sacramental ministry of the church, all of which orders the members to divine beatitude. The principle goal of Christian life in the church, therefore, is not limited to managing outcomes for growth or order, but to participate collectively in the new humanity that the body of Christ makes possible.

---

56. *In Eph.* 1 lect. 8.

57. Rendle and Mann, *Holy Conversations*, 86.

Consequently, the church fully understanding itself as Christ's body can never content itself with setting out goals that inevitably distract from the dynamic concern of the eschatological goal that is proper to its existence and purpose.[58] Aquinas's understanding of the church as a "body" overcomes the limits set by a managerial logic in reference to social bodies like corporations or other institutions. It might be the case that the ends of managerial logic (i.e., efficiency, effectiveness, control, and predictability) are suitable for those social bodies; however, the efficacy of the sacraments in effecting and maintaining the union of people with God pushes against and ultimately transcends the social categorization that would define the church by its organizational character rather than its eschatological purpose. Christ is himself the object of faith that draws together the members of his body, an organized body that he calls and forms. Though it could be argued that the church is built up by the activity of its members, their acts of virtue, and the performance of sacramental rites, what gives these activities their intelligibility is the power of Christ operative in them. To state this is to say something vastly different from describing that the church is simply the sum of work by the parts that make it up. The members of the church are never, in Aquinas's teaching, said to be related to the church as parts of a whole. Instead, the church is presented in Aquinas as a distinct and concrete community of humans (and angels), constituted by the ordering of all to one common end, the enjoyment of the beatific vision.[59]

In sum, the social character of the church is implied in the analogical use of "body," a move that maintains the church as a visible social body rather than simply a loose fellowship of like-minded people who

---

58. Pattison, *The Faith of the Managers*, 91–92. Nicholas M. Healy speaks of the church as always *in via*, on the way to its goal in the consummation of God's kingdom. Healy reads Aquinas as balancing the *performative* aspects of the church (e.g., its proclamation, practices, and precepts) with the agency of the Holy Spirit who moves us towards Christ. Healy is concerned with accounts that privilege the performance of the church over the "internal movement" of God's Spirit. See Healy, "Practices and the New Ecclesiology."

59. In the estimation of William Cavanaugh, the Body of Christ is "public" in that the celebration of the Eucharist does not simply represent a social meaning (e.g., a corporate "brand" or unique "idea"), but *makes* a social body, the church. For the Eucharist is not so much an action as an object. See Cavanaugh, "The Work of the People as Public Work," 8–9. In like manner, Catherine Pickstock summarizes the relationship of the Eucharist to the church when she speaks of the Eucharist both occurring *within* the church and giving *rise* to the church in a circular fashion. See Pickstock, "Thomas Aquinas and the Quest for the Eucharist," 178.

are organized along lifestyle choices. Unlike the modern organization and the managerial logic contained therein, the ultimate reason for the church's visibility is not found alone in social concepts. The purpose of the church is objectively given.[60] In the church's sacramental structure, where sensible signs are the means through which people are incorporated into Christ and become members of his body, an alternative logic is provided.[61] To share in the bread and wine of the Eucharist is to share in the one body of Christ, who is the source of charity and human unity. Through the Eucharistic communion, therefore, people become one with Christ and one another as a *una mystica persona*.[62] The value of this theological account is that it provides a unifying vision of the church and a word of hope for a fragmented world. For in Christ, the realities of grace and glory are placed at the center of a community the stretches across time and space. As his body, the church is the linking of "heaven and earth" performed in the sacraments that provide a proper eschatological aspect and organic link between the means of grace and the hope of glory for all people.

The Future Body

In a recent essay on the state of the church, Stanley Hauerwas notes that the current age shows clear signs of a loss of confidence by Christians, particularly those in Protestant traditions, in their ability to sustain themselves in the face of societal and cultural changes. The shrinking number of attendees has deeply influenced, Hauerwas maintains, how churches understand their role and identity within the social order. Is this the end? Hauerwas asks.[63] Even if the question is overstated, it is hard to argue that the future of churches like those identified as "mainline" is altogether certain. Continued trends of decline will not see the immediate death of major traditions like Anglicanism or Lutheranism. There remain in these

60. The objectively given purpose of the church operates as an alternative to managerialism, which, Martin Parker notes, "is an excuse for a particular form of domination, one that is taken and one that is given." Parker, *Against Management*, 210.

61. Radcliffe, "The Body of Christ," 173.

62. Swierzawski, "Christ and the Church," 247.

63. Hauerwas, "Approaching the End," 88. Hauerwas is commenting on the state of *Protestant* churches. It is worth remembering that the Protestant "mainline traditions" form the background on which this book has analyzed the concept of the church as Christ's body.

traditions structures and resources to keep church doors open for some time. Nevertheless, the "rhetoric of crisis" continues to reverberate in books, seminars, and denominational meetings, and as such, responses continue to be put forward as to how the crisis can be solved, or if not solved, at least have the effects of decline lessoned.

The ascendency of Congregational Studies as a broadly defined grouping of practical means and methods in response to the church decline represents one significant aspect of contemporary ecclesiological reflection. By way of response, instead of promoting a new set of programs and policies that might compete with those within the Congregational Studies fold, this study has focused on retrieving and exploring an alternative logic for where the church may turn for wisdom in this age. The contribution this study has sought, therefore, is to assist in the constructive efforts of articulating a theological vision that stresses the fundamental hope of a redeemed humanity gathered in unity by means of Christ's body that subsists sacramentally as the social body, the church.

As members of a redeemed community, there cannot be complacency as to how the social body of Christ is enacted through the life of *caritas* and the journey toward beatitude that gives shape and focus to the Christian life. The body of Christ is a living body and her members share in Christ's life through participation in her sacramental life that opens members to divine beatitude and friendship with members and nonmembers alike. This life of unity in Christ provides the basis for the church precisely as the renewed, redeemed humankind. Such a claim counters the "rhetoric of crisis" that sustains the efforts of some to reconfigure the church by means of a managerial logic.

Attending to an alternative ecclesial logic has, at times, meant navigating a way forward that resists deploying the speech and practices of Congregational Studies, including the notions of church growth, parish revitalization, and the range of possibilities posited by proponents of the "missional church." In one respect, precluding these particular responses to the current decline in the church has meant sounding an argument that appears counterintuitive. After all, how can avoiding notions of growth, revitalization, and mission contribute to a constructive account of the church? It is not the contention of this study that the speech and practices of such activities are inherently problematic; rather, at issue is whether employing such speech and practices means employing certain assumptions about what the church is for, and how the church exists as Christ's body. Growth, revitalization, and mission ought to be constitutive expressions to any account of the church. The caution this study has sought to address is how these expressions can be properly oriented and ordered as particular performances of Christ's body without needing to rely on the rationality of the reductive, physicalist metaphysics of a managed social body. A more ecclesial-oriented logic, this study has maintained, provides a firmer foundation than the promises of managerialism.

In the end, this and other constructive theological accounts of the church have to attend, in some way, to the position "on the ground" where Christian life is lived, and the church exists among other kinds of social bodies.[64] Therefore, by way of conclusion, it is worth picking up the question of Hauerwas: does this age mark an end for the church, in particular the mainline Protestant traditions? Is the church in *that* kind of decline? And if so, what of its future? It would seem appropriate that one more text from Aquinas might provide something of a response to Hauerwas and a final consideration for the study. The text is his Antiphon to the *Magnificat*, for Vespers on the feast of *Corpus Christi*:

> O sacred feast, in which Christ is our food, the memory of his passion recalled. The soul is filled with thanksgiving, a pledge of future glory is given to us.

This short prayer contains a précis of Aquinas's Eucharistic theology. The Eucharist is a "sacred feast," a celebration of community and food, indeed it is a celebration of Christ as "our food," based on Jesus's own declaration that he is "the living bread that has come down from heaven" (John 6:51). Jesus calls on his followers to eat this food, which is the "flesh of the Son of Man" (John 6:53) and does so on the eve of his passion, asking his disciples to do so "as a memorial of me" (Luke 22:19). Therefore, anyone who eats this food will have a pledge of "eternal life, and I shall raise him up on the last day" to "future glory" (John 6:54).

64 See, Wells, *A Nazareth Manifesto*, in particular, chapters 14 and 15. Wells use of "being with" as the basic mode of engagement expressed in the person of Jesus and the mission of the church provides a rationale for local ministry that is grounded in the particulars of location, circumstance, and resources. In seeking companionship and friendship with neighbors, strangers, and the poor, the mission of a specific church takes full account of life "on the ground" without needing to deploy techniques of growth that stem from a fear of church decline. An example of a church practicing mission in the mode of "being with" is the Community of St. Margaret the Queen in south London. Avoiding the language and practices associated with a managerial logic, this community seeks to be a church that through "prayer, hospitality, and generosity" can live with "love, grace, charity, and freedom."

Thus do Christians have reason to give thanks (Luke 22:17) as all in general do for food, but as they especially do for what Jesus calls "real food," namely himself (John 6:55).

For Aquinas, the mere bread and wine of communion bear an immense weight of meaning: basic human food is the last place you would guess to be the point of entry into the mystery of the world's creation out of nothing and its ultimate end in the eternal love that created it. It is, for sure, no overstatement to say that for Aquinas the life of the church is but an extended meditation on the meaning of bread and wine, a reflection on what they really are. When Aquinas focuses on the bread and wine, he is not merely addressing the elements associated with the Eucharist, he is making the larger claim that matter *matters*, it overflows with meaning.[65] For what are human beings but a certain kind of material item in the world, and yet animals that are meaning-making and symbol-sharing embodied souls? It is, for Aquinas, one of the wonders of what it means to be human that we are animals of a kind, ones with potential abilities to transcend our materiality through the formation of communities defined by divine *caritas*.

Meaningful animals that humans are, our bodies speak to one another, and through word and gesture, we are oriented to share in friendship. And it is through that same materiality of speech that the body of Christ is in converse with the world, the Word spoken to us as food and food given to us as Word spoken, as body speaks to body, as friend speaks to friend.[66] Thus, it is not wishful thinking to suggest that the present and future of the church is in the realm of divine friendship, where humanity is renewed and unified by unfailing grace. It is not wishful thinking, yet such a vision requires a call to action that is unsatisfied to announce anything short of divine friendship as the reason (*ratio*) for why the church is and remains where human bodies are unified through the graced humanity of Christ. To announce anything less as the church is to risk sounding a tone of resignation in an already challenging age.

65. Turner, *Thomas Aquinas*, 268.
66. Ibid., 269.

Bibliography

Adams, Marilyn McCord. *What Sort of Human Nature? Medieval Philosophy and the Systematics of Christology*. Milwaukee: Marquette University Press, 1999.

Alvesson, Mats, and Hugh Willmott. *Making Sense of Management: A Critical Introduction*. London: SAGE, 1996.

Ammerman, Nancy Tatom. *Pillars of Faith: American Congregations and Their Partners*. Berkeley: University of California Press, 2005.

Anthony, P. D. "Management Ideology." In *Critical Management Studies: A Reader*, edited by Chris Grey and Hugh Willmott, 21–28. New York: Oxford University Press, 2005.

Aquinas, Thomas. *Commentary on Aristotle's De Anima*. Edited by Kenelm Foster and Silvester Humphries. Notre Dame: Dumb Ox, 1994.

———. *Commentary on Aristotle's Metaphysics*. Translated by John Patrick Rowan. Notre Dame: Dumb Ox, 1995.

———. *Commentary on Saint Paul's Epistle to the Ephesians*. Translated by Matthew Lamb. Albany: Magi, 1966.

———. *Commentary on the Letter of Saint Paul to the Romans*. Translated by John Mortensen, Enrique Alarcón, and Fabian Larcher. Lander: Aquinas Institute for the Study of Sacred Doctrine, 2012.

———. *Commentary on the Letters of Saint Paul to the Corinthians*. Translated by Beth Mortensen Evans, John Mortensen, Enrique Alarcón, and Fabian Larcher. Lander: Aquinas Institute for the Study of Sacred Doctrine, 2012.

———. *Commentary on the Letters of Saint Paul to the Philippians, Colossians, Thessalonians, Timothy, Titus, and Philemon*. Translated by John Mortensen, Enrique Alarcón, and Fabian Larcher. Lander: Aquinas Institute for the Study of Sacred Doctrine, 2012.

———. *Knowing and Naming God: (1a. 12-13)*. Edited by Thomas Gilby. Translated by Herbert McCabe. Cambridge: Cambridge University Press, 2006.

———. "On the Principles of Nature." In *Selected Philosophical Writings*, translated by Timothy McDermott, 67–80. New York: Oxford University Press, 2008.

———. "On the Union of the Incarnate Word." In *An Aquinas Reader: Selections from the Writings of Thomas Aquinas*, edited by Mary T. Clark, 454–64. New York: Fordham University Press, 2000.

———. *On Truth*. Translated by Robert W. Mulligan, James V. McGlynn, and Robert W. Schmidt. 3 vols. Cambridge: Hackett, 1994.

———. *Quaestiones De Anima*. Translated by James H. Robb. Milwaukee: Marquette University Press, 1984.

———. *Summa Theologiae: A Concise Translation*. Edited by Timothy McDermott. New York: Christian Classics, 1989.

————. *Summa Theologiae: Questions on God*. Translated by Brian Leftow and Brian Davies. New York: Cambridge University Press, 2006.

————. *The Catechetical Instructions of St. Thomas Aquinas*. Translated by Joseph B. Collins. New York: Wagner, 1939.

Aristotle. *De Anima: Books II and III (With Passages from Book I)*. Translated by D. W. Hamlyn. 2nd ed. New York: Oxford University Press, 1993.

Ashley, Benedict M. "What Is the End of the Human Person? The Vision of God and Integral Human Fulfillment." In *Moral Truth and Moral Tradition: Essays in Honour of Peter Geach and Elizabeth Anscombe*, edited by Luke Gormally, 68–96. Dublin: Four Courts, 1994.

Ayer, A. J. *Language, Truth and Logic*. London: Penguin, 2001.

Baab, Lynne. "Myths about Communicating Congregational Identity." Accessed November 28, 2012. http://www.alban.org/conversation.aspx?id=6712.

Bacon, Francis. *The New Organon*. Edited by Lisa Jardine and Michael Silverthorne. Cambridge: Cambridge University Press, 2002.

Baglow, Christopher T. *"Modus et Forma": A New Approach to the Exegesis of Saint Thomas Aquinas with an Application to the Lectura Super Epistolam Ad Ephesios*. Roma: Pontificio Istituto Biblico, 2002.

Baker, Lynne Rudder. "Persons and the Metaphysics of Resurrection." *Religious Studies* 43.3 (2007) 333–48.

Balmer, Randall Herbert, and Lauren F. Winner. *Protestantism in America*. New York: Columbia University Press, 2002.

Bandy, Thomas G. *Mission Mover: Beyond Education for Church Leadership*. Nashville: Abingdon, 2004.

Barna, George. *Marketing the Church*. Colorado Springs: NavPress, 1988.

"The Barna Group—Report Examines the State of Mainline Protestant Churches." Accessed November 15, 2012. http://www.barna.org/barna-update/article/17-leadership/323-report-examines-the-state-of-mainline-protestant-churches.

Barnes, Corey L. "Natural Final Causality and Providence in Aquinas." *New Blackfriars* 95.1057 (2014) 349–61.

Barrow, Simon. "From Management to Vision: Issues for British Churches Negotiating Decline and Change." *International Review of Mission* 92.364 (2003) 7–17.

Bass, Diana Butler. *A People's History of Christianity: The Other Side of the Story*. New York: HarperOne, 2009.

Bauerschmidt, Frederick Christian. "'That the Faithful Become the Temple of God': The Church Militant in Aquinas's Commentary on John." In *Reading John with St. Thomas Aquinas*, edited by Michael Dauphinais and Matthew Levering, 291–311. Washington, DC: Catholic University of America Press, 2005.

Bishop, Jeffrey P. "Body Work and the Work of the Body." *Journal of Moral Theology* 2.1 (2013) 113–31.

————. "Rejecting Medical Humanism: Medical Humanities and the Metaphysics of Medicine." *Journal of Medical Humanities* 29.1 (2008) 15–25.

————. *The Anticipatory Corpse: Medicine, Power, and the Care of the Dying*. South Bend: University of Notre Dame Press, 2011.

Blankenhorn, Bernhard. "The Instrumental Causality of the Sacraments: Thomas Aquinas and Louis-Marie Chauvet." *Nova et Vetera* 4.2 (2006) 255–94.

Bostrom, Nick. "Why I Want to Be a Posthuman When I Grow Up." In *The Transhumanist Reader*, edited by Max More and Natasha Vita-More, 28–53. Chichester: Wiley-Blackwell, 2013.

Braine, David. *The Human Person: Animal and Spirit*. South Bend: University of Notre Dame Press, 1994.

Brodd, Sven-Erik. "Church, Organisation, and Church Organisation: Some Reflections on an Ecclesiological Dilemma." *Svensk Missionstidskrift* 93.2 (2005) 245–63.

Browning, Don S. *A Fundamental Practical Theology: Descriptive and Strategic Proposals*. Minneapolis: Fortress, 1991.

Brown, Warren S. "Human Nature, Physicalism, Spirituality, and Healing: Theological Views of a Neuroscientist." *Ex Auditu* 21 (2005) 112–27.

Budde, Michael L. "The Rational Shepherd: Corporate Practices and the Church." *Studies in Christian Ethics* 21.1 (2008) 96–116.

Budde, Michael L., and Robert W. Brimlow. *Christianity, Incorporated: How Big Business Is Buying the Church*. Grand Rapids: Brazos, 2002.

Bynum, Caroline Walker. *The Resurrection of the Body in Western Christianity, 200-1336*. New York: Columbia University Press, 1995.

Callahan, Kennon L. *Twelve Keys to an Effective Church*. San Francisco: Harper & Row, 1983.

Cameron, Helen. "Networks—The Blurring of Institution and Networks: How Should the Church Engage?" In *Entering the New Theological Space*, edited by John Reader and Chris Baker, 73–84. Farnham: Ashgate, 2009.

Cavanaugh, William T. "The Work of the People as Public Work: The Social Significance of the Liturgy." In *Liturgical Institute Conference Proceedings*. Institute of Liturgical Studies, 2008. http://works.bepress.com/william_cavanaugh/1/.

Cawley, Janet R. *Who Is Our Church? Imagining Congregational Identity*. Herndon: Alban Institute, 2006.

Celano, Anthony J. "The Concept of Worldly Beatitude in the Writings of Thomas Aquinas." *Journal of the History of Philosophy* 25.2 (1987) 215–26.

Chaves, Mark. *Congregations in America*. Harvard: Harvard University Press, 2004.

———. "Supersized." *Christian Century* 123.24, November 28, 2006, 20–25.

"Churches as Businesses: Jesus, CEO." *The Economist*, December 20, 2005.

Churchland, Patricia Smith. "A Neurophilosophical Slant on Consciousness Research." In *Progress in Brain Research*, edited by R. W. Guillery, S. M. Sherman, and V. A. Casagrande, 285–93. Amsterdam: Elsevier, 2005.

Churchland, Paul M. *Matter and Consciousness: A Contemporary Introduction to the Philosophy of Mind*. Rev. ed. Cambridge: MIT, 1988.

Clarke, W. Norris. *Creative Retrieval of Saint Thomas Aquinas: Essays in Thomistic Philosophy, New and Old*. Bronx: Fordham University Press, 2009.

———. *The One and the Many: A Contemporary Thomistic Metaphysics*. South Bend, IN: University of Notre Dame Press, 2001.

Congar, Yves. "The Idea of the Church in St. Thomas Aquinas." *The Thomist* 1.4 (1939) 331–59.

Cooperrider, David L., and Diana Kaplin Whitney. *Appreciative Inquiry a Positive Revolution in Change*. San Francisco: Berrett-Koehler, 2005.

Corcoran, Kevin J. *Rethinking Human Nature: A Christian Materialist Alternative to the Soul*. Grand Rapids: Baker Academic, 2006.

Costea, Bogdan, Norman Crump, and Kostas Amiridis. "Managerialism, the Therapeutic Habitus and the Self in Contemporary Organizing." *Human Relations* 61.5 (2008) 661–85.

Croft, Steven, Ian Mobsby, and Stephanie Spellers, eds. *Ancient Faith, Future Mission: Fresh Expressions in the Sacramental Tradition*. New York: Church, 2010.

Dale, Karen. *Anatomising Embodiment and Organization Theory*. New York: Palgrave Macmillan, 2001.

Dale, Karen, and Gibson Burrell. "What Shape Are We In? Organization Theory and the Organized Body." In *Body and Organization*, edited by John Hassard, Ruth Holliday, and Hugh Willmott, 15–30. London: SAGE, 2000.

Davies, Brian. *The Thought of Thomas Aquinas*. Oxford: Oxford University Press, 1992.

Davies, Mervyn, and Graham Dodds. *Leadership in the Church for a People of Hope*. London: T. & T. Clark, 2011.

Davison, Andrew, and Alison Milbank. *For the Parish: A Critique of Fresh Expressions*. London: SCM, 2010.

Dean, Kenda Creasy. *Almost Christian: What the Faith of Our Teenagers Is Telling the American Church*. New York: Oxford University Press, 2010.

———. "Faith, Nice and Easy: The Almost-Christian Formation of Teens." *Christian Century* 127.16, August 10, 2010, 22–27.

Dennett, Daniel C. *Consciousness Explained*. Boston: Little, Brown and Co., 1991.

———. *Darwin's Dangerous Idea: Evolution and the Meanings of Life*. New York: Simon & Schuster, 1995.

Descartes, René. "Passions of the Soul." In *The Philosophical Writings of Descartes*, edited by John Cottingham, Robert Stoothoff, and Dugald Murdoch, Vol. 3. Cambridge: Cambridge University Press, 1984.

———. "Synopsis of the Following Six Meditations." In *The Philosophical Writings of Descartes*, edited by John Cottingham, Robert Stoothoff, and Dugald Murdoch, Vol. 2. Cambridge: Cambridge University Press, 1984.

Diefenbach, Thomas. *Management and the Dominance of Managers*. London: Routledge, 2009.

Dillard, Peter. "Keeping the Vision: Aquinas and the Problem of Disembodied Beatitude." *New Blackfriars* 93.1046 (2012) 397–411.

Dorrien, Gary. *The Making of American Liberal Theology: Crisis, Irony, and Postmodernity: 1950–2005*. Louisville: Westminster John Knox, 2006.

Douglas, Mary. *Natural Symbols: Explorations in Cosmology*. New York: Routledge, 1996.

Doyal, Len, and Ian Gough. *A Theory of Human Need*. New York: Guilford, 1991.

Drane, John William. *After McDonaldization: Mission, Ministry, and Christian Discipleship in an Age of Uncertainty*. Grand Rapids: Baker Academic, 2008.

———. "The Church and the Iron Cage." In *McDonaldization: The Reader*, edited by George Ritzer, 2nd ed., 151–57. New York: SAGE, 2006.

———. *The McDonaldization of the Church: Consumer Culture and the Church's Future*. New York: Smyth & Helwys, 2002.

Drucker, Peter F. *Managing the Non-Profit Organization: Practices and Principles*. New York: HarperCollins, 1990.

Dulles, Avery. *Models of the Church*. Garden City: Image, 1987.

Dünzl, Franz. *A Brief History of the Doctrine of the Trinity in the Early Church*. London; New York: T. & T. Clark, 2007.

Duraisingh, Christopher. "From Church-Shaped Mission to Mission-Shaped Church." *Anglican Theological Review* 92.1 (2010) 7–28.

Dyck, Bruno, and Elden Wiebe. "Salvation, Theology and Organizational Practices across the Centuries." *Organization* 19.3 (2012) 299–324.

Eberl, Jason T. "Aquinas on the Nature of Human Beings." *The Review of Metaphysics* 58.2 (2004) 333–65.

Edwards, Mark. "Aquinas on Ephesians and Colossians." In *Aquinas on Scripture: An Introduction to His Biblical Commentaries*, edited by Thomas Weinandy, Daniel Keating, and John Yocum, 149–66. London: T. & T. Clark, 2005.

Elshtain, Jean Bethke. "The Body and the Quest for Control." In *Is Human Nature Obsolete? Genetics, Bioengineering, and the Future of the Human Condition*, edited by Harold W. Baillie and Timothy Casey, 155–76. Boston: MIT, 2005.

Enteman, Willard F. *Managerialism: The Emergence of a New Ideology*. Madison: University of Wisconsin Press, 1993.

Feingold, Lawrence. *The Natural Desire to See God according to St. Thomas Aquinas and His Interpreters*. Ave Maria: Sapientia Press of Ave Maria University, 2010.

Foucault, Michel. *Technologies of the Self: A Seminar with Michel Foucault*. Edited by Luther Martin and Huck Gutman. Amherst: University of Massachusetts Press, 1988.

Frank, Thomas Edward. "Leadership and Administration: An Emerging Field in Practical Theology." *International Journal of Practical Theology* 10.1 (2006) 113–36.

Gaukroger, Stephen. *The Collapse of Mechanism and the Rise of Sensibility: Science and the Shaping of Modernity, 1680–1760*. New York: Oxford University Press, 2012.

———. *Descartes' System of Natural Philosophy*. Cambridge: Cambridge University Press, 2002.

———. *The Emergence of a Scientific Culture: Science and the Shaping of Modernity 1210–1685*. Oxford: Oxford University Press, 2009.

———. "The Unity of Natural Philosophy and the End of *Scientia*." In *Scientia in Early Modern Philosophy: Seventeenth-Century Thinkers on Demonstrative Knowledge from First Principles*, edited by Tom Sorell, G. A. J. Rogers, and Jill Kraye, 19–34. London: Springer, 2009.

Gay, Paul du. "Alasdair MacIntyre and the Christian Genealogy of Management Critique." *Cultural Values* 2.4 (1998) 421–44.

———. *In Praise of Bureaucracy: Weber–Organization–Ethics*. New York: SAGE, 2000.

Geach, Peter. *Truth and Hope*. Notre Dame: University of Notre Dame Press, 2001.

Gill, Robin, and Derek Burke. *Strategic Church Leadership*. London: SPCK, 1996.

Gorman, Michael. "Incarnation." In *The Oxford Handbook of Aquinas*, edited by Brian Davies and Eleonore Stump, 428–35. Oxford: Oxford University Press, 2012.

Gould, Stephen Jay. *Eight Little Piggies: Reflections in Natural History*. New York: Norton, 2010.

———. *Full House: The Spread of Excellence From Plato to Darwin*. Cambridge: Belknap, 2011.

Grassl, Wolfgang. "Aquinas on Management and Its Development." *The Journal of Management Development* 29.7/8 (2010) 706–15.

———. "Mission, Vision, Strategy: Discernment in Catholic Business Education." *Journal of Catholic Higher Education* 31.2 (2012) 213–32.

Grey, Christopher. "'We Are All Managers Now'; 'We Always Were': On the Development and Demise of Management." *Journal of Management Studies* 36.5 (1999) 561–85.

Guder, Darrell L., and Lois Barrett. *Missional Church: A Vision for the Sending of the Church in North America*. Grand Rapids: Eerdmans, 1998.

Hacker, P. M. S. *Human Nature: The Categorial Framework*. Oxford: Blackwell, 2007.

———. *The Intellectual Powers: A Study of Human Nature*. Oxford: Wiley-Blackwell, 2013.

Hadaway, C. Kirk, and David A Roozen. *Rerouting the Protestant Mainstream: Sources of Growth & Opportunities for Change*. Nashville: Abingdon, 1995.

Haight, Roger, and James Nieman. "On the Dynamic Relation between Ecclesiology and Congregational Studies." *Theological Studies* 70.3 (2009) 577–99.

Hanby, Charles. *Beyond Certainty: The Changing Worlds of Organizations*. Harvard: Harvard Business, 1996.

Harrison, Peter. *The Fall of Man and the Foundations of Science*. Cambridge: Cambridge University Press, 2007.

Hauerwas, Stanley. "The End of Protestantism." In *Approaching the End: Eschatological Reflections on Church, Politics, and Life*, 87–97. Grand Rapids: Eerdmans, 2013.

Haugaard, Mark. "Reflections on Seven Ways of Creating Power." In *Directions in Organization Studies*, edited by Stewart Clegg, 4:155–82. Los Angeles: SAGE, 2010.

Healy, Nicholas M. "Practices and the New Ecclesiology: Misplaced Concreteness?" *International Journal of Systematic Theology* 5.3 (2003) 287–308.

Hiltz, Fred. "Go to the World! Go Struggle, Bless, and Pray: Bishops, Theological Schools, and Mission." *Anglican Theological Review* 90.2 (2008) 307–15.

Hobbes, Thomas. *Leviathan*. Edited by John Charles Addison Gaskin. New York: Oxford University Press, 1998.

Hobson, Theo. *Reinventing Liberal Christianity*. Grand Rapids: Eerdmans, 2013.

Holifield, E. Brooks. "Toward a History of American Congregations." In *American Congregations*, edited by James P. Wind and James W. Lewis. Chicago: University of Chicago Press, 1994.

Hoyle, Eric, and Mike Wallace. *Educational Leadership: Ambiguity, Professionals and Managerialism*. London: SAGE, 2006.

Inge, John. "Towards a Theology of Place." *Modern Believing* 40.1 (1999) 42–50.

Jackson, Norman, and Pippa Carter. "The 'Fact' of Management." *Scandinavian Journal of Management* 11.3 (1995) 197–208.

———. *Rethinking Organisational Behavior: A Poststructuralist Framework*. New York: Prentice Hall/Financial Times, 2007.

Jaeggi, Rahel. "Rethinking Ideology." In *New Waves in Political Philosophy*, edited by Boudewijn, Paul de Bruin, and Christopher F. Zurn, 63–86. New York: Palgrave Macmillan, 2009.

Jenson, Matt, and David Wilhite. *The Church: A Guide for the Perplexed*. New York: T. & T. Clark, 2010.

Jinkins, Michael. *The Church Faces Death: Ecclesiology in a Post-Modern Context*. New York: Oxford University Press, 1999.

Johnson, Phil, and Joanne Duberley. *Understanding Management Research: An Introduction to Epistemology*. London: SAGE, 2000.

Jordan, Mark D. *Rewritten Theology: Aquinas after His Readers*. Oxford: Blackwell, 2006.

Joy, Lynn S. "Scientific Explanation from Formal Causes to Laws of Nature." In *Early Modern Science*, edited by Katharine Park and Lorraine Daston, 70–105. The Cambridge History of Science. New York: Cambridge University Press, 2006.

Judovitz, Dalia. *The Culture of the Body: Genealogies of Modernity*. Ann Arbor: University of Michigan Press, 2001.

Kärkkäinen, Veli-Matti. *An Introduction to Ecclesiology: Ecumenical, Historical & Global Perspectives*. Downers Grove: IVP Academic, 2002.

Karp, Tom. "Unpacking the Mysteries of Change: Mental Modelling." *Journal of Change Management* 5.1 (2005) 87–96.

Keating, Daniel. "Aquinas on 1 and 2 Corinthians: The Sacraments and Their Ministers." In *Aquinas on Scripture: An Introduction to His Biblical Commentaries*, edited by Thomas Weinandy, Daniel Keating, and John Yocum, 127–48. London: T. & T. Clark, 2005.

Kelley, Dean M. *Why Conservative Churches Are Growing: A Study in Sociology of Religion*. New York: Harper & Row, 1972.

Kelly, Timothy. "Christ and the Church: Duo in Carne Una." PhD thesis, University of Fribourg, 2010.

Kenneson, Philip D. "Selling [Out] the Church in the Marketplace of Desire." *Modern Theology* 9.4 (1993) 319–48.

Kenny, Anthony. "Body, Soul, and Intellect in Aquinas." In *From Soul to Self*, edited by James Crabbe, 33–48. London: Routledge, 1999.

Kerr, Fergus. *After Aquinas: Versions of Thomism*. Malden, MA: Blackwell, 2002.

———. "The Varieties of Interpreting Aquinas." In *Contemplating Aquinas: On the Varieties of Interpretation*, edited by Fergus Kerr, 27–40. South Bend: University of Notre Dame Press, 2007.

Kim, Yung Suk. *Christ's Body in Corinth: The Politics of a Metaphor*. Minneapolis: Fortress, 2008.

———. "Reclaiming Christ's Body (soma Christou) Embodiment of God's Gospel in Paul's Letters." *Interpretation: A Journal of Bible & Theology* 67.1 (2013) 20–29.

Kinsella, Elizabeth Anne, and Allan Pitman, eds. *Phronesis as Professional Knowledge: Practical Wisdom in the Professions*. Boston: Sense, 2012.

Klikauer, Thomas. *Managerialism: A Critique of an Ideology*. New York: Palgrave Macmillan, 2013.

Klima, Gyula. "Man = Body + Soul: Aquinas's Arithmetic of Human Nature." In *Thomas Aquinas: Contemporary Philosophical Perspectives*, edited by Brian Davies, 257–74. Oxford: Oxford University Press, 2002.

———. "Thomistic 'Monism' vs. Cartesian 'Dualism.'" *Logical Analysis and History of Philosophy* 10 (2007) 92–112.

Kretzmann, Norman. "Philosophy of Mind." In *Thomas Aquinas: Contemporary Philosophical Perspectives*, edited by Brian Davies, 128–59. Oxford: Oxford University Press, 2002.

Ladd, John. "Morality and the Ideal of Rationality in Formal Organizations." *The Monist* 54.4 (1970) 488–516.

La Mettrie, Julien Offray de. *La Mettrie: Machine Man and Other Writings*. Edited by Ann Thomson. New York: Cambridge University Press, 1996.

Lee, Philip J. *Against the Protestant Gnostics*. Oxford: Oxford University Press, 1987.

Leftow, Brian. "Souls Dipped in Dust." In *Soul, Body, and Survival: Essays on the Metaphysics of Human Persons*, edited by Kevin Corcoran, 120–38. New York: Cornell University Press, 2001.

Levering, Matthew. "Does the Paschal Mystery Reveal the Trinity?" In *Reading John with St. Thomas Aquinas*, edited by Michael Dauphinais and Matthew Levering, 78–91. Washington: Catholic University of America Press, 2005.

———. *Jesus and the Demise of Death: Resurrection, Afterlife, and the Fate of the Christian*. Waco: Baylor University Press, 2012.

Lewis-Anthony, Justin. *You Are the Messiah, and I Should Know: Why Leadership Is a Myth (and Probably a Heresy)*. London: Bloomsbury, 2013.

Lombardo, Nicholas E. *The Logic of Desire: Aquinas on Emotion*. Washington: Catholic University of America Press, 2010.

Long, Steven. *Natura Pura: On the Recovery of Nature in the Doctrine of Grace*. Bronx: Fordham University Press, 2010.

Lowe, E. J. *Introduction to the Philosophy of Mind*. Cambridge: Cambridge University Press, 2000.

Lubac, Henri de. *Catholicism: Christ and the Common Destiny of Man*. San Francisco: Ignatius, 1988.

———. *Corpus Mysticum: The Eucharist and the Church in the Middle Ages*. Translated by Gemma Simmonds C.J. South Bend: University of Notre Dame Press, 2007.

———. *Splendor of the Church*. San Francisco: Ignatius, 1999.

Lundholm-Eades, Jim. "Best Practices in Church Management." *America* 193.19 (2005) 13–16.

MacIntyre, Alasdair C. *After Virtue: A Study in Moral Theory*. 3rd ed. Notre Dame: University of Notre Dame Press, 2007.

———. "What Is a Human Body?" In *The Tasks of Philosophy: Selected Essays. Vol. 1*, 86–103. New York: Cambridge University Press, 2006.

Malphurs, Aubrey. *Advanced Strategic Planning: A 21st-Century Model for Church and Ministry Leaders*. Grand Rapids: Baker, 2013.

Mancini, Will. *Church Unique: How Missional Leaders Cast Vision, Capture Culture, and Create Movement*. San Francisco: Jossey-Bass, 2008.

Mangham, Iain L. "Macintyre and the Manager." *Organization* 2.2 (1995) 181–204.

———. *Power and Performance in Organizations: An Explanation of Executive Process*. Oxford: Blackwell, 1986.

Marty, Martin E. *A Nation of Behavers*. Chicago: University of Chicago Press, 1980.

Mascall, Eric Lionel. *Christ, the Christian and the Church: A Study of the Incarnation and Its Consequences*. London: Longmans, Green, 1955.

Mayr, Ernst. *What Makes Biology Unique? Considerations on the Autonomy of a Scientific Discipline*. Cambridge: Cambridge University Press, 2007.

McAleer, Graham James. *Ecstatic Morality and Sexual Politics: A Catholic and Antitotalitarian Theory of the Body*. New York: Fordham University Press, 2005.

McCabe, Herbert. "Aquinas on Good Sense." *New Blackfriars* 67.798 (1986) 419–31.

———. *Faith within Reason*. Edited by Brian Davies. New York: Continuum, 2007.

———. *God Still Matters*. Edited by Brian Davies. New York: Continuum, 2005.

———. *The Good Life: Ethics and the Pursuit of Happiness*. New York: Continuum, 2005.

———. "The Immortality of the Soul." In *Aquinas: A Collection of Critical Essays*, edited by Anthony Kenny, 297–306. Garden City: Anchor, 1969.

————. *The New Creation: Studies on Living in the Church*. New York: Sheed and Ward, 1964.

————. *On Aquinas*. London: Burns & Oates, 2008.

McFarland, Ian A. "The Body of Christ: Rethinking a Classic Ecclesiological Model." *International Journal of Systematic Theology* 7.3 (2005) 225–45.

McNeal, Reggie. *Missional Communities: The Rise of the Post-Congregational Church*. San Francisco: Jossey-Bass, 2011.

McPartlan, Paul. *The Eucharist Makes the Church*. 2nd ed. Fairfax: Eastern Christian, 2006.

————. *Sacrament of Salvation*. London: T. & T. Clark, 2000.

Mead, Loren B., and Billie Alban. *Creating the Future Together: Methods to Inspire Your Whole Faith Communities*. Herndon, VA: Alban Institute, 2008.

Meeks, M. Douglas. "Hope and the Ministry of Planning and Management." *Anglican Theological Review* 64.2 (1982) 147–62.

Milbank, John. "Stale Expressions: The Management-Shaped Church." *Studies in Christian Ethics* 21.1 (2008) 117–28.

————. *Theology and Social Theory: Beyond Secular Reason*. 2nd ed. Oxford: Blackwell, 2006.

————. *The Suspended Middle: Henri de Lubac and the Debate Concerning the Supernatural*. Grand Rapids: Eerdmans, 2005.

Miller, Vincent Jude. *Consuming Religion: Christian Faith and Practice in a Consumer Culture*. New York: Continuum, 2004.

Miner, Robert C. "Recent Work on Thomas in North America." In *Contemplating Aquinas: On the Varieties of Interpretation*, edited by Fergus Kerr, 137–62. South Bend: University of Notre Dame Press, 2007.

Mintzberg, Henry. *Managing*. San Francisco: Berrett-Koehler, 2009.

————. *Mintzberg on Management: Inside Our Strange World of Organizations*. New York: Collier Macmillan, 1989.

Mission-Shaped Church: Church Planting and Fresh Expressions of Church in a Changing Context. London: Church House, 2004.

Moore, R. Laurence. *Selling God: American Religion in the Marketplace of Culture*. New York: Oxford University Press, 1995.

Moreland, J. P. "Should a Naturalist Be a Supervenient Physicalist?" *Metaphilosophy* 29.1–2 (1998) 35–57.

————. "The Mind-Body Problem." In *Science, Religion, and Society: An Encyclopedia of History, Culture, and Controversy*, edited by Gary Laderman and Arri Eisen, 2:565–74. Armonk: Sharpe, 2007.

More, Max. "The Philosophy of Transhumanism." In *The Transhumanist Reader*, edited by Max More and Natasha Vita-More, 3–17. Chichester: Wiley-Blackwell, 2013.

Morgan, Gareth. *Images of Organization*. Los Angeles: SAGE, 2006.

Moynagh, Michael, George Lings, Stuart Murray Williams, and Howard Worsley. *Emergingchurch.intro: Fresh Expressions of Church, Examples That Work, the Big Picture, What You Can Do*. Oxford: Monarch, 2005.

Mulhall, Stephen. "Liberalism, Morality and Rationality: MacIntyre, Rawls and Cavell." In *After MacIntyre: Critical Perspectives on the Work of Alasdair MacIntyre*, edited by John Horton and Susan Mendus, 205–24. Notre Dame: University of Notre Dame Press, 1994.

Murphy, Nancey C. "Nonreductive Physicalism: Philosophical Issues." In *Whatever Happened to the Soul?: Scientific and Theological Portraits of Human Nature*, edited by Warren S. Brown, Nancey C. Murphy, and Henry Newton Malony, 127–48. Minneapolis: Fortress, 1998.

———. "Physicalism without Reductionism: Toward a Scientifically, Philosophically, and Theologically Sound Portrait of Human Nature." *Zygon* 34.4 (1999) 551–71.

———. *Religion and Science: God, Evolution, and the Soul*. Harrisburg: Herald, 2002.

Nieman, James R. "Congregational Studies." In *The Wiley-Blackwell Companion to Practical Theology*, edited by Bonnie J. Miller-McLemore, 133–42. Oxford: Wiley-Blackwell, 2011.

Noll, Mark A. *America's God: From Jonathan Edwards to Abraham Lincoln*. New York: Oxford University Press, 2002.

O'Callaghan, John P. "Aquinas's Rejection of Mind, Contra Kenny." *The Thomist* 66.1 (2002) 15–59.

———. *Thomistic Realism and the Linguistic Turn: Toward a More Perfect Form of Existence*. South Bend: University of Notre Dame Press, 2003.

Oliver, Simon. "Teleology Revived? Cooperation and the Ends of Nature." *Studies in Christian Ethics* 26.2 (2013) 158–65.

Olson, Laura R. "Congregational Niche Building and Community-Based Sociopolitical Activism." *Word & World* 25.1 (2005) 34–41.

O'Neill, Colman E. *Meeting Christ in the Sacraments*. Rev. ed. New York: Alba House, 1964.

———. "St. Thomas on the Membership of the Church." *The Thomist* 27 (1963) 88–140.

Parker, Martin. *Against Management: Organization in the Age of Managerialism*. Oxford: Blackwell, 2002.

———. "Organisation, Community and Utopia." *Studies in Cultures, Organizations & Societies* 4.1 (1998) 71–91.

Pasnau, Robert. *Thomas Aquinas on Human Nature: A Philosophical Study of Summa Theologiae, 1a 75–89*. Cambridge: Cambridge University Press, 2001.

Pattison, Stephen. *The Challenge of Practical Theology: Selected Essays*. New York: Kingsley, 2007.

———. *The Faith of the Managers*. New York: Continuum, 1997.

Percy, Martyn. "'Fresh Expressions': A Journey into Implicit Theology." *Implicit Religion* 12.3 (2009) 313–32.

———. *Shaping the Church: The Promise of Implicit Theology*. Farnham: Ashgate, 2010.

———. *Words, Wonders and Power: Understanding Contemporary Christian Fundamentalism and Revivalism*. London: SPCK, 1996.

Percy, Martyn, and Ian Markham, eds. *Why Liberal Churches Are Growing*. New York: Continuum, 2006.

Perez-Ramos, Antonio. "Bacon's Forms and the Maker's Knowledge Tradition." In *The Cambridge Companion to Bacon*, edited by Markku Peltonen, 99–120. Cambridge: Cambridge University Press, 1996.

Peters, Thomas J., and Robert H. Waterman. *In Search of Excellence: Lessons from America's Best-Run Companies*. New York: Harper & Row, 1982.

Pickstock, Catherine. "Thomas Aquinas and the Quest for the Eucharist." *Modern Theology* 15.2 (1999) 159–80.

Pinches, Charles. *Theology and Action: After Theory in Christian Ethics*. Grand Rapids: Eerdmans, 2002.

Pitts-Taylor, Victoria. "Medicine, Governmentality and Biopower in Cosmetic Surgery." In *The Legal, Medical and Cultural Regulation of the Body: Transformation and Transgression*, edited by Stephen W. Smith and Ronan Deazley, 159–72. Farnham: Ashgate, 2009.

Plantinga, Alvin. "Materialism and Christian Belief." In *Persons: Human and Divine*, edited by Peter Van Inwagen and Dean W. Zimmerman, 99–141. New York: Oxford University Press, 2007.

Pollitt, Christopher. *Managerialism and the Public Services: The Anglo-American Experience*. Oxford: Blackwell, 1990.

———. "Mangerialism Revisited." In *Taking Stock: Assessing Public Sector Reforms*, edited by B. G. Peters and D. J. Savoie, 45–77. Montreal: McGill-Queen's University Press, 1998.

Pope, Stephen J., ed. *The Ethics of Aquinas*. Moral Traditions. Washington: Georgetown University Press, 2002.

Porter, Jean. "Virtues and Vices." In *The Oxford Handbook of Aquinas*, edited by Brian Davies and Eleonore Stump, 265–75. New York: Oxford University Press, 2012.

Porter, Roy. *Flesh in the Age of Reason: The Modern Foundations of Body and Soul*. New York: Norton, 2005.

Post, Stephen G. "A Moral Case for Nonreductive Physicalism." In *Whatever Happened to the Soul? Scientific and Theological Portraits of Human Nature*, edited by Warren S. Brown, Nancey C. Murphy, and Henry Newton Malony, 198–213. Minneapolis: Fortress, 1998.

Power, Michael. *Organized Uncertainty: Designing a World of Risk Management*. New York: Oxford University Press, 2007.

Putnam, Hilary. "Three Kinds of Scientific Realism." *The Philosophical Quarterly* 32.128 (1982) 195–200.

Putnam, Robert D. *Bowling Alone: The Collapse and Revival of American Community*. New York: Simon & Schuster, 2000.

Putnam, Robert D., and David E. Campbell. *American Grace: How Religion Divides and Unites Us*. New York: Simon & Schuster, 2010.

Quash, Ben. *Abiding*. London: Continuum, 2012.

Radcliffe, Fabian. "The Body of Christ: The Meaning of 'Corpus' in St. Thomas' Ecclesiology." DPhil thesis, University of Oxford, 1961.

Radcliffe, Timothy. *What Is the Point of Being a Christian?* New York: Burns & Oates, 2005.

Rasmusson, Arne. "Ecclesiology and Ethics: The Difficulties of Ecclesial Moral Reflection." *Ecumenical Review* 52.2 (2000) 180–94.

Rendle, Gilbert R., and Alice Mann. *Holy Conversations: Strategic Planning as a Spiritual Practice for Congregations*. Bethesda: Alban Institute, 2003.

Riches, Aaron. "Christology and Duplex Hominis Beatitudo: Re-Sketching the Supernatural Again." *International Journal of Systematic Theology* 14.1 (2012) 44–69.

Riem, Roland. "Mission-Shaped Church: An Emerging Critique." *Ecclesiology* 3.1 (2006) 125–39.

Rikhof, Herwi. "Corpus Christi Mysticum: An Inquiry into Thomas Aquinas' Use of a Term." *Bijdragen* 37.2 (1976) 149–71.

Ritzer, George. *The McDonaldization of Society: 20th Anniversary Edition*. London: SAGE, 2012.

Roberts, Fredric M. *Be Not Afraid! Building Your Church on Faith and Knowledge.* Herndon: Alban Institute, 2005.

Roberts, Richard H. "Order and Organization: The Future of Institutional and Established Religion." In *Managing the Church? Order and Organization in a Secular Age,* edited by Martyn Percy and G. R. Evans, 78–96. Sheffield: Sheffield Academic Press, 2000.

———. *Religion, Theology and the Human Sciences.* Cambridge: Cambridge University Press, 2001.

———. "Theology and the Social Sciences." In *Modern Theologians: An Introduction to Christian Theology Since 1918,* edited by David Ford and Rachel Muers, 370–88. Oxford: Blackwell, 2005.

Robinson, John A. T. *The Body: A Study in Pauline Theology.* London: SCM, 2012.

Roof, Wade Clark. *America Mainline Religion: Its Changing Shape and Future.* New Brunswick: Rutgers University Press, 1987.

Rosenberg, Alexander. "Reductionism (and Antireductionism) in Biology." In *The Cambridge Companion to the Philosophy of Biology,* edited by Michael Ruse and David L. Hull, 120–38. Cambridge: Cambridge University Press, 2008.

Rossi, Paolo. "Bacon's Idea of Science." In *The Cambridge Companion to Bacon,* edited by Markku Peltonen, 25–46. Cambridge: Cambridge University Press, 1996.

Roxburgh, Alan, and Fred Romanuk. *The Missional Leader: Equipping Your Church to Reach a Changing World.* New York: Wiley & Sons, 2011.

Rozemond, Marleen. *Descartes's Dualism.* Cambridge: Harvard University Press, 1998.

Russell, Letty M. "Why Bother with the Church?" In *Essentials of Christian Theology,* edited by William Placher, 241–56. Louisville: Westminster John Knox, 2003.

Sabra, George. *Thomas Aquinas' Vision of the Church: Fundamentals of an Ecumenical Ecclesiology.* Mainz: Grünewald, 1987.

Saint-Simon, Henri de. *Henri Comte De Saint-Simon 1760–1825: Selected Writings.* Translated by Felix Markham. Oxford: Blackwell, 1952.

———. *Social Organization, the Science of Man and Other Writings.* Translated by Felix Markham. New York: Harper Torchbooks, 1964.

Sargeant, Kimon Howland. *Seeker Churches: Promoting Traditional Religion in a Nontraditional Way.* New Brunswick: Rutgers University Press, 2000.

Schillebeeckx, Edward. *Christ the Sacrament of the Encounter with God.* New York: Sheed & Ward, 1987.

Schumacher, E. F. *Small Is Beautiful: Economics as If People Mattered.* New York: Harper Perennial, 2010.

Searle, John R. "Consciousness." *Annual Review of Neuroscience* 23.1 (2000) 557–78.

———. "Putting Consciousness Back in the Brain." In *Neuroscience and Philosophy: Brain, Mind, and Language,* edited by M. R. Bennett, Daniel C. Dennett, and P. M. S. Hacker, 97–126. New York: Columbia University Press, 2009.

Selznick, Philip. *Leadership in Administration: A Sociological Interpretation.* Berkeley: University of California Press, 1984.

Sennett, Richard. *The Culture of the New Capitalism.* New Haven: Yale University Press, 2006.

Shilling, Chris. *The Body and Social Theory.* 2nd ed. New York: SAGE, 2003.

———. *The Body in Culture, Technology and Society.* New York: SAGE, 2005.

Skirry, Justin. *Descartes and the Metaphysics of Human Nature.* New York: Bloomsbury, 2005.

Slater, Don. *Consumer Culture and Modernity*. Oxford: Blackwell, 1997.

Smith, Anne Kates. "Make Working at Home Work." *Kiplinger's Personal Finance* 67.1 (2013) 61–65.

Smith, Christian. "Implications of National Study of Youth and Religion Findings for Religious Leaders." In *With Energy, Intelligence, Imagination and Love: Leadership in Youth Ministry*, 59–68. Princeton: Princeton University Press, 2005.

Smith, Christian, and Melinda Lundquist Denton. *Soul Searching: The Religious and Spiritual Lives of American Teenagers*. New York: Oxford University Press, 2005.

Smith, Daniel P., and Mary K. Sellon. *Pathway to Renewal: Practical Steps for Congregations*. Herndon: Alban Institute, 2008.

Snider, Alvin. "Cartesian Bodies." *Modern Philology* 98.2 (2000) 299–319.

Soros, George. *Open Society: Reforming Global Capitalism*. New York: PublicAffairs, 2000.

Spellers, Stephanie. "The Church Awake: Becoming the Missional People of God." *Anglican Theological Review* 92.1 (2010) 29–44.

Starbuck, William. "The Origins of Organizational Theory." In *The Oxford Handbook of Organization Theory: Meta-Theoretical Perspectives*, edited by Haridimos Tsoukas and Christian Knudsen, 143–82. New York: Oxford University Press, 2003.

Stark, Rodney, and Roger Finke. *The Churching of America, 1776–1990: Winners and Losers in Our Religious Economy*. New Brunswick: Rutgers University Press, 1993.

Stinchcombe, Arthur L. "Reason and Rationality." In *The Limits of Rationality*, edited by Karen Schweers Cook and Margaret Levi, 285–317. Chicago: University of Chicago Press, 2008.

Stump, Eleonore. *Aquinas*. New York: Routledge, 2003.

———. "Aquinas's Metaphysics of the Incarnation." In *The Incarnation: An Interdisciplinary Symposium on the Incarnation of the Son of God*, edited by Stephen T. Davis, Daniel Kendall, and Gerald O'Collins, 197–220. New York: Oxford University Press, 2004.

Suttle, Tim. *Shrink: Faithful Ministry in a Church-Growth Culture*. Grand Rapids: Zondervan, 2014.

Swierzawski, Waclaw. "Christ and the Church: Una Mystica Persona in the Pauline Commentaries of St. Thomas Aquinas." In *S. Tommaso Teologo*, edited by Antonio Piolanti, 239–50. Roma: Libreria Ed. Vaticana, 1995.

Swinburne, Richard. "From Mental/Physical Identity to Substance Dualism." In *Persons: Human and Divine*, edited by Peter Van Inwagen and Dean W. Zimmerman, 142–65. New York: Oxford University Press, 2007.

Taylor, Charles. *The Ethics of Authenticity*. Cambridge: Harvard University Press, 1992.

———. *Modern Social Imaginaries*. Durham: Duke University Press, 2004.

Thweatt-Bates, Jeanine. *Cyborg Selves: A Theological Anthropology of the Posthuman*. Farnham: Ashgate, 2012.

Torrell, Jean-Pierre. *Saint Thomas Aquinas: The Person and His Work*. Translated by Robert Royal. Washington: Catholic University of America Press, 2005.

———. *Saint Thomas Aquinas, Vol. 2: Spiritual Master*. Translated by Robert Royal. Washington: Catholic University of America Press, 2003.

Townley, Barbara. *Reason's Neglect: Rationality and Organizing*. New York: Oxford University Press, 2008.

Trabbic, Joseph G. "The Human Body and Human Happiness in Aquinas's *Summa Theologiae*." *New Blackfriars* 92.1041 (2011) 552–64.

Turner, Bryan S. "The Body in Western Society." In *Religion and the Body*, edited by Sarah Coakley, 15–41. Cambridge: Cambridge University Press, 2000.

Turner, Denys. *Thomas Aquinas: A Portrait*. New Haven: Yale University Press, 2013.

Vaccari, Andrés. "Dissolving Nature: How Descartes Made Us Posthuman." *Techne: Research in Philosophy & Technology* 16.2 (2012) 138–82.

Van Gelder, Craig. "Rethinking Denominations and Denominationalism in Light of a Missional Ecclesiology." *Word & World* 25.1 (2005) 22–33.

Vann, Gerald. *Morals Makyth Man*. New York: Longmans, Green and Co., 1938.

Velde, Rudi Te. *Aquinas on God: The "Divine Science" of the Summa Theologiae*. Farnham: Ashgate, 2007.

Vita-More, Natasha. "Life Expansion Media." In *The Transhumanist Reader*, edited by Max More and Natasha Vita-More, 73–82. Chichester: Wiley-Blackwell, 2013.

Walsh, Liam. "The Divine and the Human in St. Thomas's Theology of Sacraments." In *Ordo Sapientiae et Amoris*, edited by Carlos Josaphat Pinto de Oliveira, 321–52. Fribourg: Universitatsverlag Freiburg Schweiz, 1993.

Wang, Stephen. *Aquinas and Sartre: On Freedom, Personal Identity, and the Possibility of Happiness*. Washington: Catholic University of America Press, 2009.

Wannenwetsch, Bernd. "Inwardness and Commodification: How Romanticist Hermeneutics Prepared the Way for the Culture of Managerialism—A Theological Analysis." *Studies in Christian Ethics* 21.1 (2008) 26–44.

Ward, Graham. *The Politics of Discipleship: Becoming Postmaterial Citizens*. Grand Rapids: Baker Academic, 2009.

Ward, Pete. *Liquid Church*. Carlisle: Paternoster, 2002.

Watkins, Clare. "The Church as a 'Special' Case: Comments from Ecclesiology Concerning the Management of the Church." *Modern Theology* 9.4 (1993) 369–84.

Wawrykow, Joseph P. *God's Grace and Human Action: "Merit" in the Theology of Thomas Aquinas*. South Bend: University of Notre Dame Press, 1996.

Weber, Max. *Economy and Society: An Outline of Interpretive Sociology*. Edited by Guenther Roth and Claus Wittich. Berkeley: University of California Press, 1978.

Webster, John. "Theologies of Retrieval." In *The Oxford Handbook of Systematic Theology*, edited by Kathryn Tanner, Iain R. Torrance, and John Webster. New York: Oxford University Press, 2007.

Wells, Samuel. *A Nazareth Manifesto: Being with God*. Malden: Wiley and Sons, 2015.

———. *God's Companions: Reimagining Christian Ethics*. Oxford: Wiley & Sons, 2008.

Westberg, Daniel. *Right Practical Reason: Aristotle, Action, and Prudence in Aquinas*. Oxford: Oxford University Press, 1994.

Wheeler, Michael. "God's Machines: Descartes on the Mechanization of Mind." In *The Mechanical Mind in History*, edited by Phil Husbands, Owen Holland, and Michael Wheeler, 307–30. Cambridge: Bradford, 2008.

White, Robert N. *Managing Today's Church*. Valley Forge: Judson, 1981.

William R. Hoyt. *Effectiveness by the Numbers: Counting What Counts in the Church*. Nashville: Abingdon, 2007.

Williams, A. N. *The Ground of Union: Deification in Aquinas and Palamas*. New York: Oxford University Press, 1999.

Williams, Rowan. *Faith in the Public Square*. New York: Bloomsbury, 2012.

Willmott, Hugh. "Rethinking Management and Managerial Work: Capitalism, Control, and Subjectivity." *Human Relations* 50.11 (1997) 1329–59.

Wimberly, Jr., John W. *The Business of the Church*. Herndon: Alban Institute, 2010.

————. "The Challenges of Incarnational Life." *Management & Leadership in the Church Blog*. Accessed November 28, 2012. http://managingministry.com/2010/06/25/the-challenges-of-incarnational-life/.

Wittgenstein, Ludwig. *Philosophical Investigations*. Edited by Peter M. S. Hacker and Joachim Schulte. Translated by G. E. M. Anscombe. 3rd ed. Chichester: Wiley-Blackwell, 2009.

Wolin, Sheldon S. *Politics and Vision: Continuity and Innovation in Western Political Thought*. Expanded. Princeton: Oxford University Press, 2004.

Index